Base Towns

RECENT TITLES IN

OXFORD STUDIES IN CULTURE AND POLITICS
Clifford Bob and James M. Jasper, General Editors

Base Towns

Local Contestation of the U.S. Military in Korea and Japan

CLAUDIA JUNGHYUN KIM

OXFORD
UNIVERSITY PRESS

OXFORD
UNIVERSITY PRESS

Oxford University Press is a department of the University of Oxford. It furthers
the University's objective of excellence in research, scholarship, and education
by publishing worldwide. Oxford is a registered trade mark of Oxford University
Press in the UK and certain other countries.

Published in the United States of America by Oxford University Press
198 Madison Avenue, New York, NY 10016, United States of America.

Library of Congress Cataloging-in-Publication Data
Names: Kim, Claudia Junghyun, author.
Title: Base towns : local contestation of the U.S. military in Korea and Japan / Claudia Junghyun Kim.
Other titles: Local contestation of the U.S. military in Korea and Japan
Description: New York, NY : Oxford University Press, [2023] |
Includes bibliographical references and index.
Identifiers: LCCN 2022037308 (print) | LCCN 2022037309 (ebook) |
ISBN 9780197665275 (hardback) | ISBN 9780197665299 (epub)
Subjects: LCSH: Military bases, American—Korea (South)—Public opinion. |
United States—Armed Forces—Korea (South) | United States—Military relations—Asia. |
Korea (South)—Military relations—United States. |
Military bases, American—Japan—Public opinion. | United States—Armed Forces—Japan. |
Japan—Military relations—United States. |
Military bases, American—Foreign countries. | United States—Armed Forces—Asia—History. |
Military bases, Foreign—Political aspects.
Classification: LCC UA26 .K6 K554 2023 (print) | LCC UA26 .K6 (ebook) |
DDC 355.7095195—dc23/eng/20220805
LC record available at https://lccn.loc.gov/2022037308
LC ebook record available at https://lccn.loc.gov/2022037309

DOI: 10.1093/oso/9780197665275.001.0001

Printed by Integrated Books International, United States of America

To Mom, Dad, Sis, and Isak

Acknowledgments

First and foremost, I am immensely indebted to my mentors at Boston University: Thomas Berger, William Grimes, and Taylor Boas. They are my *onshi*, and they will always have my deepest gratitude. Each of them has had concrete influence on my career—and thus my life. They are role models that I can only hope to emulate.

I thank Shin Fujihira, Susan Pharr, Christina Davis, Amy Stockton, and Emma Duncan at the Program on U.S.-Japan Relations at Harvard University's Weatherhead Center for International Affairs, where I was a postdoctoral fellow for 2019–2020. While at Harvard, I had the great privilege to organize a book workshop and receive feedback from Daniel Aldrich, Terrence Roehrig, and Takako Hikotani. I am sure they can see how their comments helped restructure the book. I also thank Taishi Muraoka and Elijah Greenstein for their camaraderie.

My very special thanks go out to Clifford Bob, the coeditor of the Oxford Studies in Culture and Politics and one of the best writers in political science. He helped me take a fresh look at my book manuscript. Two anonymous reviewers at Oxford University Press further shaped this book, and I hope they will be able to see their influence in the final product. I also thank my editor, James Cook.

Many people generously offered feedback on various parts of the book at its many different stages. At the Emerging Scholars in Grand Strategy Workshop at the University of Notre Dame, I received extensive feedback from Adam Liff, Sebastian Rosato, Michael Desch, Eugene Gholz, Rosemary Kelanic, Daniel Lindley, Joseph Parent, Maddison Schramm, Thomas Cavanna, Renanah Joyce, Andrew Sjareko, Alex Lin, and Dani Nedal. At a workshop organized by the U.S.-Japan Program at Harvard University, Jennifer Lind offered valuable comments. At the Joint Consortia National Dissertation Workshop on Contemporary East Asia at the University of Southern California, William Marotti, Susan Hwang, and Stanley Rosen shared their insights from different disciplinary perspectives. At the Social Science Research Council Korean Studies Dissertation Workshop, Suzy Kim, Youngju Ryu, and Robert Oppenheim helped me think about how my work fits within Korean Studies. I also thank the late Bill Gamson (whose very last social movements seminar I was lucky to attend), Joshua Shifrinson, Alexander Cooley, Andrew Yeo, Andrew Bacevich, Sheila Smith, Soeya Yoshihide, David Leheny, Connor Mills, Bruce Jentleson, Anne Sartori, Sato Manabu, Gabe Masaaki, Miyagi Taizo, Oguma Eiji, Hosoya Yuichi, Swen Hutter, Susan Eckstein, Taishi Muraoka, Noriyuki Shikata, Christopher Ahn, Vivian Shaw, Amy Chin, Chanaka Jun Takazawa, Yuko Kawato, Tomoki Kuniyoshi, John Gerring, Laura Blume, Pilar Giannini, Hao Chen, Aki Nakai, Ingu Hwang, Seo-hyun Park, and Hye Young Kang. I also thank Scott Walker for creating the maps and Jerome Li and Ye Qianying for their research assistance.

My colleagues in Hong Kong have offered advice on the seemingly nebulous book publication process. In particular, I thank Dan Lynch, Brad Williams, Renaud Egreteau, and Diego Fossati for their valuable and timely advice. I also thank Yuk Wah Chan, Tom Patton, Jaemin Shim, Su Yun Kim, Soo Ryon Yoon, Edmund Cheng, Dongshu Liu, Sean Starrs, and Mark Thompson for their encouragement.

Of course, this book would not have been written without the generosity of the people I interviewed and spent time with during my fieldwork. I sincerely thank each and every one of them, and I hope they will forgive me for not being able to list some eighty names here. My special thanks go out to Shin Soo-yeon, Goo Jung-suh, Bae Jong-jin, Kim Dong-ryeol, Park Seok-jin, Takahashi Toshio, Shinozaki Masato, Asada Shigeki, Tomita Eiji, Nīkura Yasuo, and Fukumoto Michio. I know that this book will never repay the debt I owe to these individuals, but I hope that it will play a small role in communicating at least some of their ideas and aspirations to the world.

Lastly, I thank my parents, my sister, and my husband. This book is dedicated to them.

Contents

Abbreviations

2ID	Second Infantry Division
CFA	Commander Fleet Activities
DLP	Democratic Labor Party
DPJ	Democratic Party of Japan
FRF	Futenma Replacement Facility
JCP	Japan Communist Party
KCPT	Pan-National Solution Committee to Stop the Expansion of U.S. Bases in Pyeongtaek
LDP	Liberal Democratic Party
LPP	Land Partnership Plan
MCAS	Marine Corps Air Station
NAF	Naval Air Facility
SACO	Special Action Committee on Okinawa
SDF	Self-Defense Forces
SDP	Social Democratic Party
SOFA	Status of Forces Agreement
THAAD	Terminal High Altitude Area Defense
UPP	Unified Progressive Party
USFJ	US Forces Japan
USFK	US Forces Korea
YRP	Yongsan Relocation Plan

Conventions

I have used the Revised Romanization System for Korean romanization and the modified Hepburn system for Japanese romanization. Korean and Japanese names are written in their proper order (last name first and given name last), except in cases where individuals use Western name order in Western-language publications.

Tables, Figures, and Maps

Tables

Figures

Maps

1

Introduction

U.S. Military Base Towns in Korea and Japan

At Rodriguez Live Fire Complex, the largest American firing range in Asia just 12 miles south of the border dividing South and North Korea, residents of the surrounding communities tolerated the daily clangor of combat for six long decades. The mostly elderly and conservative populations seemed determined to avoid causing any trouble, even as stray bullets fell in residential areas and cattle suffered miscarriages from the sounds of explosions. Nor did the people in these communities complain about the forest fires caused by errant shells, which almost seemed like a routine annual event. They said little when what they thought was an earthquake—they called 119 to report it—turned out to have been the military blowing up numerous unexploded bombs all at once. They remained tight-lipped despite suspicions of groundwater contamination and concerns about the falling prices for local farm produce. Their silence was a long time in the making: even when an accidental blast from an unexploded shell instantly killed nine residents in 1980, no one protested.

By the end of 2014, however, they had had enough. Residents of Changsu, Yeongjung, Idong, and Yeongbuk—the four rural townships in the northern city of Pocheon abutting the 3,390-acre training complex—began mobilizing. Residents climbed up a nearby mountain, a frequent target of firing exercises, to act as voluntary human shields against the shooting exercises. They placed straw bales at thirty locations surrounding the base and set them ablaze. They threatened to occupy the base, block its gate with farm tractors, and even suspend base water supplies. They set up a tent within a stone's throw of the base, from which they began to stage unprecedented, community-wide protests. These elderly conservatives, who once seemed to accept their life alongside the firing range, quickly evolved into the biggest headache for the U.S. Forces Korea (USFK). Even in the most heated moments of protest, however, they took pains to present their movement in a certain way: the movement, they believed, had to appear "pure"—unadulterated by supposedly

Base Towns. Claudia Junghyun Kim, Oxford University Press. © Oxford University Press 2023.
DOI: 10.1093/oso/9780197665275.003.0001

"radical" politics—to gain legitimacy. They were protesting stray bullets, not American militarism.[1]

What do these unlikely activists tell us about the communities hosting U.S. military bases abroad and the lives of the people in them? The sudden bout of activism in this formerly acquiescent community might be puzzling to national policymakers engaged in high-level alliance politics. For anyone paying close attention, however, Pocheon is hardly an anomaly. The Rodriguez range, after all, is merely one of the many U.S. military bases and installations dotting South Korea (hereafter Korea) and Japan—two of the largest U.S. base hosts in the world. As the United States shuffles and reshuffles people and machinery among its bases half a world away, introduces new ordnance and military technologies to them, and expands and reduces their acreage, host communities across the two countries have seen varied spurts of localized anti-base contestation. Some of the most intense moments of contention have come from the least likely places. In the Japanese host cities of Sagamihara and Zama, for example, locals went from calling Camp Zama, which is home to the U.S. Army Japan, a "very quiet base" to locking arms in a human chain to surround what they began to denounce as a "control tower of war." Similarly, Pyeongtaek and Iwakuni, despite their reputations as friendly hosts characterized by pro-base conservative politics in Korea and Japan, respectively, experienced strong anti-base challenges they had never seen before. Drastic transitions have also occurred in the opposite direction. In Dongducheon and Uijeongbu, two heavily militarized Korean cities south of the Demilitarized Zone, once-heated anti-base activism has gradually subsided. Seoul's Yongsan Garrison, once a magnet for nationalistic uproar, sees fewer picketers today. Underneath the monolith of the network of U.S. military bases abroad, local actors continue to both contest and embrace the physical manifestations of American power projection on the ground.

These fluctuations over time and across different U.S. military base host communities raise larger questions: When do we see social movements against the American military overseas, and what explains their varying intensity? Why do some locals seem to find peace with war machines and war exercises in their backyard, while others resist them? And when protests do occur, are they about stray bullets and forest fires, or are they about American hegemony? With the official number of U.S. bases and military installations outside the U.S. and U.S. territories standing at 514 (Department of Defense 2018), a number that excludes many existing bases (Vine 2015, 4), and as Washington continues to rely on its global basing network for power projection, these questions remain pressing ones. Anti-American nationalism might be one way to explain America's contested garrisons overseas (Katzenstein and Keohane 2007), but such simplification does little justice to much more nuanced local dynamics (Moon 2012, 17–20). Even in ostensibly anti-American host countries, many bases are accepted by most residents, whereas others become lightning rods for local anger. Similarly, episodes of large-scale, high-intensity anti-base activism that tend to garner attention (Lutz 2009; Yeo 2011; Holmes 2014; Kawato 2015) are not representative of the everyday life of base towns. The differing responses to U.S. military bases at the subnational level—with key domestic and international conditions held constant, and with bases producing similar negative and positive externalities—remain a puzzle.

To address this puzzle, I examine the contentious politics surrounding twenty U.S. military bases across Korea and Japan for the period 2000–2015. In particular, I look at municipalities hosting these bases and differing levels of community acceptance and resistance over time. I call these communities "base towns," following the Japanese expression *kichi no machi* (and the Korean expression *gijichon*, although that term tends to evoke images of smaller villages and military prostitution), to highlight distinct local political dynamics centering on the American presence (Kovner 2009; Moon 2012; Höhn and Moon 2010; Gillem 2007). In explaining how local actors in base towns contest or refrain from contesting this symbol of American military primacy, I shed light on the shifting contexts they exploit to build their movements, both successfully and unsuccessfully. In particular, I look at the following: how activists variously take advantage of the major changes these bases go through (i.e., status quo disruptions); adopt resonant, if surprisingly mundane, movement frames (i.e., movement framing); and attract third-party support from local political elites (i.e., elite allies). Activist actions, strategies, and dilemmas in these contexts translate into fluctuating levels of oppositional mobilization across host communities.

In tracing the trajectories of the base towns, I shed light on marginalized actors in domestic and international politics—far removed from elite decision-making processes, and yet living with their consequences—who sometimes manage to complicate the operations of America's military behemoth. As this book goes on to demonstrate, some host communities are much more vocal than others, and formerly compliant communities can suddenly turn against bases they have long tolerated. Sometimes local challengers successfully mobilize; other times, they struggle to retain even their existing movement membership. Sometimes they win broader public sympathy; other times, they are dismissed as a bunch of clueless anti-American zealots. Delving beneath the surface of interstate alliance politics and finding consistent patterns in these varied local experiences is my primary goal.

The Contentious Politics of Overseas Basing

I take a social movement approach to the contentious politics surrounding U.S. military bases in Korea and Japan at the subnational level. Scholars of international security may be skeptical about the aim of this book. Often, the sheer immensity of the U.S. basing network—according to one estimate, the number of golf courses alone on U.S. overseas bases stands at 170 (Vine 2015, 4)—is simply taken for granted (Schmidt 2020). Local responses to U.S. military bases overseas, when they are discussed at all, tend to be brushed off as a mere "third-order issue" on the margins of high-level alliance politics (Armitage and Nye 2012, 14). Local voices of discontent, from this perspective, are an occasional blip in the otherwise cohesive narratives of American superpower. Policymakers and defense officials, as a result, lack an understanding of the drivers of community acceptance of, and resistance to, the bases that they establish and guard.

I argue that contentious base politics, despite the prevalent skepticism, deserve attention as a social force shaping domestic and international politics. From the American strategic standpoint, the U.S. overseas basing network enables continued power projection in regions of key security and economic interest (Posen 2003; Pettyjohn and Kavanagh 2016). Opposition within host states, however, can delay, disrupt, and even thwart U.S. military initiatives. At the national level, host state discontent can spawn devastating consequences for both peacetime and wartime basing access. In the Philippines, the U.S. military was forced to leave Subic Bay Naval Station, once the largest U.S. naval facility in the Pacific, after nationalist Filipino senators, backed by a strong anti-base coalitional movement, voted to terminate a basing agreement in 1991. The full withdrawal in 1992, often described as a victory of people power, ended ninety-four years of the U.S. presence in this former American colony (Yeo 2011, 35). In Turkey, a popular movement against the Iraq War prodded its national political elites into denying basing access to the United States in 2003 (Holmes 2014, 187). In Ecuador, President Rafael Correa, buttressed by a strong anti-base movement, refused to renew the lease for a base in Manta—the only condition demanded for a change of heart being an Ecuadorean base in Miami (Yeo 2011, 86). As a result, after spending $60 million, the U.S. military withdrew in 2009 from what it considered a strategic base for the war on drugs (Lostumbo et al. 2013, 102). Washington's subsequent negotiations with Peru, Panama, and Colombia to open a formal base to replace the Manta base failed; even when government authorities wanted to host U.S. bases, they feared domestic opposition from civil society and opposition politicians newly emboldened after democratization (Bitar 2016, 7–8).

Even when high-level, interstate base politics remains stable, low-level politics of opposition sometimes proves to be surprisingly influential. In fact, some experts worry about the future prospects for American basing rights— and by extension, American power projection—in Korea and Japan, two enduring security partners (Erickson and Mikolay 2012, 83). This seemingly overblown concern has historical precedents. In mainland Japan, several communities in the 1950s successfully resisted land confiscation and construction of U.S. facilities: Uchinada of Ishikawa Prefecture, Mt. Asama of Nagano Prefecture, and Mt. Myōgi of Gunma Prefecture (Hayashi 2012, 93). The expansion of Tachikawa airfield in Sunagawa, western Tokyo, served as a harbinger of mass protests in 1960 against the U.S.-Japan security treaty (Molasky 2015, 67–68). In Sasebo, a port call by the USS *Enterprise* in 1968 provoked such combative opposition that no other nuclear-powered aircraft carrier could visit Japan until 1983 (Havens 1987, 150–51).

More recently, local opposition to the construction of a Marine air facility in Okinawa, Japan's southernmost island prefecture, has managed to stall what has been a top policy agenda for Washington and Tokyo for more than twenty-five years. As currently conceived, the envisioned facility is already constrained in its operational capacity, since concerns about local opposition, rather than considerations for strategic needs, dictated its design (Harding 2021). Local discontent there has also pushed the allies to draw up plans to send Okinawa-based Marines to Guam, Hawaii, and Australia, directly influencing the U.S. force posture. In Korea, a high-profile environmental campaign in 2000 pressured the allies into adding an environmental clause to the Status of Forces Agreement (SOFA), a legal framework for U.S. military operations on foreign soil, some thirty-five years after it was signed. Militant resistance to U.S. base consolidation in the Korean city of Pyeongtaek in the mid-2000s, meanwhile, heavily politicized what the U.S. military intended as a strategic, operational initiative; defense analysts see this contentious episode as a major peacetime challenge to the U.S. force posture (Pettyjohn and Kavanagh 2016, 137). Most recently, a surge in local opposition in Pocheon, a point of departure for this book, led the USFK commander to publicly complain about lacking "reliable, accessible training areas" essential for "war fighting readiness" (Sisk 2020). After the authorities moved some of the live-fire training involving Apache helicopters from Pocheon's embattled Rodriguez range to Pohang, residents in this southern military city staged drive-through protests at the height of the pandemic. As protests spread from one community to another, the defense ministry announced in 2021 its plans to look for a third training location—a move bound to antagonize yet another locality. Alaska and Japan have also been named as potential candidates for overseas training. "[D]omestic political pressures are the main driver of limitations on training," warned a former USFK commander (Brooks and Leem 2021).

Conceptualized as a social movement, base opposition typifies a David-and-Goliath struggle in which localized collective action targets an exceedingly powerful international opponent enjoying the full backing of the national government. Anti-base opposition also resembles anti-infrastructure movements in its rejection of concentrated local costs (i.e., negative externalities) forced onto marginalized localities for the sake of diffuse public benefits (i.e., national defense) (Aldrich 2009; C. J. Kim 2021b). With the odds stacked against the challengers—they lag far behind their target in terms of resources, institutional access, visibility, and influence—they strategize to maximize what little comparative advantage they may temporarily gain. Given the global reach of the U.S. military basing network, one may assume that anti-base activists primarily target global audiences. However, many base opponents seem surprisingly inward-looking: more often than not, they take advantage of local—as opposed to global or domestic—opportunities and articulate their grievances in the seemingly mundane language of the everyday. This unique focus on the local differentiates anti-base activists from many other contestants of global targets, such as antiwar or anti-globalization activists, whose claims are nationally and internationally oriented.[2]

This surprising primacy of the local in a movement targeting a global superpower indicates conscious strategizing on the part of anti-base activists—but who are they? I variously use the terms "activists," "latent adherents," and "base opponents" throughout the book to distinguish between activists—some of them professional and semi-professional—and other residents in host communities who join protests only occasionally, if at all. "Activists" are already staunchly opposed to U.S. military bases, usually for political or philosophical reasons, and spend a lot of time and energy in organizing protests, discussing rhetorical strategies, and courting third-party support. On the other hand, other residents, whom I call "latent adherents," may hold grievances but usually stand by. Activists are always alert for opportunities to mobilize opposition, but whether latent adherents with dormant grievances join the opposition depends partially on activist efforts to find common ground with them. As the book will demonstrate, sizable oppositional mobilization, as measured by protest turnout, occurs on relatively rare occasions when activists and their latent adherents join forces; when this happens, I use the catch-all term "base opponents." In courting latent adherents, activists often subordinate their more radical movement goals—closing down bases and booting troops out, for example—to more immediate, pragmatic demands that form the basis of everyday local grievances.

The focus on varying protest levels across subnational host communities over time—in part a product of varied interactions between anti-base devotees and their latent supporters—responds to the call by McAdam and Boudet (2012) to avoid a common pitfall in social movement research: focusing solely on large, sustained, and successful movements. By virtue of hosting U.S. military bases, all host communities are potentially "at risk for mobilization" (McAdam and Boudet 2012, 24)—but not all actually mobilize. And even when they do, the intensity and persistency of such mobilization attempts vary widely. Of the twenty American military bases I study for the period 2000–2015 in this book, five face what I categorize as high contestation, which, as I will show in the following chapters, arises only occasionally and typically loses steam over time. For these five bases that rile up local populations, there are six others that do not generate much attention from residents. The rest stand somewhere in between. As social movement researchers increasingly demonstrate, powerful, large, and high-profile movements are in reality "wildly atypical of mobilization attempts" (McAdam and Boudet 2012, 23). Similarly, unlike the stylized image of highly disruptive protests, most anti-U.S. military base protests have become routinized and predictable.

The subnational, longitudinal approach I take in this book captures the picture that emerges when one not only looks at highly contested bases across different countries, but also across a range of bases within each country over time. This new picture presents underexplored drivers of local base politics, in which the critical link between activists and residents shapes periods of commotion and quiescence in base towns. To be sure, the subnational focus is not meant to suggest that there are no cross-national differences among host states. In Korea and Japan, the U.S. military presence has drastically different roots, as the brief historical overview below will show. Americans descended on Korea in 1945 as liberators who ended the Japanese colonization, and they returned to the peninsula in 1950 to join the Korean War on behalf of the South. When their occupation began in Japan, on the other hand, Americans were conquerors of a defeated, suddenly docile nation. Base politics in Korea and Japan also developed in different social and political contexts, as detailed in the next chapter. Anti-base contention in the former is a byproduct of student activism of the 1980s, which saw the U.S. presence as a buttress of authoritarian rule and an obstacle to national unification. In Japan, base opposition is part of the broader post–World War II pacifist tradition. Individual movement cycles seem shorter in Korea, if occasionally punctuated by intense outbursts that command attention. By contrast, localized anti-base activism in many Japanese localities has persisted for decades, although an overwhelming focus on Okinawa, once a virtual U.S. military colony where base opposition persists, eclipses the experiences of base towns on the Japanese mainland (Hein and Selden 2003; Tanji 2006; Inoue 2007; McCormack and Norimatsu 2012). Despite these cross-national differences, there are meaningfully consistent patterns of anti-base mobilization and demobilization at the subnational level—systematic comparisons of which will draw a much richer portrait of faraway U.S. military base towns than what the current literature offers.

The Argument in Brief

Embracing the multifaceted nature of contentious base politics at the subnational level, this book eschews a monocausal explanation of why local opposition varies in its intensity and frequency. Instead, based on mobilization patterns for the period 2000–2015 in Korean and Japanese communities hosting twenty U.S. bases, I show that activists successfully build broad-based movements and mount significant opposition when they variously (1) exploit disruptions to the quotidian life in base towns; (2) adopt culturally resonant yet mundane movement frames; and (3) win endorsement— sometimes given enthusiastically and sometimes opportunistically—from

3 IVs → DV.
theory-proposing (not testing)

local elites. Whether and to what extent activists and latent adherents find common ground in these contexts determines the varying magnitude of contestation in host communities. What ultimately emerges from the disparate experiences of a wide range of host towns is the primacy of the local in antibase movements—that is, strong activist beliefs in building locally grounded campaigns against the world's mightiest military.

(1) **Status Quo Disruption:** The first finding of the book is that local challengers take advantage of volatility, rather than stasis, in the local life surrounding U.S. military bases. It is not the unvarying presence of military bases, but rather major disruptions to the status quo at long-standing bases, that sparks mobilization. In the Korean city of Daegu, Nam District residents on a bus along Route 1, for example, do not bother to look out the window when the bus pulls to a stop literally named the "8th U.S. Army"; for many, the three Army bases in the district blend into the background. However, when major changes occur to these long-standing installations, such as expansion, relocation, reduction, and closure, the American military monolith—as well as the quotidian life built around it—is suddenly rendered fluid. For base opponents, this sudden volatility presents both a threat that disrupts the normality in base towns and opportunities for oppositional mobilization. Although the "quotidian disruption" (Snow et al. 1998) may initially seem to be a threat that unravels the familiar status quo, there is an oft-overlooked temporal element that I argue makes it a fleeting source of opportunities: as the disruption of normality begins, activists are able to exploit a window of opportunity before the disruption becomes a possible new normal. While activists strive to keep the window open, they can peddle their causes more loudly and convincingly to a larger audience than usual. During this transitory period, mobilization peaks. Those harboring grievances often jump at the first hint of looming status quo disruption, perceiving it as an exceedingly rare opportunity—something of a "rupture" or a "crack" in the system (McAdam and Boudet 2012, 97)—to shape the future trajectory of the bases in motion.

While a status quo disruption of any kind shakes up the quotidian normality of base towns, it exhibits itself in two broad patterns with differing implications for mobilization. First, opponents mobilize against major disruptions that imply a more intrusive U.S. presence (e.g., base expansion), which allows them to newly emphasize grievances, deprivations, and the collective identity of host communities. The literature, with its tendency to focus on large-scale base contestation, has overwhelmingly focused on this first type of status disruption. Status changes, however, can occur in the opposite direction. When changes imply a less intrusive U.S. presence (e.g., base reduction), and when opponents positively evaluate status reduction as meaningful progress in addressing grievances, they demobilize. Albeit in the context of uneven power relations, opponents typically see base expansion as a loss, and base reduction as a gain. These dual patterns, meanwhile, come with a caveat: the perception of loss or gain is a relative—as opposed to an absolute—one. The magnitude of status quo changes, therefore, does not always correspond to that of local counter-responses.

(2) **Movement Framing**: The second finding is that activist discourses surrounding U.S. military bases are driven by rhetorical pragmatism, as opposed to ideological or nationalistic dogmatism. For all the stereotypes of angry anti-American protesters—imagine a burning effigy of George W. Bush, which did appear at some Korean protest events—local anti-base mobilization often revolves around surprisingly mundane matters. As the unlikely activists contesting the Rodriguez range remind us, ear-splitting noise and broken windows, rather than the purported evil empire, form the basis of everyday grievances in base towns. Accordingly, activists often focus on the everyday politics of how the global intrudes on local lives, thereby maximizing movement resonance both locally and nationally. Those contesting the Atsugi naval air base in Japan, for example, have made a conscious decision to cite noise pollution from the base as a reason to reject Japanese public broadcaster NHK's mandatory subscription fees; everybody understands that aircraft noise disturbs television watching, and everybody wants to avoid paying NHK. It is more difficult, by contrast, to mobilize people by describing the same noise pollution problem as an outcome of American imperialism and Japanese subservience.

Activists may be variously motivated by nationalism, pacifist ideology, and pragmatism in their opposition (Calder 2007, 84), but they are usually mindful of the varying efficacy of their rhetorical strategies. Playing up pragmatic grievances associated with bases, instead of fanning the flames of nationalistic or ideological convictions, proves to be a more effective strategy in facilitating local anti-base mobilization. In this sense, anti-base activists as frame entrepreneurs deviate from the rhetorical tendency of other aggrieved local actors to globalize their local grievances (Gordon and Jasper 1996; Bob 2005; Tsutsui 2017). This rhetorical pragmatism—or deliberate parochialism—serves as a rhetorical safe haven for activists, since their seemingly radical agenda of challenging the U.S. military, and thereby challenging a critical pillar of national security, becomes something more neutral, cool-headed, and palatable when couched in the language of the everyday.

A caveat, however, is warranted: this rhetorical safe haven, while effective for greater mobilization involving latent adherents and more tolerable to the authorities, can also become a rhetorical trap. Pragmatic framing on the part of activists is bound to invite pragmatic solutions from policymakers, which inadvertently precludes the kind of radical changes to which many activists aspire. Pragmatism will get broken windows fixed, for example, but it stops short of mounting more fundamental challenges against the world's most powerful military. By limiting the realm of possibilities to practical, everyday issues, pragmatic framing risks inviting changes that are, at best, incremental and cosmetic. Rhetorical pragmatism, in this sense, inadvertently preserves the very power relations that activists strive to subvert (e.g., Gaventa 1982).

(3) **Local Elite Allies:** The third finding is that activists strategically court local political elites, who occasionally emerge as surprisingly influential veto players in interstate base politics. While the default instinct of local elites (e.g., mayors) is to stay away from base politics, once involved, they intensify base opposition in the localities they govern. Elite involvement signals to fence-sitters that the locally elected representatives endorse anti-base causes, which instantly legitimates the movement in the eyes of latent adherents. Furthermore, local elite dissent often evolves into a conflict between the central and the local government, which in turn broadens the scope of the base conflict and turns it into a broader question of local autonomy and democracy (Mulgan 2000). Winning elite support, in this sense, reinforces the primacy of the local. In Okinawa, Japan, the alliance between activists and their local representatives—and the rare contest between Okinawa and Tokyo that can ensue as a result—should be at least partially credited for the resilient opposition to the construction of a Marine air facility in the northern city of Nago.

Elites, however, do not exist as a mere background for activists; they have their own agency, preferences, and interests (Jasper 2006, 5). Some are opportunists, who co-opt the movement by capitalizing on local grievances as political leverage in their negotiations with the central government. Some of them actively refuse to ally with traditional "leftist" activist groups—purported troublemakers with supposedly radical demands—and instead cherry-pick conservative civic groups for top-down, rather than bottom-up, anti-base mobilization. The opportunists, by using the movement for their parochial interests and moderating movement goals, help perpetuate, rather than unravel, the status quo (McAdam 1982). This risk of co-optation seems higher for communities that lack a tradition of strong civic opposition, furthering their quiescence. Even when local elites become loyal movement allies, these elite enthusiasts are not always a boon for the anti-base movement in the long run. As the enthusiasts embrace the uncompromising stances that devoted activists demand of the elites, local elite dissent invites retaliation from the central government. The ensuing local-central conflict galvanizes anti-base devotees but alienates bystanders over time, eventually turning the latter against the anti-base cause. Dedicated elite allies, in this sense, can inadvertently invite community polarization and erode the kind of broad-based local support that activists sought to attain by courting elites in the first place.

The common thread linking these mechanisms is the agency of the central actors in subnational base politics—activists, latent adherents, and local political elites—as they shape base-community relations and their many twists and turns. Focusing on their agency offers a departure from an overly structuralist account of social movement studies (Jasper 2006). Activists do not respond reactively when status changes are imposed on them; rather, they are alert to and act on mobilization opportunities, often pre-emptively. Local residents are not just spectators of anti-base protests; their presence forces activists to adjust their strategies. Latent adherents' often reluctant support determines whether there can be a relatively broad-based campaign. Local elites, for their parts, are much more than a backdrop; not only do they respond to activist overtures in a calculating way, but the nature of their involvement also shapes responses from the central government. At first glance, these actors appear to be natural allies. They can point to each other, for example, to claim the legitimacy of anti-base causes, which might then help them gain something useful—policy changes for base opponents and votes for elites, among others. In reality, however, they join hands only occasionally, which is when broad-based mobilization becomes possible.

Country Selection

Korea and Japan

I look at social forces within Korea and Japan, the two treaty-bound U.S. allies without which America's status as a Pacific power cannot be sustained.

Together, they host nearly 40 percent of the officially acknowledged U.S. military installations overseas: 83 and 121 sites, respectively, out of the global total of 514 (Department of Defense 2018). The importance of U.S. forward presence in Korea and Japan is likely to endure, given their proximity to the largest U.S. rival: China.

These countries offer instructive cases in contentious base politics, as they remain loyal allies at the interstate level and yet are prone to ebbs and flows in local protests—including militant protests against some of the most strategically important American bases overseas. With Korea's wartime operational control in the hands of Washington and with Japan's constitution banning the country's remilitarization, the two Asian allies are arguably more dependent on U.S. security commitments than any other allied nations. As American overseas bases are routinely touted as "living proof of the American commitment" (Hincks 2018), base opponents in Korea and Japan face a particularly hostile environment. Still, both countries have seen social movement groups contest the U.S. presence, sometimes for decades. Indeed, defense analysts have voiced concerns over "sustained and serious public opposition" in Korea and Japan (Lostumbo et al. 2013, 105), and some even worry about losing basing rights as a result (Erickson and Mikolay 2012, 83). This contrasts with Germany and Italy, the two other major U.S. base hosts, where relations between the U.S. military and host populations are less conflictual (Rassbach 2010, 127; Nexon and Wright 2007, 267).

The temporal scope of 2000–2015 coincides with the global repositioning of U.S. forces beginning in the early 2000s, or "the most sweeping changes in the U.S. military posture abroad in half a century" (Campbell and Ward 2003, 95). These changes affected a host of U.S. military base towns across Korea and Japan at roughly the same time, creating a unique opportunity to trace their local consequences. The period also ensures that the countries under examination are affluent democracies that have long maintained stable, institutionalized bilateral alliance partnerships with the United States. Established democracies, scholars argue, make the best base hosts when compared to either transitioning democracies (Cooley 2008) or autocracies (Pettyjohn and Kavanagh 2016). Similarly, alliances as an institution often guarantee stable relationships among the member states (C. J. Kim 2021a). From an ideational point of view, Korea and Japan are enduring security partners whose strategic priorities remain fundamentally in synch with those of the United States (Yeo 2011). In particular, a nuclear North Korea and an assertive China are persistent sources of security concerns for all three parties, which reinforces the consensus on the need to maintain the U.S. presence in the region. American foreign and defense policies as they apply to the region, such as the "Pivot to Asia" and the "Indo-Pacific" as the latest geostrategic buzzwords, similarly influence the two host nations.

And yet, despite these similarities, localities within these countries have exhibited varying levels of anti-base protests. The micro-level approach I take illustrates varieties of base contestation within a given country that is both an established democracy and a faithful security partner, with key external conditions, such as democracy, national wealth, institutionalized alliances, and the enduring presence of external security threats, held constant. While my primary focus is on mobilization outcomes (i.e., protest levels), rather than movement outcomes (i.e., basing policy outcomes), the longitudinal scope of the book allows us to follow movement cycles—as movements arise, peak, and dissipate—along with their varying influence on policy.

A Brief History of U.S. Military Bases in Korea and Japan

How did these bases come about in Korea and Japan, and why did they crop up in some places but not in others? Military bases on foreign soil are often the spoils of war, and those in Korea and Japan encapsulate both the contingency and the path-dependency of military basing. World War II, an important watershed for the rise of the United States as a peerless "base nation" (Vine 2015), subjected these two Asian nations with widely disparate trajectories—the colonized and the colonizer—to the same fate: U.S. military occupation. The Korean War, which transformed both into staunch U.S. Cold War allies, solidified and legitimized U.S. forward deployment in Asia (Calder 2007, 21–25). Despite drastic political, economic, and social changes in Korea and Japan over time, the U.S. presence has persisted for more than seven decades with remarkable stability, shaping not only the historical trajectories of the host states but also the lives of countless people in host communities.

The origins of the imposing American presence in Korea, however, seem more accidental than planned in nature. In the immediate aftermath of World War II, Americans intended to oversee the Japanese surrender in Korea, rather than build permanent military outposts there. Washington rushed to assume the task in the South, with troops arriving at the port of Incheon on September 8, 1945, in what their commander called a "scramble move" (Cumings 2011, 104). For Koreans south of the 38th Parallel, the American arrival meant that they had to watch the Japanese flag at the Office of the Governor-General of Korea, the headquarters of the Japanese colonial government in Seoul, simply replaced with the American flag. Yongsan Garrison in Seoul, once home to the Japanese following the Russo-Japanese War, saw its occupants replaced with the U.S. Seventh Infantry Division. The U.S. Army Military Government in Korea became "the only lawful government," thwarting aspirations of self-determination by the Provisional Korean Government (H. Kim 1988). Some 70,000 American troops were initially stationed in this strange, foreign land, where mutual contempt characterized the daily interactions between the new occupiers and the long occupied (Matray 1995; Stueck and Yi 2010). Some Americans, including Franklin D. Roosevelt, thought the occupation should last for forty years. The prevailing anti-imperialist sentiments in the aftermath of the war, coupled with pleas to bring American troops back home, however, meant that it would last only for three years (Immerwahr 2019, 232–34). Following the establishment of the first postwar Korean government in the South and the Soviet withdrawal from the North in 1948, Americans left the country in 1949, leaving behind 500 military advisors.

The departure proved to be short-lived, however, with the outbreak of the Korean War in 1950 spurring Washington's rise as a basing power in Korea. North Korea's surprise attack in June 1950, which gave the peninsula sudden geostrategic importance in the context of the emerging Cold War competition, resulted in the influx of more than 320,000 American troops and the construction of new bases. Once the war ended with a ceasefire and a divided peninsula, the bases stayed, many of them standing between the land border with North Korea—the most heavily guarded border in the world—and the capital city of Seoul. Uijeongbu, Dongducheon, Pocheon—three cities in northern Gyeonggi with some of the heaviest U.S. presence—were all crucial battlegrounds during the war, acting as the roadblocks in North Korea's advance to Seoul. In southern Gyeonggi, what eventually became Osan Air Base was constructed after the famous Battle of Bayonet Hill. Americans also took over many former Japanese military outposts. Kunsan Air Base in Gunsan used to be a branch of Japan's Kamikaze-training Tachiarai army flight school (Allied Geographical Section, South West Pacific Area 1945). Camp Humphreys, the largest U.S. overseas base today, was once a Japanese airfield (Pyeongtaek City 2018). Combined, these bases occupied some 73,000 acres of land (*Hankyoreh* 1988).

Where American bases ended up in Korea, therefore, was determined largely by the necessities of the unforeseen war and the expediency of Japanese colonial residues. While eight combat divisions were reduced to two immediately after the conflict, and then to one during the Nixon years, the fundamental force structure of U.S. Forces Korea remained grounded in the experience of the Korean War (Roehrig 2014, 69–70). It is not so surprising, then, that American policymakers and military officials came to view the U.S. force posture in the country as a "glaring anachronism" (Campbell and Ward 2003, 99). By the early 2000s, various policymakers and military officials, including Secretary of Defense Donald Rumsfeld, began to bemoan U.S. bases in Korea for being "virtually frozen" where they were during the bygone days of the Korean conflict, "all over the place," and "antiquated and inefficient" (Roehrig 2014, 73–75). This assessment, coupled with the global initiative to reposition U.S. forces abroad in response to 9/11, led to major plans to relocate, close down, and expand some of these longstanding bases—the reverberations of which are still felt throughout Korea (see chapter 2).

In neighboring Japan, the U.S. occupation began when General Douglas MacArthur, as the Supreme Commander for the Allied Powers, descended on what was a Kamikaze-training base built just seven years prior by the Japanese Imperial Navy. As the Kamikaze base transitioned to Naval Air Facility (NAF) Atsugi, the U.S. military took over numerous other Japanese military facilities, both immediately after World War II and during the Korean War (Hayashi 2012). For example, Camp Zama, home to the U.S. Army Japan, sits on the site of the Japanese Imperial Military Academy. Yokosuka Naval Arsenal and Sasebo Naval Arsenal of the Imperial Japanese Navy became Commander Fleet Activities (CFA) Yokosuka and CFA Sasebo, respectively. In Okinawa, where one third of the population perished in the 1945 Battle of Okinawa, including those who followed Tokyo's order to commit suicide, locals were released from detention camps only to see their homes destroyed for base construction and expansion. A Japanese airfield created just before the battle was immediately captured by the Americans and evolved into Kadena Air Base. What is now Marine Corps Air Station (MCAS) Futenma was also constructed at that time with an attack on the mainland in mind, although Japan's subsequent surrender made it redundant (Shimoji 2011). The Korean War, "a gift of the gods" in the words of Yoshida Shigeru and "divine aid" according to the Bank of Japan chief (Immerwahr 2019, 361), confirmed the usefulness of Japan as a rear base and "established . . . the basic profile of

U.S. bases" (Calder 2007, 24). Okinawans, who would find themselves under America rule until 1972, recall the massive U.S. base expansion at the time with the expression "bayonets and bulldozers," alluding to the forcible nature of large-scale land expropriation. Kadena Air Base, for example, was hastily expanded during the war to accommodate the formerly Guam-based 19th Bombardment Group.

By the time the U.S. occupation of Japan proper ended in 1952, 2,824 American installations occupied some 334,333 acres of land in mainland Japan; by 1959, after the departure of the Army in 1957, the number decreased to 83,027 acres (Koyama 2008, 6). Richard Nixon's initiatives to reduce the U.S. military presence in Asia, meanwhile, materialized in 1973 in the form of the Kanto Plain Consolidation Plan. The plan, which consolidated military bases and housing facilities in the increasingly urban and populous areas surrounding Tokyo, helped defuse anti-base sentiments on the mainland. For example, Tachikawa Air Base, the site of the fierce leftist anti-base resistance in the latter half of the 1950s, was one of the six major bases returned to Japan as part of the consolidation (Koyama 2008). As a result of this large-scale drawdown, former base towns in the mainland have found new identities. Few today remember that Roppongi, Harajuku, and Ginza, the flashy "centres of consumer culture" in Tokyo, were once home to American bases, barracks, and military housing (Yoshimi 2003).

Base reduction on the mainland, however, came at the cost of base concentration in Okinawa, a formerly an independent kingdom annexed by Japan in 1879. In the words of a former prime minister whose political career stalled over Okinawan base issues, it was "as if what is unwanted but necessary for the mainland could simply be carted away to Okinawa" (Interview, Hatoyma Yukio, June 19, 2017). But as implausible as it may sound today, Washington did not always envision a permanent base presence on Okinawa (Toriyama 2003). The amount of land occupied by U.S. bases in 1952 was actually 10.9 times larger in the mainland than in Okinawa (*Okinawa Times* 2019). However, as American rule continued in Okinawa—initially by the U.S. military government (1945–1950), followed by the U.S. civil administration (1950–1972)—the bases there also endured and expanded. With a flurry of base construction in the 1950s, the entire island of Okinawa, in the words of an American diplomat, turned into "one continuous American base"—a spectacle that "ha[s] to be seen to be believed" (Sarantakes 2000, 69). As the American occupation of Okinawa drew to an end by 1972, 87 U.S. installations stood on 70,822 acres of the land, accounting for 58.7 percent of all land used by the U.S. military in Japan (Okinawa Prefectural Government 2017, 6). Despite the promise of "*hondonami*" at the time of Okinawa's reversion to Japan, which meant that the U.S. presence in this formerly occupied territory would shrink to the mainland levels, quite the opposite happened. By 2007, the number stood at 74.3 percent of the national total (Okinawa Prefectural Government 2008). The American footprint has since declined, although not as much as base opponents would have liked: the latest number stands at 33 installations and 46,229 acres of the land in Okinawa, or 70 percent of the land used by the U.S. military nationwide (Okinawa Prefectural Government 2020). Despite some reductions in recent years, Okinawa, which makes up 0.6 percent of the Japanese territory, continues to shoulder a disproportionately heavy "base burden" (*kichi futan*). Political—if lackadaisical—commitments to reducing this localized burden, coupled with strategic initiatives to realign the U.S. force posture throughout Japan, propel the changing configuration of American military bases in the country.

As these bases in Korea and Japan persist, the international threat environment has evolved and presented the U.S. military with new missions. In the face of China's increasing military assertiveness, the U.S. presence has a new-found role as a stabilizer—an "arbiter play[ing] a policing role" (Christensen 1999, 50). North Korea's nuclear and missile capabilities remain another perennial source of security threats, which in turn encourages Korea and Japan to bolster their military capabilities not just independently but also jointly with the United States (Hughes 2009). In this context, the American rebalance to Asia reinforces the status quo where much of the American supremacy in the region—and the stability it purportedly ensures—depend on its alliance ties and forward basing (Glaser 2015). As Korea continues to look to Washington for reassurances about the uncertain future of the Korean peninsula, and as Japan pushes the boundaries of its antimilitarist norms as an increasingly active American military partner, the bases are here to stay for the foreseeable future. And as they stand as semi-permanent fixtures in host communities, many base town residents are bound for—and increasingly born into—a life alongside them.

Key Actors in Subnational Base Politics

While interstate basing decisions are a product of international security, their physical manifestation on foreign soil makes them a domestic political issue.

Contentious politics surrounding American military bases abroad thus involves international, national, and subnational actors, including basing and host nations, central and local governments, host community residents, and activists. The following actors—with base opponents and local elites as central actors, and the rest in the background—shape the subnational base politics in Korea and Japan today.

(1) **Base Opponents**: I use this term to describe people who oppose U.S. military bases, either individually or as part of a group, and either as a full-time occupation or on a voluntary basis. The term incorporates both activists (i.e., those fully committed to acting upon the cause) and latent adherents (i.e., those who may occasionally join in opposition). Large-scale mobilization becomes possible when activists and latent adherents come together. The relative rarity of broad-based mobilization in turn attests to the difficulty of turning latent adherents into active opponents.

(1-1) **Activists**: Activists hold deep convictions about anti-base causes and publicly express their views in various forms, including protests, marches, sit-ins, lawsuits, and petitions. Some build their entire professional careers around opposing bases; for example, Korea's Base Peace Network (Giji pyeonghwa neteuwokeu), a loose network of five civic groups in Seoul, Gunsan, Pyeongtaek, and Uijeongbu, consists of full-time career activists. Japanese anti-base activism involves more grassroots organizations and non-career activists, but centralized professional organizations with explicit partisan allegiances do exist: the Japan Peace Committee, affiliated with the Japan Communist Party (JCP), and the Peace Movement Center, affiliated with the Social Democratic Party (SDP), both of which boast local branches throughout the country. Still, the very physical presence of bases in local communities means that these activists are mostly locally based themselves. Some are born-and-raised natives or have lived in base towns for decades, while others are transplants. What constitutes "local," though, can be ambiguous at times. A Seoul-based activist on a mission to stop the expansion of a firing range in the Korean city of Paju, for example, once spent two years farming alongside locals in a rural village (Interview with Park Seok-jin, June 22, 2016). In Pyeongtaek, where a militant movement emerged in the mid-2000s against base expansion, dozens of activists officially moved their legal residence to the city to resist eviction. Although critics of anti-base activists like to cast these voluntary transplants as outside agitators, their very presence further attests to the primacy of the local in anti-base activism.

Variously motivated by nationalism, pacifist ideology, and practical concerns (Calder 2007, 84), activists assign different meanings to the imposing U.S. presence. Some explained to me that military bases are a militarist tool intended ultimately to "kill people," and others told me that they are proof that "Japan is a slave of the United States." These ideational differences, to be sure, do not necessarily preclude a coalitional movement; a national umbrella coalition against the expansion of Camp Humphreys in Pyeongtaek, for example, brought together activists of all stripes—indignant nationalists, visionary pacifists, and clear-eyed pragmatists. In propagating their anti-base beliefs, though, activists are mindful of the local resonance of such beliefs. In the words of one Korean activist, anti-base movements driven exclusively by professional activists, and not by "those who suffer the most," cannot sustain themselves; activists, in this sense, see their role as something limited to "helping" latent adherents "take ownership" of the movement (Interview with Kim Pan-tei, June 15, 2016). In order to play this facilitating (if slightly paternalistic) role, activists serve as strategic frame entrepreneurs and filter out the kind of language that may alienate fellow local residents. Activists' framing choices can therefore deviate from their true motivation: those spurred into action by radical anti-militarist beliefs, for example, may still find it easier to talk about tangible everyday grievances to mobilize the local communities.

(1-2) **Latent Adherents**: U.S. military bases elicit a complex set of images and emotions in the minds of base town residents. Sometimes bases violently assert themselves into host communities, such as when a U.S. F-8 Crusader jet, en route to NAF Atsugi from Kadena Air Base, crashed and killed four civilians in 1964. Other times they insinuate themselves into the daily lives of local residents, as the Spam luncheon meat spotted in the local cuisine in Okinawa and Uijeongbu attest. Even the latest global pandemic linked U.S. forces to their host populations: American personnel, who continued to travel for their assignments in Pyeongtaek and Okinawa since pandemic-induced border shutdowns meant little to them, became part of the local Covid-19 statistics.

Base town residents may hold grievances about the U.S. presence, but they seldom get involved. Despite the belief that we live in a "movement society" where protests have become a routine part of conventional politics (Meyer and Tarrow 1997), many non-activists, suspicious of activists and their agenda, remain reluctant to get involved (Luke et al. 2018). In localities where many small businesses cater to the U.S. military, such as Korea's

Dongducheon or northern Pyeongtaek, anti-base proselytizing gets particularly tricky. "You may be able to demand a wholesale troop withdrawal in places without bases," says Lee Cheol-hyeong, a longtime Pyeongtaek activist. "But you can't do that in base towns. Locals get immediately skeptical" (Interview, June 18, 2016). In rural areas with elderly, conservative residents—downtown Gunsan might be a bustling shopping district, for example, but Okseo, a county abutting Kunsan Air Base, is a sleepy town heavily populated by the elderly—activists also tread carefully to fend off suspicions.

On rare occasions when social movement skeptics do mobilize, they portray their participation as a "reluctant" and "accidental" one (Gullion 2015; Arrington 2016; Luke et al. 2018). It is hardly surprising, then, that when latent adherents join anti-base movements, their opposition is often about a wide range of negative externalities military bases entail, rather than about American global hegemony: noise pollution, environmental contamination, accidents involving U.S. personnel, and insufficient government compensation. The practical nature of these everyday grievances often forces activists to subordinate their aspirations for radical changes—"a world without the military," for example (Interview with Kang Sang-won, June 11, 2016)—to the more immediate, parochial goals that local residents pursue. In this sense, latent adherents are the ones who shape activist strategies, not the other way around—a finding that directly contradicts the frequent vilification of activists as agitators manipulating locals. But even then, some latent adherents still refuse to work with professional activists and instead form their own groups, often for fear that leftist politics will adulterate the supposed "purity" of local grassroots initiatives.

(2) **Local Political Elites**: Locals up in arms about U.S. military bases in their backyard often turn to their local—not national—representatives as a first resort, hoping for an intervention. Local governments are a channel of communication—what the Japanese would call *madoguchi* (literally, "window")—for residents who wish to file complaints against the U.S. military. In the Okinawan city of Nago, for example, residents can still register base-related grievances with the city office after hours by dialing a direct-dial emergency number; city officials, whose mobile phones are connected to the emergency number, respond swiftly to these requests, sometimes in the middle of the night (Interview with Nago officials, September 15, 2016).

Local elite support, however, is not easy to come by. Often, activists with maximalist goals and local elites prone to compromises fail to meet in the middle. Activists in Nago and the Korean city of Uijeongbu attempted to "recall" their pro-base mayors in 1998 and 2002, respectively, for the mayors' apparent willingness to countenance U.S. military consolidation. The name of one Nago-based grassroots group at the time, the Association of Citizens Angry at Mayor Kishimoto (Kishimoto shichō ni okkotteiru shimin no kai), bespeaks the frustration with the city government that chose to dismiss the 1997 anti-base referendum. Mutual hostility is not uncommon. Uijeongbu mayor Kim Mun-won, facing pressure to keep his election promise to hold an anti-base referendum, called the police on activists multiple times (Interview, anonymous, July 12, 2016).

While the first instinct of local elites is to stay away from base politics, they sometimes become anti-base claimants themselves—either after much courting from activists or on their own initiatives. As municipal governments oversee the administrative units where bases are located, mayors and governors can influence bureaucratic and technical aspects of bases when it comes to their construction, relocation, and operation. When Okinawa's late governor Ōta Masahide exercised his administrative authority and refused to grant land leases for U.S. bases in 1995, for example, Okinawan base issues quickly became politicized. Local elites' obstructions of the allies' basing policy often results in a conflict between the local and central governments, which creates elite cleavages that activists can exploit (even if ultimately to their detriment, as we shall see later). Base opponents in Japanese localities ranging from Iwakuni to Nago, for example, found their cause suddenly gain national and even international political salience when their mayors turned against base relocation. In rare instances, as in the Korean city of Dongducheon, local elites may actually be the ones leading mobilization in a top-down manner, as opposed to following activists. In typical Korean local government behavior, city-led anti-base initiatives mobilize politically conservative and pro-government—meaning noncontroversial—civic groups and exclude their traditional leftist—meaning controversial—counterparts. Elite preferences for politically moderate civic groups give activists another incentive to engage in impression management—and another reason that the movement's supposedly radical ideas are tamed, at least in their public presentation.

(3) **The Public**: The presence of oppositional mobilization does not equal the presence of general discontent. After all, the U.S. Osprey tiltrotor aircraft, a subject of universal antipathy among anti-base activists, boasts a "fan club" in none other than Okinawa—the place most frequently associated with anti-base sentiments. In Seoul's Gwanghwamun, the political center of the

country that is also home to the U.S. embassy, no one bats an eye at the sight of a gathering of anti-American activists just a stone's throw away from another gathering of pro-American Korean War vets with a banner reading, in English, "Thanks Runs Forever." At Camp Humphreys, once a magnet for protesters, many of whom are sympathetic to North Korea, a large banner makes a plea: "Bomb North Korea!"

Unfortunately for base opponents, they are destined to belong to a movement where the "goal orientations of reference publics depart significantly, in direction or intensity, from the goals of protest groups" (Lipsky 1968, 1146). Nationwide public opinion polls in both countries have shown a majority supporting the continued U.S. military presence. An annual poll in Korea between 2012 and 2019 showed consistent support—ranging from 67 to 82 percent—for a continued U.S. presence (Asan Institute for Policy Studies 2019). Even in 2003, a survey that came on the heels of mass protests over a U.S. military accident that killed two teenagers showed an absolute majority holding favorable views of the United States (Moon 2012, 20). In Japan, various polls indicate a general acceptance of the U.S. presence, although clear divisions exist between mainlanders and Okinawans (NHK Broadcasting Culture Research Institute 2017). Even when we set aside the issue of the U.S. military, the Japanese public's apparent aversion to social movements, which some allege borders on "phobia" (Higuchi 2021), bodes ill for activists. The public, in this sense, serves as an important background actor that further informs activist strategies.

(4) **Host State Governments**: Host state governments—Korea and Japan in this study—facilitate the continued U.S. presence, widely considered an effective deterrent against North Korea and, increasingly, China. The two longtime U.S. allies are something of poster children for American interventionalist expansionism: stories of the former's rags-to-riches success and the latter's militarist-to-pacifist transformation serve to highlight salubrious aspects of American foreign policy, of which the forward military presence is an integral part.

The anti-base cause will rarely find a vocal champion among national political elites. The United States and its military loom disproportionately large in the worldview of host state political elites, almost as if Washington constitutes the entirety of foreign relations. From Syngman Rhee's fixation with extracting U.S. security commitments in the form of a military alliance to the continued pleas to delay the transfer of wartime operational control that remains in the hands of Washington, Korean elites remain faithful to the

American presence that they associate with security and prosperity. From the Yoshida doctrine of postwar security dependence to the increasing military ambition synchronized with the U.S. regional strategy, Japanese elites dutifully follow the rules set by their erstwhile enemy. It is unthinkable today, for example, that the term *dōmei* (alliance) was once such a loaded term in the context of Japan's imposed anti-militarism that Japanese leaders actively avoided using it to describe U.S.-Japan relations until the 1990s (McCormack and Norimatsu 2012, 63).

As an agent of the U.S. military, host states are tasked with ensuring the continued cooperation of subnational localities. Although they increasingly feel compelled to seek local consent, such consent is often little more than a formality. Many base-related decisions follow the "decide-announce-defend" model (O'Hare, Bacow, and Sanderson 1983), in which the allies announce their decisions and then seek local understanding after the fact. What base scholars call compensation politics (Cooley and Marten 2006; Calder 2007) comes into the picture here, as the central government dangles monetary rewards—and the threat to withdraw them—in front of the financially vulnerable localities. Some get carrots, and others get sticks. Residents of Okseo, a rural county bordering Kunsan Air Base in the Korean city of Gunsan, frequent a public bathhouse and a small library housed together in a community building named *soeum pihae bokjihoegwan*—literally, "a welfare facility built as consideration for noise pollution." Iwakuni residents saw a similar community hall built in the 1970s when U.S. bases in Japan served as a launchpad for the Vietnam War. More recently, though, they found themselves on the receiving end of the stick when the state subsidies earmarked for a half-built city office building evaporated as a punishment for the mayor's opposition to the fortification of MCAS Iwakuni. Conversely, local governments may actively protest bases in the hope of extracting financial concessions from the central government. Pocheon, home to the Rodriguez firing range, is demanding a new subway line connecting the city to Seoul, citing the heavy American presence as a cause of the stagnant local economy. The host states, facing these varying local interests, continue to cajole and threaten as they seek to protect the most conspicuous symbol of U.S. security commitments.

(5) **Basing State (U.S.)**: U.S. basing rights in Korea and Japan are codified in the two separate mutual defense treaties originating from the Korean War and World War II, respectively. Despite a few moments of disturbance—such as Jimmy Carter's attempt in 1977 to withdraw all troops from Korea, and the

mass movement that resisted the renewal of the U.S.-Japan security treaty in 1960—the alliances and the U.S. military presence they institutionally guarantee remain incredibly stable. State visits by American presidents are newsworthy anywhere, but such visits to Korea and Japan often involve their grand appearances at major American bases—a home away from home. On his 2019 visit to Korea's Osan Air Base, Donald Trump walked out of Marine One to greet the cheering crowd of troops, with Lee Greenwood's song "God Bless the USA" playing in the background: "I'm proud to be an American where at least I know I'm free."

American base officials rarely, if ever, interact directly with base opponents (Yeo 2011, 25). As those familiar with base-community relations say of protesters at Yongsan Garrison: "What happens at Gate 3 is outside (the USFK's) jurisdiction" (Interview, anonymous, June 23, 2016). At the same time, the U.S. military exclusively oversees what goes on behind fences, although host communities often bear the brunt of such extraterritoriality. In one such example, information obtained through the Freedom of Information Act (FOIA) shows that there were eighty-four cases of oil leaks at Yongsan Garrison between 1990 and 2015, most of which were never reported to Korea (Green Korea United 2017). Separate FOIA requests demonstrate that members of the U.S. Marine Corps in Okinawa are advised not to inform the Japanese authorities of "nonemergency and/or politically sensitive incidents," such as environmental accidents (Mitchell 2016). Host communities, as a result, are left to quarrel over remediation and redevelopment of base sites, even after bases close and American troops leave (C. J. Kim 2018). Most recently, as national borders were shut down amid the global pandemic, American troops proved that such borders, for them at least, remain porous. As troops continued to relocate to Korea and Japan, they shaped local health dynamics. On August 5, 2020, for example, 121 of 161 infection cases counted in Pyeongtaek were traced back to the USFK (Pyeongtaek City 2020). The conduct of the U.S. military, formulated internationally and implemented locally, has ripple effects on host communities in myriad ways.

Figure 1.1 illustrates how activists, latent adherents, and local political elites engage in their anti-base claims-making. Far from being natural allies, they come together only occasionally; the intersection of the three circles thus holds the most potential for broad-based anti-base mobilization. The thick arrows indicate the direction of claims on the part of these actors. They may press their claims against the U.S. military, such as when they stage rallies

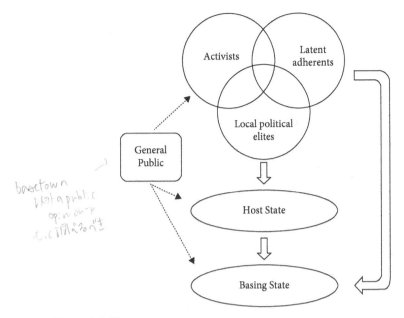

Figure 1.1 Key actors

in front of the bases or deliver letters to base officials; although, as mentioned above, the U.S. military rarely interacts directly with the protesters. They also direct their demands to the host state government, such as when they sue the central government for compensation for noise pollution at American air bases. The dotted arrows indicate the direction of influence that comes from the general public, whose opinion occasionally influences the behavior of anti-base actors as well as that of the host state and the U.S. military.

Plan of the Book

In the pages that follow, I draw on fieldwork interviews, participant observation, and protest event data to illustrate how these key actors shape the trajectories of base towns across Korea and Japan. Chapter 2 lays out theoretical grounds for the varying contexts in which activists and latent adherents come together. It also offers an overview of the political, historical, and social contexts of Korea and Japan in which anti-base contentions occur. Chapters 3, 4, and 5 illustrate the ebbs and flows in protest mobilization as they correspond to each of the three contextual factors, respectively: exploiting moments of disruption in base towns; relying on deliberately parochial rhetoric; and courting local elites whose political calculations diverge from their own. The concluding chapter discusses dilemmas facing activists: while their strategies do help them build a more broad-based movement, such choices may still come with unintended consequences in the long run. The book ends with a prediction for the future of base-community relations in Korea and Japan. Ultimately, the landscape of contentious base politics portrayed in this book contextualizes and adds nuance to two familiar narratives surrounding the U.S. military presence overseas: the narrative of seamless alliance management, which writes off local discontent, and the narrative of beleaguered American outposts, which fails to capture the much more varied experiences of base towns.

2

Explaining Protest (De)mobilization

U.S. military bases dotting Korea and Japan, the two pillars of the U.S. Indo-Pacific Command, have witnessed waves of protest mobilization and de-mobilization at their gates. Between 2000 and 2015, bases in such disparate places as Iwakuni, Pyeongtaek, and Zama saw a sudden surge, and then a steep drop, in local protests. Other American outposts in Dongducheon, Uijeongbu, and Seoul, meanwhile, experienced a general abatement in contestation. Still others in Jinhae, Gotemba, and Pohang remained practically invisible. These trends in part corresponded to the evolving profile of American military outposts during the same period: many bases were on the move, leaving their longtime hosts behind and imposing themselves on new communities. Many others, to the dismay of some residents and the delight of others, stayed put. Activists throughout Korea and Japan almost unanimously attempted to influence the fate of these bases in motion. At the same time, some seasoned activists left the protest scene, while others became newly involved. Some of them sought to rethink their strategies to boost dwindling interest in anti-base causes, whereas others did not seem particularly troubled by their increasing political isolation. Local political elites occasionally rose to fame for their unusually strong anti-base views; but many remained aloof.

Existing explanations of the contentious politics of U.S. military bases abroad, which focus on regime types, robust alliance ties with the U.S., and enduring regional security threats, do not account for these variegated local experiences. Instead, I look at shifting local contexts that base opponents exploit to build an opposition campaign, which sometimes balloons into a sizable anti-base movement and sometimes fizzles out. Of all the base towns subjected to potential mobilization attempts (McAdam and Boudet 2012), those that mount significant challenges to the formidable symbol of American military might are the ones where activists and latent adherents manage to join hands.

Base Towns. Claudia Junghyun Kim, Oxford University Press. © Oxford University Press 2023.
DOI: 10.1093/oso/9780197665275.003.0002

Explaining Anti-Base (De)mobilization

Conceptualizing Local Anti-Base Opposition

The disparate municipality-level and movement-specific contexts that activists use to their advantage speak to the complicated social processes, relationships, and strategic dilemmas inherent in collective action. Major changes to long-standing bases are an externally imposed, structural condition that base opponents must confront. Movement framing, on the other hand, comes out of decision-making processes internal to the movement, albeit under certain external constraints. Local elite allies arise from a confluence of factors both external and internal to the movement. In looking at how base opponents exploit these dissimilar contextual factors, I respond to the call by social movement scholars to depart from an overly structuralist account of social movement studies and instead highlight actors and their agency (Jasper 2006). Status quo disruption may be externally given, but activists are the ones who seize on these status changes to mobilize opposition. The window of opportunity associated with status disruption does not automatically open, nor does it stay open; activists have to make use of the window and fight—if often unsuccessfully—to extend it. When it comes to movement frames, activists debate the varying resonance of different frames and sometimes strategically subordinate their proclivities for more radical rhetoric to latent adherents' preference for moderation. Local elites have their own agency, and their interests may or may not align with those of the activists. In exploiting these contextual factors to their advantage, activists practice the primacy of the local—the cardinal principle in anti-base activism—by seeking common ground with other base town residents and building broad-based mobilization. Activists are neither completely powerless in influencing base politics, nor are they the sole determinant of base dynamics.

In the following pages, I discuss each of the three contextual factors by situating them in the social movement literature and then in the context of Korean and Japanese politics and society. There is no distinctive hierarchical order to the three factors in terms of causal significance; the book posits an additive relationship in which the presence of more factors results in greater contestation. As detailed in the appendix, the magnitude of oppositional mobilization—the outcome of interest—is based on the aggregated protest turnout for 2000–2015, as opposed to protest frequency, although the latter will be referenced throughout the book.

Status Quo Disruption

Major changes to long-standing U.S. military bases represent the disruption of taken-for-granted normality in host communities, or what social movement scholars call "quotidian disruption" (Snow et al. 1998). Although long-standing bases blend into everyday life in host communities (Enloe 2014, 132–33; Lutz 2009, 32), bases in motion—those that expand, scale down, relocate, and close—disrupt preexisting expectations established around them.

Social movement scholars typically view quotidian disruption as a source of threat that provokes oppositional mobilization seeking the status quo ante (Snow et al. 1998). More recently, scholars have begun to see quotidian disruption as a source of both threat and opportunity (McAdam et al. 2010). Despite this structural account, activists do not simply react to such disruption; instead, its influence on social movement dynamics depends on whether and how activists seize on and exploit this external shock. In the context of base politics, such major changes as base expansion and relocation come as a result of interstate decisions—something imposed on local actors from above. Local opponents, rather than merely respond reactively to this imposition, proactively and preemptively organize against the changes in the offing. They do so because status changes render the established order "flexible and vulnerable to the political assaults of excluded groups" (Eisinger 1973, 28), offering a rare moment in which the structural conditions sustaining American military bases—heretofore semi-permanent fixtures in local communities—suddenly become fluid. Activists seize on this "crack in the system—an opportunity of some kind" (McAdam and Boudet 2012, 97) and organize opposition. Opposition in this context often has an emotional element: as sudden changes to one's familiar surroundings arouse "feelings of dread and anger," activists strive to channel the former into the latter, and the latter into collective action (Jasper 1997, 106–7).

An undertheorized temporal element in quotidian disruption further highlights the role of activist agency in exploiting this structural condition. Disruption of normality, over time, becomes a new normal. Before the new normal sets in, the transitory period of disruption opens a window of opportunity, during which activists can newly emphasize preexisting grievances, or "highly salient deprivations" (Useem 1998, 227), with more immediacy and urgency (Meyer and Reyes 2009, 227). The timeline associated with the window of opportunity, however, means that such urgency has an eventual expiry date; activists therefore need to make use of this temporary political opening before it closes (Kingdon 1984). For this reason, once activists mobilize to take advantage of the short-lived fluidity, their next goal is to keep the window of opportunity open as long as possible. It is no coincidence, in this sense, that those opposing the construction of an offshore Marine facility in northern Okinawa have put forth a number of reasons—environmental damage, active earthquake fault lines, and the fragile seabed, among others— why the landfill required for the construction should stop. They have been effective in delaying, if not completely halting or undoing, the construction for more than twenty-five years.

To be sure, scholars have focused on only one type of status quo disruption, when in fact status disruption varies in nature. Major changes to military bases, in practice, do not only include the kind that implies a larger, more intrusive U.S. presence, such as base construction and expansion. They also include changes that herald a reduced, less obtrusive U.S. presence, such as relocation, partial reduction and retrieval, and closure. Newly salient deprivations in base host communities are a feature of base expansion, which represents a loss to base opponents. Conversely, base relocation, reduction, and closure that entail the removal or attenuation of specific sources of grievances represent a relative gain—albeit a gain still rooted in uneven power dynamics. As people generally fear losses more than they enjoy equivalent gains (Kahneman and Tversky 1979; Samuelson and Zeckhauser 1988), activists find it easier to mobilize more latent adherents over perceived losses, such as those provoked by base expansion, than over potential gains (Snow et al. 1998).

These patterns—base expansion and mobilization, and base reduction and demobilization—are in turn qualified by what McAdam (1982, 34) calls "variability in the subjective meanings that people attach to their 'objective' condition." People, after all, react differently to objectively similar deprivations; whether they act on deprivations depends on whether they perceive them to be serious enough to warrant resistance. In the context of base politics, opponents mobilize only when they perceive base expansion to be enough of a loss to merit costly organizing efforts and participation. Likewise, they have to see base reduction as an alleviation of key grievances, or a relative gain, to cease protest activities. As I go on to show in chapter 3, these perceptional differences explain why community responses to status disruptions do not neatly correspond to the magnitude of the physical changes they entail.

U.S. Base Realignment and Status Quo Disruption in Korea and Japan
American military bases in Korea and Japan, as detailed in the historical overview in chapter 1, find their origins in Japan's ultimately thwarted imperialism and the U.S.'s relentless expansionism. Once planted on foreign soil, these bases went on to shape countless local lives. As they took shape, bases destroyed existing communities and created new ones. As they stayed, they exerted violence and provided subsistence. Having survived historical exigencies, occasional political uncertainties, and bouts of popular anger, these long-standing U.S. outposts gradually came to be seen as permanent fixtures in host communities, blending into the background of everyday life.

Then the bases suddenly became fluid. As the international threat environment went through unanticipated changes, U.S. force posture evolved. The end of the Cold War triggered a review of U.S. forward posture, which resulted in closing down or handing over to host states some 60 percent of American overseas bases in the first half of the 1990s (U.S. Department of Defense 2004, 5). The shock of the 9/11 terrorist attacks added to the realignment initiatives in the early 2000s, culminating in the Global Defense Posture Review (GDPR) in 2004. Introduced by the George W. Bush administration, the GDPR sought to revamp the U.S. global defense posture and make American forces more agile in their responses to new security threats. This global mission—greater in scope than changes made to the U.S. military after the Vietnam War and the Cold War (Campbell and Ward 2003, 95)—involved major base reductions and consolidations in Europe and East Asia (Pettyjohn 2012, 87–91).

The geopolitical changes that necessitated the posture review brought about concrete local consequences in Korea and Japan. In Korea, where bases that stood frozen on former battlefields began to look grossly outdated for "twenty-first-century threats" (Campbell and Ward 2003, 99), U.S. force redistribution came in two forms. The first initiative, called the Land Partnership Plan (LPP), predates the GDPR but later merged with its goals: consolidating "tiny bases all over the place" that were becoming "very expensive, very inefficient, (and) completely unnecessary" (Interview with Robert G. Loftis, May 9, 2016). Under the 2002 LPP, the U.S. military pledged to reduce the number of major bases from forty-one to twenty-three by returning some 33,500 acres of occupied land, or around 55 percent of all land—60,775 acres as of 2002. In exchange for the substantial land return, Korea was to newly grant the U.S. military 1,260 acres of land. The authorities branded the LPP as a breakthrough in minimizing negative externalities of the U.S. footprint. Seoul's foreign ministry, for example, noted that the plan would "address longstanding (local) grievances" and contribute to "balanced regional development" (Ministry of Foreign Affairs of Republic of Korea 2002). The revised LPP in 2004, which fully embraced the GDPR, heralded even more dramatic changes: the plan now involved the southward reloca-tion of the Second Infantry Division (2ID) near the land border with North Korea. Even more land—totaling 42,208 acres—was set to return, but on the condition that some 2,850 acres of land in the city of Pyeongtaek, the relocation site some forty-three miles south of the capital, would be newly granted to the U.S. military. Officials celebrated the revised plan with similar rhetoric, stating that it would "greatly reduce inconveniences" in local host communities; the Pyeongtaek land to be given away, they explained, was "ap-propriately sized," all things considered (Sook Kim 2004).

The second, closely related initiative from 2004, named the Yongsan Relocation Plan (YRP), sought to move Yongsan Garrison, at the time home to the Eighth Army and the USFK headquarters, out of Seoul. Unlike the LPP, which embodied U.S. strategic priorities, the YRP at least partially reflected Korean political elites' long-standing wish to rid the densely populated me-tropolis of an obtrusive symbol of foreign dominance: the base, located in the heart of the nation's capital, saw the Chinese, the Japanese, and the Americans as its successive occupants in its storied history of over a century. The relocation initiative originated from the 1987 election pledge by Roh Tae-woo, which coincided with Korea's democratic transition. In an ironic parallel to North Korea's *Juche* (self-reliance) trope, Roh called for Yongsan Garrison's relocation in the name of *mijok jajon* (national self-reliance). The allies signed a memorandum of understanding to move the base to Pyeongtaek as early as 1990, only to see the North Korean nuclear crisis, coupled with the high costs associated with the move, sink the plan. When the relocation agenda resurfaced in the early 2000s, it aligned perfectly well with the GDPR, with Pyeongtaek as a new military hub slated to host both the 2ID and Yongsan Garrison. The allies used language similar to their ac-count of the LPP to describe the Yongsan deal, citing "efficient use of land" as a major justification for the move (Ministry of Foreign Affairs of Republic of Korea 2004). A plan to turn the post-relocation Yongsan site into a public park—once tentatively called *minjok gongwon* (the nation's park)—was long in the making. "We can now finally secure space in the urban center that will rival Central Park of New York City," a high-ranking foreign ministry official touted the idea (Sook Kim 2004).

While these changes provoked fierce parliamentary debates over their military and political implications, base town residents were more interested in the immediate impact on their lives. For them, the biggest implication of the LPP and the YRP was that multiple bases in Gyeonggi Province—Gyeonggi literally means an area surrounding Seoul—and Yongsan Garrison in Seoul were to relocate to Pyeongtaek, a city in southern Gyeonggi. The reshuffling was expected to shrink the U.S. footprint in northern Gyeonggi, where a disproportionately heavy U.S. Army presence served as a tripwire just below the border; 87 percent of the land granted to the U.S. military is located in Gyeonggi, with most bases located in the northern half (D. S. Kim 2010). The drawdown, however, came at the cost of a massive military buildup in Pyeongtaek, which already hosted Camp Humphreys and Osan Air Base. To accommodate the influx of troops, the two already obtrusive U.S. bases occupying this port city's southern and northern parts, respectively, had to expanded.

In Japan, a similar mixture of strategic imperatives and political considerations resulted in two U.S. force posture initiatives: a broad realignment of U.S. Forces Japan (USFJ) as part of the GDPR, and a separate plan dating back to the 1990s to scale down—although many activists reject this characterization—the American footprint in Okinawa. A 2005 report by the allies, titled *U.S.-Japan Alliance: Transformation and Realignment for the Future*, combined the two agendas. The authorities described the plan as an effort to increase interoperability between U.S. forces and the Japanese Self-Defense Forces (SDF) and "reduc[e] burdens on local communities, including those in Okinawa" (Ministry of Foreign Affairs of Japan 2005). Finalized plans, detailed in a 2006 report titled *United States–Japan Roadmap for Realignment Implementation*, reiterated the initiatives with some technical modifications. These changes, which came without much of a national debate, represented a quiet transformation of the U.S.-Japan relationship: the Cold War–era goal of defending Japan has been superseded by the new goal of supporting U.S. global military strategy (Frühstück 2007, 187).

In addition to consolidating forces at Camp Zama and MCAS Iwakuni, the blueprint included what was already an irritant for the alliance: moving MCAS Futenma, a highly contested base in central Okinawa, to northern Okinawa. The idea stems from the U.S.-Japan Special Action Committee on Okinawa (SACO), established in 1995 to mollify the Okinawans after the infamous rape of a twelve-year-old girl by three U.S. servicemen. The rape, to be sure, was only a trigger that inflamed long-standing grievances about the heavy concentration of U.S. bases on Okinawa, home to nearly one fourth of all U.S. military facilities and half the American personnel in Japan (see chapter 1). Ostensibly to alleviate Okinawa's "base burden," a 1996 SACO report concluded that Futenma, encircled by a dense population, should be replaced with a sea-based facility in a less populated area off the island's east coast (Ministry of Foreign Affairs of Japan 1996). Henoko, a coastal hamlet in the northern city of Nago, was chosen as the relocation site. This decision to relocate Futenma within Okinawa, not off the island as many had hoped, opened a can of worms, and the ever-elusive pursuit of the Futenma Relocation Facility (FRF) began. By 2005, the already unpopular relocation plan was included in the broader realignment agenda. The allies' 2005 report, calling Futenma's return "long-desired," demanded "acceleration" of its relocation to Henoko (Ministry of Foreign Affairs of Japan 2005). Today, more than twenty-five years after the initial SACO decision, the FRF project is still moving at a snail's pace while antagonizing just about all parties involved. A longtime observer of Okinawan base politics succinctly summarizes the dissonance among the three key actors involved in the FRF quagmire: "Okinawa looks at it politically, Japan thinks it's a policy issue, and the U.S. thinks it's an operational issue" (Interview with Robert D. Eldridge, June 12, 2017).

Movement Framing

Movements seeking to redress similar grievances can still yield different outcomes due to the different framing strategies that activists employ (Snow et al. 1986, 464–81). Social movement frames are a product of activist agency, as they construct and adjust the meaning they assign to social problems, often with the aim of maximizing the resonance of movement causes (Gamson and Meyer 1996; Rothman and Oliver 1999; McCammon et al. 2007).

Anti-base frames come in various flavors: nationalistic protests express indignation at the supposed breach of national sovereignty and ethnic unity; ideological protests invoke anti-militarist, pacifist ideals; and pragmatic protests challenge everyday grievances, such as pollution and crimes (Calder 2007, 84; C. J. Kim and Boas 2020). While these three framing strategies coexist in anti-base activism, a lot of anti-base rhetoric, it turns out, fails to live up to the stylized image of irate anti-American protesters ripping the Stars and Stripes apart and setting them alight. (This was not a particularly surprising sight in Korea back in 2002, when a fatal accident involving American soldiers ignited national anger.) Instead, most anti-base discourses are

almost deceptively mundane. As I show in chapter 4, protest discourses resonate better when they draw on humdrum, everyday local experiences, which
requires pragmatic, as opposed to dogmatic, rhetoric. Activists, therefore,
often subordinate their more radical aspirations to the pragmatic concerns of
latent adherents. In this sense, base opponents as frame entrepreneurs largely
defy the tendency of other aggrieved actors in the world to universalize their
local grievances for outside support (Bob 2005; Tsutsui 2017).

This deliberate rhetorical parochialism is partially a political necessity for
these marginalized political actors: with a focus on urgent, practical, immediately relatable concerns, base opponents, like many other activists leading
localized activism, can ward off accusations of ulterior political motives
(Gullion 2015, 115–16). Leftist-nationalist activists in Korea, for example,
routinely invite suspicions that they are far too sympathetic to the brutal
North Korean regime. Similarly, septuagenarian protesters in Okinawa face
accusations that they are politically motivated outsiders, or even worse,
Chinese stooges. In this sense, pragmatic frames facilitate impression management and better mobilize third-party support (Luke et al. 2018). At the
same time, rhetorical pragmatism is also a superior mobilization strategy
when compared to its two alternatives. It allows activists to tailor what may
appear to be an abstract, distant ideal to specific grievances in base towns
so as to have greater empirical credibility, relatability, and cultural resonance (Snow and Benford 1988, 208–11). The authorities can easily ignore
accusations made against the alleged evil empire, but they are forced to respond to charges of, for instance, a violation of environmental laws. Small
victories that pragmatic approaches occasionally attain, such as compensation for noise pollution, also prevent cynicism and defeatism endemic to
movements with distant goals.

At first glance, this conscious insularity seems to support one side of
the scholarly debate on the efficacy of social movement frames: some advocate for broader frames that supposedly have greater mobilization capacity (Gerhards and Rucht 1992, 580), whereas others tout specific,
well-articulated, and narrower frames that appeal to people's everyday
experiences (Snow and Benford 1992, 141; Cress and Snow 2000). The
beauty of rhetorical pragmatism, however, is also its pitfall—something
that scholars advocating for narrower frames neglect. As activists and
policymakers participate in, and continuously reinforce, rhetorical practices
constrained by deliberate pragmatism, they confine themselves to a narrow
discursive space where immediate grievances prevail over aspirations for

more fundamental changes—even when many activists are motivated by radical goals in the first place. Within the contours of base discourses shaped by pragmatism, activists may be able to address everyday grievances, such as fixing broken windows, but not distant goals, such as closing down the bases. Over time, pragmatic challenges become the only acceptable form of anti-base challenges that merit responses from the authorities, which helps perpetuate, rather than subvert, the entrenched power relations (Gaventa 1982). Therein lies the dilemma facing activists: subordinating their maximalist aspirations to the more immediate grievances of latent adherents for the sake of broad-based mobilization may ultimately defeat the original purpose of their activism.

Origins of Anti-Base Frames in Korea and Japan

In the following pages, I situate the three predominant rhetorical approaches that activists adopt—those that variously emphasize nationalism, anti-militarist pacifism, and pragmatism (Calder 2007, 84; C. J. Kim and Boas 2020)—in the context of Korean and Japanese societies.

a. Nationalism. Nationalism has an anti-colonial streak in Korea, a nation where Woodrow Wilson's idea of national self-determination inspired a mass uprising against Japan's brutal colonial rule (1910–1945). Early traces of post–World War II resentment toward the United States can be found in the 1945–1948 occupation era, as the arrival of the purported liberators resulted instead in a divided peninsula. The division that has since been perpetuated was a puzzling outcome for many, given that Korea, unlike Germany, Japan, and Italy, was not "a party of belligerency during the war" (H. Kim 1988, 62; see also Cumings 2011, 104). The subsequent resurrection of the Japanese and pro-Japanese collaborators, the continuation of the colonial structure, and the denial of self-rule added to the skepticism toward the once-celebrated liberators. The disgruntled Koreans, who lacked the kind of obsequiousness that Americans came to associate with the Japanese (Carruthers 2016, 109), soon earned themselves the moniker "Irish of the orient" (Carruthers 2016, 182–83). It was not meant to be a compliment. John Reed Hodge, who led the U.S. occupation, complained soon after landing in the new protectorate that Koreans, fixated with the idea of independence, would "happily open guerrilla warfare against occupying troops of any nation" (Stueck and Yi 2010, 188).

After the 1950–1953 Korean War, where more than 33,000 Americans died in battle, feelings of indebtedness toward the U.S. prevailed. Korea's authoritarian leaders, buttressed by carefully nurtured anti-communism, the proselytizing mantra of state-led developmentalism, and support—if at times grudging—from Washington, stifled dissent for decades. But a sea change occurred after the May 1980 Gwangju Massacre, in which the authoritarian government of Chun Doo-hwan killed hundreds of dissenting civilians. With the popular suspicion that the United States tacitly approved the bloodshed (Sunhyuk Kim and Lee 2011; Shin 2006), the American military presence came to symbolize its "political endorsement" of the repressive regime, as it did in many other host states (Cooley 2008, xii). Gwangju became a traumatic memory; in a telling 1985 survey, elite students attending Seoul National University singled out the massacre, not the Korean War, as the "worst tragedy in Korea's modern history" (*Dong-a Ilbo* 1988). Many young student activists, as a result, went from admiring the United States as a symbol of democracy to seeing anti-Americanism as an axiomatic element in their struggle for democracy (N. Lee 2007, 118). The long-standing taboo associated with criticizing the United States, the erstwhile savior, was shattered, and "Yankee go home!" became a mundane protest slogan. Offices of the U.S. Information Service throughout the country came under attack, with students setting fire to the U.S. cultural centers in Gwangju and Busan in 1980 and 1982, respectively, and occupying the Seoul branch in 1985. Even rock music, popularized via the U.S. Armed Forces Korea Network radio, became "imperialist"; at an annual Seoul National University festival in 1981, a student rock band named Galaxy was confronted on stage by some 300 anti-government activists (Kang 2015).

The outburst of anti-American sentiments then converged with the "reimagining" of the self-avowedly anti-imperialist North Korea as an idealistic alternative (N. Lee 2007, 127–44). Increasingly, the United States came to be seen as a root cause of Korea's national division and an impediment to reunification. Korea's authoritarian leaders, with the backing of the United States, could point to the national division as a justification for the perennial state of security emergency and repression of dissent; ending that division, then, was a logical solution for many who fought for democracy (Sunhyuk Kim 2000, 46–47; Paik 1993, 72). The unique, seemingly incompatible association between pan-Korean ethnic nationalism and the political left was born out of this political context and has since characterized much of the anti-base movement in the country. Indeed, many first-generation anti-base activists in Korea trace their roots to the leftist-nationalist "NL" (national liberation) faction in the democracy movement, which advocated for a nationalist struggle to end the American dominance, as opposed to a class struggle as espoused by the rival "PD" (people's democracy) faction. Some of these activists were members of the National Committee of University Student Representatives (Jeondaehyeop), a powerful student coalition established at the height of the 1987 democracy movement and best known internationally for organizing an unauthorized trip to North Korea in 1989.

Japan's postwar national identity, meanwhile, also evolved under the influence of the United States, as the Americans went from a wartime enemy to a triumphant occupier and then to a domineering ally. Right-wing anti-American sentiments reek of resentment toward the "emasculat[ing]" postwar occupation (1945–1952) and the U.S.-Japan security treaty, as well as wartime atrocities blamed—"unfairly"—on Japan (Glosserman 2005, 35). As early as the 1950s, conservative-nationalist voices targeted the increasingly unpopular U.S. military bases in the mainland. Nakasone Yasuhiro, who went on to become the prime minister three decades later, cautioned against a Japan that is "overtaken by hundreds of military bases" and "overrun by mixed-race children and *panpan* (street prostitutes)" (Shimabuku 2019, 36). The theatrical suicide of writer Mishima Yukio in 1970—he committed seppuku after giving an ill-received speech about how Japan's SDF, which is supposed to serve only defensive purposes under the country's war-renouncing postwar constitution, should become a "national military" and "break out of the U.S. hegemony"—attests to the right-wing aversion to American supremacy (Igarashi 2000, 194–96). Ishihara Shintaro, a right-wing novelist-turned-governor who once pledged to evict the U.S. military from Yokota Air Base in western Tokyo, offers a more recent example. It is hardly surprising, then, that such polar opposites as Okinawa's grassroots anti-base groups and right-wing organizations like the Association to Honor the Spirits of the Fallen Heroes (Eirei ni kotaeru kai) may converge on their rejection of the American military predominance (Frühstück 2007, 76).

The Japanese political left, despite their universalistic pacifist rhetoric, are not devoid of nationalist sentiments either. The Japanese version of pacifism reflects the national desire to transition from "losers of war" to "winners of peace" (Dower 1999, 493–94), with antiwar pacifism as a yearning for autonomy (Suzuki 2015, 100–1) and a form of popular nationalism (McVeigh 2000, 26). Even the JCP, the only party that opposed Japanese wartime aggression, once described itself as the "true patriotic party" and espoused nationalism as a means of "anti-U.S. patriotism" (Oguma 2014, 216). Even in Okinawa, where many resent Tokyo for treating them as a pawn (*suteishi*) in its security relations with Washington, the "reversion" movement aimed at ending the prolonged U.S. occupation and returning Okinawa to mainland Japan was partially a pursuit of "*minzoku* (national) unification": the unification of the Japanese ethnic nation divided by the U.S. occupation of Okinawa, which continued even after the rest of Japan regained its sovereignty in 1952 (Oguma 2014, 236–38). To suppress anti-American sentiments, occupation authorities tried, to no avail, to ethnically differentiate Okinawans from mainlanders by evoking the island's past as the independent Ryukyu Kingdom (1429–1879). In this sense, the clashing images of an ideal Japanese national identity—an unconstrained military power for the political right; a self-righteously pacifist state for the left; and for Okinawans, a cohesive nation inclusive of Okinawa—had their common roots in nationalism.

Okinawa's identity discourses, meanwhile, experienced a telling shift after the end of the U.S. occupation in 1972. In a slap in the face for many, Tokyo's pre-1972 promises to reduce the U.S. military footprint on Okinawa did not materialize. A sense of betrayal, and the perception of continued discrimination against Okinawa, prevailed. As a result, Okinawa went from yearning for a return to "motherland Japan" before 1972 to emphasizing "*Okinawan* national identity" after 1972 (Dietz 2016, 213). This newly salient indigenous identity—or what some see as a regional variation of nationalism (Interview with Oguma Eiji, May 29, 2017)—became an undercurrent of anti-base sentiments. The Japanese national flag, once waved as a show of protest against the U.S. military prior to Okinawa's reversion, became unpopular enough in Okinawa by the 1980s that Tokyo felt it necessary to order its display at Okinawan schools (Smits 1999, 155); by then, the national flag had come to symbolize Japanese militarism and Okinawan victimization, as an Okinawan grocer told the world when he famously set it ablaze during a national sports tournament in 1987 (Dietz 2010). Similarly, *uchinanchu*, a term in the endangered local language that distinguishes Okinawan natives from *yamatonchu*, or Japanese mainlanders, became a frequent feature of Okinawan anti-base discourses. It is no coincidence, then, that *uchinanchu* served as a protest slogan for a thousand Okinawans who set fire to American military vehicles and raided Kadena Air Base in what is known as the 1970 Koza Riot (Shimabuku 2019, 119–23). Today, there remains a marginal yet passionate plea for Okinawan independence. A middle-aged Okinawan man I shared a bus ride with enthusiastically described to me a vision for an independent Okinawa: it will be a self-sufficient economy driven by the already-thriving tourism industry and the supposedly lucrative redevelopment of U.S. base sites. The sentiment was echoed by some others I have met. "Of course we want to change the situation (about U.S. military bases) as constituents of the Japanese state, but if that's impossible, we (can) go back to Ryukyu," says Taira Shinchi, an Okinawan activist who likens Okinawa to Japan's internal colony. "Bye-bye Japan, *sayōnara* (goodbye)" (Interview, September 21, 2016).

b. Pacifism. Due to the conflation of democratic yearnings, pan-Korean nationalism, and anti-American sentiments that underlay much of anti-base activism in Korea, universalist pacifist ideology is a relatively recent addition to Korea's base protest scene. Cockburn (2012) categorizes the country's anti-militarist activism, which she argues dates back to the 1990s, into three types: general anti-militarist activism, activism against specific wars (especially the Gulf War and the wars in Afghanistan and Iraq), and everyday peace advocacy. Initially a response to the U.S. military presence, the peace movement evolved to include the domestic military as another target. Activists now regularly censure their own government for issues ranging from the purchase of U.S. weapons to an increase in defense spending (Cockburn 2012, 191). According to activists, the Iraq War led to a generational change within the anti-base movement; the new generation of "peace activists," as they prefer to be called, are freer from the nationalistic preoccupations that have long characterized their predecessors. Many now distance themselves from traditional anti-American nationalism, calling it "dangerous" and "degenerate" (Interviews with Park Kyung-soo, August 23, 2016; Goo Jung-suh, June 13, 2016; Park Seok-jin, June 22, 2016). Even in 2002, when mass protests raged over an accident involving the U.S. military that killed two teenage girls, the anti-base coalition movement saw a fringe group calling for the complete removal of the U.S. military as an "isolated" group with an "unrealistic" goal (C. Lee 2002).

To be sure, pacifist rhetoric itself is not entirely new. "Antiwar, anti-nuke" (*banjeon banhaek*) slogans were just as frequently heard as anti–Chun Doo-hwan chants at the peak of student activism in the 1980s. Still, even the ostensibly anti-militarist rhetoric carried anti-American overtones. When university students refused to take part in mandatory military training, a popular cause that took two student protesters' lives in 1986, it was more of a refusal to serve as "mercenaries for Yankees" than an active commitment to pacifism (N. Lee 2007, 118–20). Indeed, the two Seoul National University students who died for the cause named their dissident group the Special Committee against Military Training and U.S. Imperialists'

Military Base-ification of the Korean Peninsula (Jeonbangipso hullyeon jeonmyeon geobu mit hanbando mije gunsagijihwa gyeolsajeojireul wihan teukbyeorwiwonhoe). Similarly, a 1986 protest song warns of a "nuclear storm" threatening "national survival" and cries out, in the true spirit of the 1980s, "antiwar, anti-nuke, Yankee go home!" For many student activists at the time, "anti-Americanism" was a means to "resurrect the nation wrecked by pro-Americanism" (*Joongang Ilbo* 1986). Because base opposition in Korea took root in this leftist-nationalist tradition, many activists to date tend to call for peace *with North Korea* when making antiwar pleas—thereby mixing supposedly universal pacifist ideals with nationalistic language and geographically confining their peace agenda to the Korean peninsula. Even the anti–Iraq War movement saw a confluence of new pacifism and lingering anti-American nationalism. For example, the Korean Action against Dispatch of Troops to Iraq (Pabyeong bandae gungmin haengdong), an umbrella antiwar coalition, consisted of member organizations that were explicitly nationalistic in their orientations. They would, for example, call for "autonomy and peace" (*jaju pyeonghwa*)—as opposed to the more commonly used expression "antiwar and peace" (*banjeon pyeonghwa*).

Japan's postwar pacifism, on the other hand, has deeper roots that nonetheless seem riddled with contradictions. Japan's pacifist, war-renouncing constitution that anti-base activists assiduously seek to protect today was imposed by the U.S. military—the very entity activists simultaneously challenge. The U.S. occupation authorities, for their part, soon regretted their forcible demilitarization of Japan, as the emergent Cold War suddenly required that the former enemy become a key security partner. At the same time, the U.S.-imposed democracy went on to animate the Japanese left, while fervent support for remilitarization came from the far right—accused war criminals among them (Takeshi 1985, 355; Cockburn and Ikeda 2012, 155–56). Conflicting demands for demilitarization and remilitarization have since raised the perennial question of what constitutes Japan's "normal" status (Hook 1996, 2–3).

Despite these internal contradictions, postwar Japan won a reputation for being a pacifist state (*heiwa kokka*) with an institutionalized anti-militarist culture (Berger 1998; Katzenstein 1996). According to this conventional wisdom, anti-militarist traditions are shaped not just by peace-loving, alliance-bashing "left-idealists," but also by pragmatic, merchant-minded "centrists" and nationalistic, resentful "right-idealists" (Berger 1998, 55–66). While all three groups have shaped the tradition that has prevented the outright remilitarization of Japan, anti-base protests are strictly dominated by leftist-idealists and exclude the rest. The kinds of anti-militarist beliefs held by these activists differ from, for example, Japanese leaders' acquiescence to pacifism as a postwar survival strategy (Takeshi 1985, 328). Conservative nationalists, after all, used demilitarization and democratization as a means to encourage the American occupation authorities of the GHQ (General Headquarters) to "Go Home Quickly," as Japan's postwar prime minister Yoshida Shigeru liked to say (Welfield 1988, 40). This steadfast universal pacifism, however, sometimes rings hollow. The master narrative of World War II that equates the Japanese with victims, not victimizers, undergirds the Japanese peace movement (Dower 1999, 493–94; Orr 2001), which inadvertently helps reinforce the revisionist agenda.

Okinawan peace narratives, meanwhile, developed separately from the mainland narrative that centers on the experience of Hiroshima and Nagasaki (Figal 2001, 40–41). Despite vastly different origins, victim identification is just as salient in Okinawa. The Ryukyu Kingdom independently ruled what is now Okinawa from the fifteenth to the nineteenth century until the 1879 Japanese annexation; the transition "from kingdom to colony" is still bitterly remembered (Smits 1999, 144–46). The 1945 Battle of Okinawa, during which up to one third of the islanders perished at the hands of the Americans and the Japanese, has provided an "ideological resource" for postwar base opposition in Okinawa (Tanji 2006, 37).[1] The battle is often invoked alongside the alleged pacifism of the Ryukyu Kingdom to accentuate and condemn the present-day American militarism forced upon Okinawa—a myth, according to critics, that romanticizes its premodern past for political purposes (Smits 2010). Regardless of its inaccuracy, the narrative persists today in a way that meaningfully shapes anti-base sentiments on the island. Still, Okinawan pacifists see individual American service members as future partners in antiwar initiatives, not enemies to be driven out. All these bases dotting Okinawa would have to be shut down, activists believe, if no American volunteers to serve in the military (Interview, Taira Shinchi, September 21, 2016).

   c. Pragmatism. Despite occasional skepticism, mainstream narratives in Korea of the United States as a protector remain ingrained in the public mind. The country's political legitimization and identity construction, after all, came largely from pro-American anti-communism—to the point where Pyongyang regularly belittles Seoul as a "puppet regime beholden to American imperialists" (Shin 2006, 155–56). With the entrenched belief in American benevolence and the virtue of the U.S. military presence as a deterrent against North Korea, challenging American military bases on nationalistic or ideological grounds remains an uphill battle. As a result, anti-base activists—those who care about generating public support, or at least minimizing antagonism—propagate their messages in ways that do not directly clash with the dominant cultural narratives surrounding the U.S. presence.

The contemporary political landscape, in which traditional leftist-nationalists are trapped in an ever-decreasing political space, adds to the dominance of pragmatism as a rhetorical necessity. As Korea democratized, many former dissidents, including those who threw homemade bombs at the U.S. embassy in Seoul, became part of institutionalized, mainstream politics. The political ascendance of former democracy activists—they have become lawmakers, cabinet ministers, and presidents—not only attests to successful democratization, but also reveals finer distinctions within the left half of the political spectrum that is often lumped together under the broad *jinbo* (progressive) umbrella. The mainstream liberal camp that does not demonize American primacy—if anything, in vying for the presidency, it does its best to prove its loyalty to Washington—contrasts with the increasingly marginalized group of leftist-nationalists who continue what today borders on knee-jerk criticism of the United States. The political space for leftist-nationalists has further dwindled in recent years, after the Unified Progressive Party (UPP), the bastion of leftist-nationalist politics, was forcibly disbanded in 2014 after one of its lawmakers allegedly plotted a pro-North Korean insurrection. The UPP saga frustrates even like-minded activists, who now face even more stigmatization as a result: "Look around—the world has changed. It's not 1945 anymore. There's no need for an underground revolt!" (Interview, anonymous, July 11, 2016). Activists say they do see less of the typical, nationalistically charged anti-base rhetoric after the UPP's fall. Pragmatism, which facilitates the dual tasks of impression management and grassroots resonance, fills this conspicuous void. As one activist put it: "Locals don't care about American hegemony; they care about their everyday life."

Japanese base opponents, facing fewer immediate threats from North Korea, can better afford to employ traditional antiwar rhetoric that aligns perfectly well with their political orientations. Still, opponents face numerous hurdles in a country with a seemingly inherent disdain for overt political expressions (Pharr 1992). Activists, for example, face a fair amount of vilification: as the territorial dispute with China rages over the Senkaku/ Diaoyu islands, whose administrative authority lies with the Okinawan city of Ishigaki, base opponents' efforts are maligned as a scheme to boost Chinese influence. Familiar allegations—which some Japanese academics *interesting)* and policymakers repeated to me over the years—are that protesters are on the Chinese payroll, and that they are not actually from Okinawa. Indeed, when I first attended a morning rally at MCAS Futenma, a heavily contested Marine base in central Okinawa, a Japanese police officer immediately questioned me: "Are you from outside the prefecture?" (Later, when I followed an activist to his rooftop overlooking the base, I found two policemen driving slowly by and photographing us. Apparently, I made it onto what protesters half-jokingly call the "blacklist."[2]) Even Japan's Public Security Intelligence Agency has publicly alleged Chinese influence in Okinawa's independence movement, although critics dismiss the claim as a fabrication (*Okinawa Times* 2017). Added to the incentive to avoid this smear campaign is the widespread political apathy that seems to take for granted the conservative political dominance, a surefire guarantor of the status quo in base politics. This apathy coincides with a decline in leftist social movements and the erosion in the salience of pacifism as a tenet (Iida 2002). In the face of right-wing hostility, dormant civil society, and the seemingly impenetrable conservative rule, Japanese base opponents struggle to carve out a political space of their own. Pragmatic framing, which couches the ostensibly subversive anti-base agenda in the more palatable language of quality-of-life issues, helps them do just that.

The use of pragmatic framing in Japanese anti-base protests is more prevalent than what the literature may suggest—especially in Okinawa, whose experience as a base town is treated as sui generis and whose dissent is equated with the practice of pacifism. While pacifism is an underlying sentiment buttressing anti-base activism in Okinawa, clear variations in the level of local contestation facing a host of U.S. facilities scattered across the island show that the supposedly universal anti-militarism does not translate into equal amounts of contention. Not all bases are contested in Okinawa, and the ones that are tend to be attached to specific, tangible grievances that activists tap into. Much of Okinawan activism targets particular byproducts of the U.S. military presence, such as noise, pollution, and crimes, not the presence itself (Dietz 2016, 215). The overwhelming emphasis on bases as a "burden" suggests that anti-base activism, if not underlying antiwar sentiments, focuses on reducing specific grievances grounded in everyday experiences.

At the same time, the primacy of the local—that is, activist beliefs that anti-base activism should be grounded in local experiences, with local residents at the center of the movement—aligns best with rhetorical pragmatism. An idealized view of localized social movements, which exists in both Korea and Japan, pictures "average citizens . . . spontaneously creating new forms of democratic organization in the best traditions of grass-roots egalitarian democracy" (Krauss and Simcock 1981, 212). In a similar vein, civil society actors are supposed to be "pure," "innocent," and preferably apolitical (Arrington 2016). Diehard nationalists and stubborn pacifists fail to pass the "model protester" smell test. It is no coincidence, in this sense, that seemingly nonpolitical groups like Gate 22, an association of artists seeking to shape the future of Seoul's Yongsan Garrison, are invited to public forums to speak on the issue, while leftist-nationalist groups, with their long tradition of decrying the base as a colonial relic, are left out.

Local Elite Allies

Political leaders and protesters share mutual interests in working toward a common cause: the former get to act as true champions of the people, and the latter gain an elite ally (Tarrow 2011, 168). Elites at the local level—I focus on municipal leaders in this study—are key actors in contentious base politics, where distinctions between high-level and low-level politics are particularly salient. The in-betweenness of local governments, simultaneously "self-governing bodies" and "subdivisions in a hierarchical system of administration" (Steiner 1980, 19), presents local elites with a dual challenge: ensuring the well-being of local residents and complying with central government demands in managing the U.S. presence (Smith 1999).

Activists court elite support, if often unsuccessfully, to reinforce the primacy of the local. Elite endorsement instantly legitimates the otherwise politically sensitive anti-base agenda in the eyes of latent adherents and thereby helps build a more broad-based movement. As the anti-base cause goes from a narrow activist pursuit to a local cause célèbre, many fence-sitters reluctant to voice their grievances are encouraged to join in. Elite involvement also broadens the scope of conflict, in part by inviting the central government to "assert its predominance" over defiant localities and thereby highlighting the central-local power imbalance (Mulgan 2000, 161). Military bases, due to their concentrated local costs (i.e., base-related grievances) and diffuse public benefits (i.e., national security), easily lend themselves to gripes about regional discrimination (Aldrich 2009; C. J. Kim 2021). Subnational base

NIMBY

politics then expands into a larger debate on local autonomy, or even more broadly, the quality of democracy, which in turn generates support from local populations interested in defending those broader values (Smith 1999; Mulgan 2000).

While social movement research often reduces elite allies to a component of the political opportunity structure (for a critique, see Jasper 2006, 5), local elites have their own agency, with varying interests and preferences that often diverge from those of activists. They may embrace the anti-base agenda to widen their electoral base. As one Korean activist explains: "We may not be able to supply enough votes to elect certain mayoral candidates, but we do have enough power to campaign against them." Other local elites may see base-related grievances as an opportunity to engage in pork-barrel politics. Stories of local grievances can easily become stories of local sacrifices for national security—as grounds for demanding more resources from the central government. Still others, though their number is low, seem committed to the anti-base cause to an extent that makes them almost indistinguishable from activists. Elite allies in contentious base politics, in other words, range from opportunists who co-opt the movement for their own interests to enthusiasts who seem to fully embody the movement cause.

Even the most fervent elite support, however, is not always a boon for activists. Even as elites legitimate and amplify the anti-base cause, their influence can be detrimental in the longer run. The opportunists, by appropriating the movement cause, moderate movement goals and ultimately help protect, rather than subvert, the status quo (McAdam 1982). As the opportunists presume the inevitability of the continuing American presence in the localities they govern, they serve as another constraint on activists' pursuit of radical change. The enthusiasts, while faithful allies of the movement, often invite retaliation from the central government precisely due to their devotion to the cause. A prolonged local-central conflict may animate the anti-base movement and galvanize its most devoted supporters, but it risks alienating latent adherents over time. Once an instant shot in the arm for the movement, elite devotion over time can ultimately turn base town residents against the cause. Indeed, as I show in chapter 5, electoral setbacks for dissenting mayors in Japan, which were a blow to the anti-base movement in localities they govern, came on the heels of their much-publicized disputes with the central government. The elite dynamics we witness in contentious base politics therefore contradicts much of the social movement literature that treats elite allies as an automatic source of opportunities.

Local Autonomy and U.S. Military Bases in Korea and Japan
How localities approach base issues is closely linked to the practice of local autonomy, a legally guaranteed right for municipalities in both countries. While local governments remain indisputably weaker vis-à-vis the central government in both countries, subnational base politics occupies a peculiar place in inter-governmental relations as a potential hotbed of center-local conflict. The dual nature of local autonomy—at once a "bulwark against the tyranny of the centre" and a means by which local elites prioritize their "parochial" interests over state interests (Rhodes 1999, 27)—is on full display in subnational base politics.

Local autonomy is a relatively recent addition to Korea's young democracy, which contributes to the lack of local elite involvement in base politics. During the authoritarian era, national political elites partially relied upon the U.S. military presence to legitimize their authority and secure regime survival (Cooley 2008, 106). Authoritarian rulers maintained tight control over base towns in order to maintain the "continued tolerance, if not eager support," of the U.S. presence (Moon 2012, 74). With local government heads nominated by the central government, and with the police state suppressing political dissidents, local opponents had nowhere to turn to—much less attain local elite allies.

The sea change came with Korea's democratization, which revived the constitutionally granted, and yet hitherto ignored, rights of local autonomy. A series of sweeping reforms resurrected and revised the Local Autonomy Act in 1988, and reinstituted local councils and local elections in 1991 following a hiatus of three decades. The 1999 law on the transfer of central authority, as well as the 2004 law on decentralization, added to the rapid empowerment of local governments. These changes coincided with the establishment of groups devoted solely to the issue of local autonomy, such as the National Association of Mayors, the Governors' Association, and the National Association of Local Council Chairs. These "radical" changes threatened to challenge the predominance of central authority (Bae and Kim 2013, 262). Some even contend that Korean local political elites, thanks to the ample autonomy they ostensibly enjoy, "express their parochial (anti-base) views in uninhibited fashion" and render base politics "more confrontational and chaotic" than elsewhere (Calder 2007, 226).

Despite any impression to the contrary, however, Korean municipalities tend to stay out of base politics, which they say should belong to high politics. They are reluctant to voice their opinion on issues that directly affect their

cultural explanation

interests, such as delayed water and electricity bills that hurt their coffers (*Hankyoreh 21* 2000). Their silence is akin to self-censorship, according to a frustrated former activist (Interview, anonymous, July 11, 2016): "Let's say a mayor initiates an anti-American drive. You think the government would cheer him on?" In rare instances where local political elites do complain, they often use the word "sacrifice" (*hisaeng*)—host communities have been sacrificed for national security interests, which they portray as a case of concentrated costs at the local level and diffuse public benefits at the national level. What is implied here is that such sacrifices should be rewarded with "compensation" (*bosang*), usually in the form of economic assistance from the state. When twelve municipalities came together in 2000 to officially protest U.S. bases, for example, the sole aim of the otherwise bold initiative was to pressure the state into shelling out compensation. Similarly, when local governments commission research reports on U.S. bases, such reports prominently feature the estimated economic loss incurred because of the American presence, with an implicit suggestion that the state owes the local government the amount in question. Ultimately, local governments water down their opposition by making their continued tolerance of the U.S. presence conditional on financial compensation. Local elite defiance, in this sense, is often a self-serving tactic aimed at maximizing financial gains while preserving the status quo, rather than a genuine attempt to fundamentally transform subnational base politics.

pragmatic

Japanese local governments, meanwhile, have similarly experienced increasing power vis-à-vis the central government. The postwar Constitution and the Local Autonomy Law, both dating back to 1947, permitted direct elections of governors, mayors, and city assemblies, and led to the creation of organizations such as the National Governors' Association, which has run a study group on U.S. base issues. (One may find it ironic that the introduction of local autonomy by the U.S. military authorities has facilitated local leaders' opposition to U.S. military infrastructure.) Further progress in the 1990s and the 2000s, such as the 1995 Decentralization Promotion Law and the 1999 Omnibus Decentralization Law, awarded local governments even more independent authority. "The central government used to issue orders, which local governments would then have to follow," said Ōta Masahide, who became a symbol of local government anti-base dissent when he, as Okinawa governor, refused to grant land leases for U.S. bases in 1995.[3] "With the new law on local autonomy, we didn't have to any longer, as we were now of equal status" (Interview, September 6, 2016).

Japanese host communities, at least when compared to their Korean counterparts, seem willing to exercise greater levels of local autonomy, either independently or in close association with civic groups. For Japanese municipalities, "burden" (*futan*) is the watchword, which evokes the image of all the grievances and perceived opportunity costs associated with hosting bases. Burden, as commonly narrated in anti-base discourses, requires an "alleviation" (*keigen*), which necessitates changes that are potentially of a more structural nature than mere compensation offered in exchange for the continuation of the status quo. Moreover, many Japanese localities are at least rhetorically committed to anti-militarism, which, in theory, is consistent with pacifist anti-base ideals. Some actually go out of their way to obstruct the implementation of basing policy, even at the risk of forgoing economic subsidies the state doles out in exchange for local cooperation.

The rhetorical commitment, a common denominator for Japanese municipalities, stems from both Japan's postwar pacifist tradition and the worldwide trend. The National Council of Japan Nuclear Free Local Authorities (Nihon hikakusengen jichitai kyōgikai), established in 1984 following Manchester City Council's anti-nuclear declaration in 1980, offers one such example. By 1987, one third of all Japanese municipalities declared themselves to be nuclear-free. Member municipalities include cities hosting U.S. bases, such as Sagamihara, Yamato, Ginowan, Nago, and Okinawa. Other host cities, such as Yokosuka, Sasebo, Zama, Ayase, Gotemba, and Kadena, issued the pronouncements without joining the council. Most statements express an ambiguous commitment that could be taken as merely performative, but some manage to be more specific. Nago's statement dating back to 1982, for example, directly targets a specific U.S. facility, known as the Henoko Ordnance Ammunition Depot: "We the residents of Nago refuse to live alongside the Henoko nuclear ammunition storage facility and demand the immediate denuclearization of the area we live in" (National Council of Japan Nuclear Free Local Authorities 2018). A similar anti-nuclear initiative in Japan, Mayors for Peace (Heiwa shuchō kaigi), was established in 1983 by the mayors of Hiroshima and Nagasaki, two cities of obvious symbolic significance. As of 2021, the group boasted 1,734 Japanese member municipalities and 15 Korean localities—again, including those that host American military bases.

In principle, local elites can invoke these stated principles to regulate certain operations at American bases and port facilities used to store or carry nuclear weapons and materials. In practice, however, they never mount the kind of challenge against U.S. military practices that could, if subjected to scrutiny, directly clash with Japan's official denuclearization policy. At the national level, Japan's breach of its own three non-nuclear principles—no possession, no production, and no introduction of nuclear weapons—has long been an open secret. At the local level, these declarations "continue a dubious Japanese peace movement tradition" that offers vague lip service to anti-militarist ideals but no solid guidance for action (Takahara 1987, 52–53). Cities like Yokosuka and Sasebo, which once committed themselves to becoming "peace" ports, have actively participated in the "bland and unconvincing denials" repeated by the Japanese government that the passage of American nuclear-powered warships does not violate the country's non-nuclear tenet (Morrison 1985, 23). Even when the visit of the nuclear-powered USS *Enterprise* in 1968 provoked militant protests in Sasebo, the city actually "lobbied hard to . . . have the honor of this great ship's visit," and arranged for a choir to sing at the Sasebo station to welcome the sailors (Havens 1987, 148). The city government has since claimed to be acting in good faith by refraining from asking the U.S. military to verify that there are no nuclear weapons aboard its warships. The city leadership, in the words of a city councilwoman, is little more than a "yes man" (Interview with Waseda Noriko, September 23, 2016).

While the wide divergence between rhetoric and reality is the order of the day, there remain a few outliers. Okinawan municipalities have been obvious anomalies at least since the mid-1990s, "strategizing in much the same way as" anti-base activists (Smith 2006, 25). As a Korean activist marvels (Interview with Shin Soo-yun, June 8, 2016): "The Okinawan government is doing what we activists are trying to do in Korea." The Study Group on Okinawan Self-Governance (Okinawa jichi kenkyūkai) epitomizes the island prefecture's aspirations for self-determination, as its members seek diplomatic negotiation rights so that Okinawa can bypass Tokyo and negotiate directly with the United States (Dietz 2010, 196). One telling document from 2011 lists the mayors of every Okinawan municipality, their party affiliation and "political views," and, most important, their stance on the Futenma relocation; the document concludes that 48 out of 48 municipality heads as of April 2011 opposed the relocation within the prefecture, and that 28 of them went so far as to oppose the U.S.-Japan alliance itself (Okinawa Prefectural Government 2011). The prefectural government has also studied the U.S.-Japan SOFA, with the intention of influencing a traditional diplomatic issue long out of bounds to local governments. A series of referenda on the base question—the first one in 1996 made the Japanese government fear its "inestimable" political consequences (Takao 1999, 91), and the latest one in 2019 forced the government to hasten the pace of the long-delayed FRF construction—is an overt attempt to shape the allies' decisions. Shrewd politicians also know how to assert indigenous Okinawan identity as a way to press their anti-base agenda. It comes as little surprise that the late Okinawa governor Onaga Takeshi, who was a fierce anti-base advocate, opened his press conference in Tokyo in May 2015 with a greeting delivered in a language few in the room understood: the endangered Ryukyuan language.

Case Selection

Sites of Investigation

Military bases range from carbon copies of American suburban towns implanted on foreign soil to smaller, less obtrusive "lily pads" in remote areas (Vine 2015, 45). Acknowledging the various forms of bases, this book focuses on sizable bases that defense analysts consider particularly important for strategic reasons (Lostumbo et al. 2013). Different branches of the military— the Army, Air Force, Marine Corps, and Navy—are represented, with their various negative externalities (e.g., noise at an air base, nuclear-powered warships at a naval base, etc.), although the following chapters will show that contestation does not automatically follow from the nature or the severity of particular grievances. Locations of the bases and population densities in the host communities also vary, although base protests are not solely a function of location either. The smallest installations and facilities were excluded to rule out the possibility that wide variations in base sizes could become a source of bias.[4] Table 2.1 lists the twenty bases under study (see maps 2.1 and 2.2), which face varying degrees of local challenges: some routinely appear in international media as a symbol of the beleaguered U.S. presence, while others almost never get headlines, even in local media.

Case Summary

Table 2.2 summarizes the cases, demonstrating multiple pathways to base contestation. It shows how the varying contexts activists make use of to

Table 2.1 List of bases

Bases in Korea	Municipality	Province
Yongsan Garrison	Seoul[a]	Seoul
Camp Humphreys	Pyeongtaek	Gyeonggi
Camp Red Cloud	Uijeongbu	Gyeonggi
Rodriguez Live Fire Complex	Pocheon	Gyeonggi
Camp Casey	Dongducheon	Gyeonggi
Osan Air Base	Pyeongtaek	Gyeonggi
Camp Walker	Daegu	Daegu
Kunsan Air Base	Gunsan	North Jeolla
Camp Mujuk	Pohang	North Gyeongsang
CFA Chinhae	Jinhae/Changwon[b]	South Gyeongsang

Bases in Japan	Municipality	Prefecture
MCAS Futenma	Ginowan	Okinawa
Camp Schwab	Nago	Okinawa
Kadena Air Base	Kadena Town, Chatan Town, and Okinawa City	Okinawa
MCAS Iwakuni	Iwakuni	Yamaguchi
CFA Yokosuka	Yokosuka	Kanagawa
NAF Atsugi	Ayase and Yamato	Kanagawa
Camp Zama	Zama and Sagamihara	Kanagawa
Yokota Air Base	Fussa City, Tachikawa City, Akishima City, Musashi-Murayama City, Hamura City, and Mizuho Town	Tokyo
CFA Sasebo	Sasebo	Nagasaki
Camp Fuji	Gotemba	Shizuoka

[a] When it comes to Seoul, I only look at protest events taking place in the district of Yongsan, given the enormous size of the metropolis of 10 million residents and various protest events directed at the U.S. but not at its military (e.g., regular protests at the U.S. embassy) in other parts of the city.

[b] The city of Jinhae became Jinhae District in the city of Changwon in 2010.

pursue mobilization result in differing levels of anti-base protests. Protest event data for 2000–2015, discussed in detail in the appendix, are based on national and local media reports, activist-run blogs and websites, hand-written memos kept by activists, and various activist publications, such as leaflets and booklets. High, moderate, and low contestation levels (the right-most column of the table) correspond to the total number of protesters, as opposed to protest frequency, at each base over sixteen years.[5] To clarify the

CHINA

NORTH KOREA

Rodriguez Live Fire Complex

Camp Red Cloud

Camp Casey

Yongsan Garrison

Osan Air Base

SOUTH KOREA

Camp Humphreys

Camp Mujuk

Kunsan Air Base

Camp Walker

● Air Force Base

★ Army Base

▲ Marine Corps Base

■ Naval Base

Commander Fleet Activities Chinhae

JAPAN

0   100 mi

0   100 km

Map 2.1 U.S. Military Bases in Korea from Table 2.1

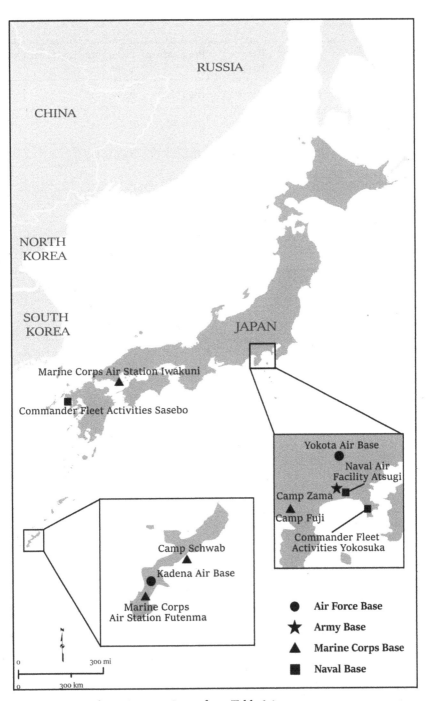

Map 2.2 U.S. Military Bases in Japan from Table 2.1

Table 2.2 Case summary

Bases	Country	Status disruption	Pragmatism	Local elite allies	Contestation
MCAS Futenma	Japan	Reduction (0)	High (1)	Present (1)	
Camp Schwab	Japan	Expansion (1)	High (1)	Present (1)	
Camp Humphreys	Korea	Expansion (1)	High (1)	Present (1)	High
CFA Yokosuka	Japan	Expansion (1)	Low (0)	Present (1)	
NAF Atsugi	Japan	Reduction (0)	High (1)	Absent (0)	
Kadena Air Base	Japan	No change (0)	High (1)	Present (1)	
MCAS Iwakuni	Japan	Expansion (1)	High (1)	Present (1)	
Yongsan Garrison	Korea	Reduction (0)	Moderate (0)	Absent (0)	
Yokota Air Base	Japan	Expansion (1)	Moderate (0)	Present (1)	
Camp Zama	Japan	Expansion (1)	Low (0)	Present (1)	Moderate
Camp Casey	Korea	Reduction (0)	High (1)	Present (1)	
Camp Red Cloud	Korea	Reduction (0)	High (1)	Absent (0)	
CFA Sasebo	Japan	No change (0)	Low (0)	Absent (0)	
Camp Walker	Korea	Reduction (0)	Low (0)	Absent (0)	
Kunsan Air Base	Korea	Expansion (1)	High (1)	Absent (0)	
Osan Air Base	Korea	Expansion (1)	High (1)	Present (1)	
Rodriguez Live Fire Complex	Korea	No change (0)	Moderate (0)	Present (1)	
Camp Fuji	Japan	No change (0)	Low (0)	Absent (0)	Low
CFA Chinhae	Korea	No change (0)	Low (0)	Absent (0)	
Camp Mujuk	Korea	Expansion (1)	Low (0)	Absent (0)	

relationship between the three contextual factors and the resulting contestation levels, 1 is assigned to the correlates of greater contestation—namely, status disruption in the form of base expansion, the prevalence of pragmatic framing, and the presence of local elite allies. All other conditions—base reduction, nationalistic and ideological framing, and the absence of local elite allies—are marked as 0. On average, highly contested bases have a score of 2.2, meaning more than two conditions are present in the host community. Moderately contested bases have a score of 1.5, and minimally contested bases stand at 0.8. Altogether, they show an additive relationship between these contextual factors and the contestation levels.

In a preview of chapters 3–5, I briefly visualize protest levels observed in three sets of host communities. First, figures 2.1 and 2.2 show protest count and turnout over time at two U.S. military bases: Camp Humphreys and CFA Yokosuka. These bases, which form the backbone of the American power projection in Asia, have gone through status changes of widely disparate natures—physical and symbolic—but saw similar spurts of relatively broad-based, large-scale mobilization. Camp Humphreys, which saw hardly any challenge before news of a base expansion hit its host city, went on to draw tens of thousands of protesters—elderly farmers among them—each year between 2004 and 2006. CFA Yokosuka, a proud symbol of cordial base-community relations, was met with unexpectedly high opposition when a nuclear-powered aircraft carrier, anathema to nuclear-averse pacifists in town, replaced its conventionally powered predecessor. While Yokosuka's relatively high protest turnout depends largely on the mobilization of those already mobilized (namely, an assortment of leftist groups that continue to hold regular events), the spike in protest turnout in 2008 and 2015 coincided with the deployment of the USS *George Washington* and the USS *Ronald Reagan*, respectively.

Second, figures 2.3 and 2.4 show protest count and turnout over time at Rodriguez Live Fire Complex and MCAS Futenma. These bases are selected to highlight the mobilizing capacity of pragmatic framing. The sudden transition of the Rodriguez range from a virtually uncontested base to the latest flashpoint in base-community relations by the end of 2014 was made possible only by local residents' fixation on rhetorical pragmatism. The flare-up we see in 2015 followed a rash of near-miss accidents involving stray shells, which finally pushed the elderly local farmers to mobilize. These unlikely activists, as we saw in the previous chapter, strove to highlight their "purely" pragmatic grievances. High levels of contestation at MCAS Futenma, meanwhile,

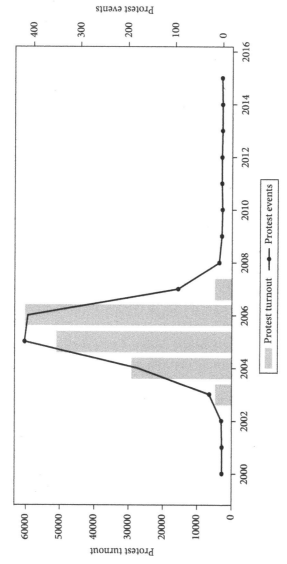

Figure 2.1 Protests against Camp Humphreys (2000–2015)

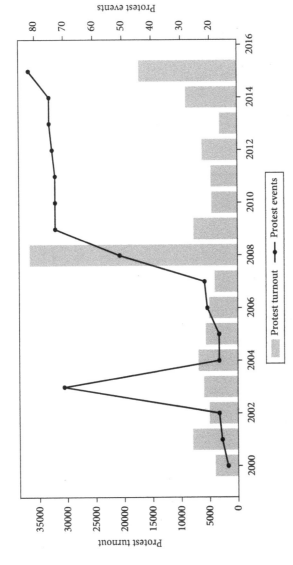

Figure 2.2 Protests against CFA Yokosuka (2000–2015)

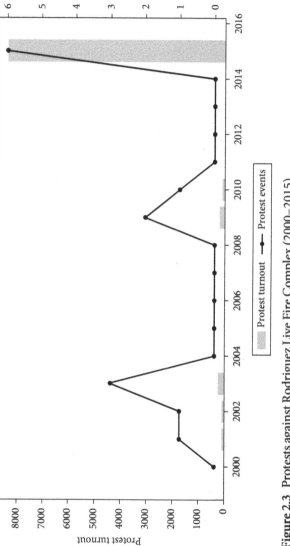

Figure 2.3 Protests against Rodriguez Live Fire Complex (2000–2015)

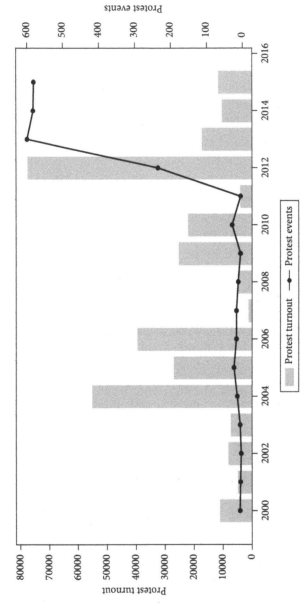

Figure 2.4 Protests against MCAS Futenma (2000–2015)

are another reminder that everyday grievances can continue to fuel anti-base activism even when the base in question is scheduled to relocate elsewhere. While other bases slated for relocation have seen a steady decline in opposition, MCAS Futenma remains an exceptional case where contestation has only intensified: the controversial deployment in 2012 of the MV-22 Osprey tiltrotor aircraft stoked local fears about everyday safety, touching off new waves of dissent against the base forever awaiting its departure. Similarly, the high protest turnout in 2004 followed the crash of a Marine helicopter on the campus of a local university.

Third, figures 2.5 and 2.6 show protest count and turnout over time at MCAS Iwakuni and Camp Casey, the two U.S. bases that saw boycotts by the mayors of their host cities. When Iwakuni's mayor turned against the fortification of the Marine base, the hitherto unquestioned U.S. presence in this nondescript town made national and international headlines. His ultimately failed rebellion between 2005 and 2007 drove much of the anti-base contestation observed during the same period. Dongducheon's mayors, for their part, mobilized some of the least likely protesters—shopkeepers and pro-American conservative civic groups—to protest the economic doldrums in the city, which they blamed on the heavy American presence. Two phases of elite-led, top-down mobilization in 2004 and 2014 coincided with a noticeable uptick in protest turnout, although 200 days of one-person protests in 2014 were not counted as protest events (see the appendix). While local elites range from anti-base enthusiasts to opportunists, they do meaningfully shape contentious base politics when they stake their political fortunes on it.

In the following chapters, I introduce each of the three contextual factors and examine the corresponding patterns of anti-base mobilization and demobilization. I occasionally make references to "protest towns" and "quiet towns" to contrast high and low levels of contention across different host communities: In "protest towns," activists achieve the rare feat of relatively large-scale, sustained mobilization against the imposing American military presence. In "quiet towns," by contrast, mobilization almost never, or only belatedly, occurs. The rest stand somewhere in between these two extremes.

Stories of these towns will complicate many of the common assumptions about correlates of base contestation. To begin, civic capacity, which scholars often attribute to mobilization capacity, does not seem to determine contestation levels. Seoul, despite the heavy concentration of powerful NGOs, has seen a lull in anti-base activism, whereas Gunsan, a Korean city of 267,000, is home to the longest-running anti-base rallies in the country. If, as some have

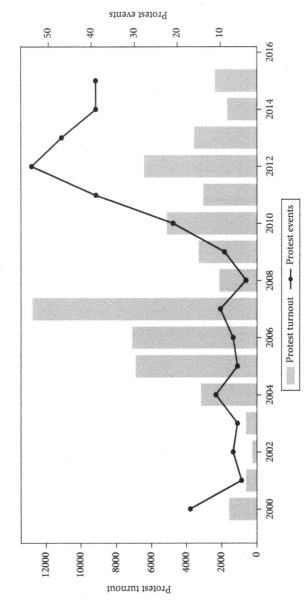

Figure 2.5 Protests against MCAS Iwakuni (2000–2015)

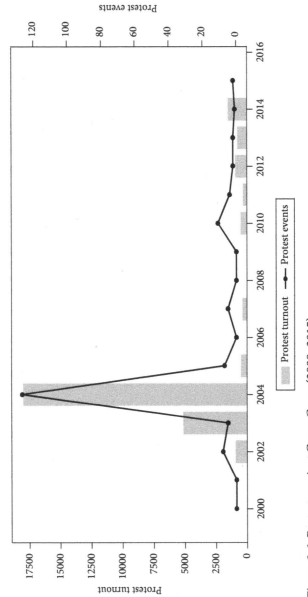

Figure 2.6 Protests against Camp Casey (2000–2015)

hypothesized, frequent civil-military contacts as measured by population density dictate base frictions, then Yongsan Garrison in central Seoul, with a city population density among the highest in the world, would have won the trophy. The presence of intense grievances does not automatically translate into intense or frequent protests, as some sixty years of silence about the daily shooting exercises at Rodriguez Live Fire Complex in Pocheon attest. Similarly, politics, as opposed to the frequency of aircraft accidents, explains why MCAS Futenma in Okinawa faces much greater contestation than its colossal neighbor, Kadena Air Base, and why the former is considered "the most dangerous base in the world," when in fact the latter is more accident-prone (Okinawa Prefectural Government 2017, 103). The relatively low-profile U.S. naval presence in Yokosuka, as well as the cordial civil-military relations in the city, did not stop anti-base activists from turning CFA Yokosuka into a highly contested base, if briefly. In addition, contrary to the common perception that attributes the economic benefits associated with military bases to stable civil-military relations, many opponents in Korea and Japan, including their elected local representatives, view the bases as a hurdle to local economic growth. In Dongducheon, one of the poorest cities in Korea where a disproportionately high number of small businesses cater to the U.S. presence, city officials have protested the delayed departure of Camp Casey. Okinawa, the poorest Japanese prefecture where many benefit from land leases and state subsidies, still likes to remind base supporters that American bases only account for 5 percent of its prefectural GDP. Going subnational—and following local actors and tracing their interactions—uncovers the intricacies of contentious base politics.

3

Bases in Motion

Four thousand five hundred twenty-nine. The number on the sign jumped out at me as I approached the Tent Village (*tento mura*), a famed protest camp overlooking the emerald-green waters off northern Okinawa, on September 11, 2016. The sign, where opponents tally each passing day since their first protest dating back to 2004, indicated that my visit fell on the 4,529th day of the daily sit-in against the construction of an offshore U.S. Marine facility in the seaside Henoko district. Despite the reputation of the protest camp as the epicenter of the struggle against American military bases on foreign soil, it was a quiet day. A handful of locals sat around, sipping tea, chatting, and greeting occasional visitors. When I returned to the hut three days later, it was another slow day. We drank some more tea, and we chatted some more. On the day I returned to the tent for the third time, a storm warning had been issued. We retreated to what was named Tent 2, another protest encampment farther away from the shore. Sitting around, some of the locals folded T-shirts printed with an image of the endangered dugongs swimming in Henoko waters. Others dozed off. The colossal weight of the number—over 4,500 days of protests and counting, rain or shine—pressed down not only upon tense moments of confrontation, but also upon a countless number of seemingly tedious, slow days like these. They had never imagined, the people at the hut told me, that they would see four digits on the sign.

If it is any consolation to them, neither did the policymakers. The new offshore runways stretching from Camp Schwab, a U.S. Marine base in Henoko, have yet to be built more than twenty-five years after the allies officially put forward the idea in the late 1990s. The new facilities are meant to replace MCAS Futenma, a subject of much local resentment, whose continuously delayed relocation to Henoko has hurt U.S.-Japan ties. How have these sit-inners—along with kindred spirits who, since 2014, have been staging similar sit-ins at the gate of Camp Schwab—managed to turn a policy priority for the U.S.-Japan alliance into a two-decade-old policy quagmire? In this chapter, I explore major status quo changes surrounding U.S. military bases and how activists seize upon the opportunity to mobilize against them, both

Base Towns. Claudia Junghyun Kim, Oxford University Press. © Oxford University Press 2023.
DOI: 10.1093/oso/9780197665275.003.0003

successfully and unsuccessfully. Bases in motion—those that expand, scale down, relocate, and close—disrupt preexisting expectations established around long-standing military bases (Lutz 2009, 32). U.S. base realignment initiatives (see chapter 2), which have shaken up the quotidian life in many base towns, offered an exceedingly rare moment of fluidity and uncertainty. Activists in key base towns preemptively mobilized against looming status disruption, oftentimes even before the allies officially announced realignment plans. When they managed to join hands with latent adherents, their challenges evolved into what defense analysts call major peacetime challenges to the U.S. military presence (Pettyjohn and Kavanagh 2017, 137). Even the mightiest of these challenges, however, has been mostly about delaying—rather than undoing—the eventual status transition.

Expanding Bases, Swelling Opposition

In towns chosen as candidates for an enlarged U.S. presence, activists jumped at the chance to mobilize against what they successfully branded as a status disruption threat, both physical and symbolic. As activists and latent adherents joined hands to fight off base expansion and the disruptions it supposedly entailed, broad-based anti-base movements ensued. If activists anywhere are on the alert for opportunities to mobilize, activists in the headline-making protest towns of Nago and Pyeongtaek managed to do so with the support of latent adherents. Likewise, activists in Yokosuka, easily among the friendliest host towns in the world, achieved the rare feat of mobilizing broad, city-wide support for its opposition campaign, even when the changes facing the naval base were more symbolic than physical. Once the authorities began to execute the status change, the anti-base struggle evolved into one focused on keeping the window of opportunity open. Nago has succeeded in doing so—indefinitely. Pyeongtaek activists managed to extend the clock, but not for as long. Outside these headline-hitting towns, activists also managed to seize on threatened status expansion in Iwakuni, Sagamihara, and Zama, turning these hitherto acquiescent host towns into front-page news. Behind the quiet façade of these communities, activists showed, lurked lingering apprehensions that they could ignite. Unable to extend the window associated with the transition, however, activists could not sustain high-intensity activism as status changes became the new normal.

Camp Schwab (Nago, Japan) and Camp Humphreys
(Pyeongtaek, Korea): Physical Disruption

Base opponents in the fiercest protest towns, such as Nago and Pyeongtaek, know how to capitalize on local grievances suddenly imposed by status quo changes. Without their efforts to turn the threat of quotidian disruption into an opportunity for mobilization, Camp Schwab and Camp Humphreys, two of the most contested American bases overseas, would have kept their former low profiles. Instead, activists managed to appeal not only to anti-base devotees but also to latent adherents, turning these formerly quiet towns into unlikely anti-base battlegrounds. Once mobilized, opponents in Nago and Pyeongtaek strove to ward off the eventual status transition. Their subsequent fates, however, differed. At Camp Schwab, activists have successfully delayed the FRF construction, a prerequisite for the relocation of MCAS Futenma (see chapter 2), extending the critical window for more than two decades. With the threat of status disruption perpetually in the offing, the opposition in Nago is going as strong as ever. At Camp Humphreys, activists did manage to delay the construction, but not for long enough.

The uproar surrounding proposed construction in the northern Okinawan city of Nago since 1997 is a sea change from the quiescence that once prevailed in this city. Indeed, Nago citizens once seemed content with their pre-relocation status quo. When Okinawans collectively rose against the extensive land expropriation by the U.S. military in the 1950s, the district of Henoko in Nago ran against the tide and went pro-base. It signed a rare deal with the Americans, albeit reluctantly, to allow the construction of Camp Schwab, thereby dampening the Okinawa-wide anti-base movement at the time. The destitute village chose economic benefits over a united Okinawan front against U.S. military bases, and economically thrived as a result—at least until the U.S. presence dwindled after the Vietnam War (Inoue 2004, 87–88; Williams 2013). Rent payments for landowners and jobs on the base became as important as ever for the economically struggling Henoko, so much so that Henoko dismissed Governor Ōta Masahide's initiative to scale down the U.S. presence in 1994 as "*meiwaku*" (nuisance) (Rabson 2012). Villagers even threw a party for troops returning from the Gulf War, calling them "neighborhood sons" (Williams 2013, 965).

What turned this sleepy town into an anti-base battlefront, then, was not the initial decision to host Camp Schwab, but the decision that came some four decades later to disrupt the long-established normality surrounding it.

Once Nago turned against the relocation of MCAS Futenma from Ginowan to Nago, as well as the FRF construction that would accompany the move, it became a rogue town that threatened to derail alliance management. It even contributed to the political fall of Hatoyama Yukio, who stunned the world by crushing the long-ruling Liberal Democratic Party (LDP) at the polls in 2009 with a new vision for Japan—which included a promise to move Futenma out of Okinawa. Just eight months in office, however, the prime minister stepped down in part for failing to do so. Just how much of a quagmire the Futenma relocation has become is also indicated by the fact that its supporters and critics do not even agree on how to define the always-ongoing yet never-completed status change. For supporters, the proposed changes amount to an expansion of the already existing base that is Camp Schwab, whereas for critics, it represents the construction of a completely new base. The latter characterization—*shin kichi kensetsu*—is predominantly used among anti-base activists and like-minded Okinawan government officials; according to them, new runways and military port facilities to be built as a replace-ment for Futenma add completely new functions to Camp Schwab, a base for live-fire and amphibious assault training, and therefore constitute a new base. The disagreement persists. "You can call it expansion, strengthening, or strengthening of base functions, but don't call it a new base," says Robert D. Eldridge, an academic who formerly worked for the U.S. Marine Corps in Japan. "Protesters try to create certain impressions" (Interview, June 12, 2017). The allies' 2006 realignment blueprint portrays the change as "adjustments" and "reconfiguration . . . of Camp Schwab facilities" (Ministry of Foreign Affairs of Japan 2006), presenting the view that the FRF does not represent a new base.

Even as base supporters and critics squabble over the definition, no one disputes the fact that activists have managed to turn this particular status change into what is today the world's most high-profile anti-base movement. In particular, the coastal district of Henoko, a community of fewer than 2,000 residents and the site of construction, has become an icon of anti-base resist-ance. Local activism began in 1997, soon after the allies released the SACO report in an apparent attempt to placate Okinawans irate over the 1995 rape case (see chapter 2). In response, local residents organized a grassroots group called the Society for the Protection of Life (Inochi o mamoru kai) and began monitoring developments at the planned site of a 1,500-meter, sea-based facility. Other groups sprung up, such as the Society of Nago Citizens Opposed to the Heliport (Heripōto iranai Nago shimin no kai) and the

All-Nago Citizens' Group against the Heliport (Heripōto kichi o yurusanai minna no kai) (Tanji 2006, 167). The emphasis at the time on the heliport belied the immensity of the envisaged expansion (Tanji 2006, 162), which some say amounts to "the largest concentration of land, sea, and air military power in East Asia" (McCormack 2014). As opposition sprouted, challengers pushed for a Nago-wide anti-base referendum. The vote in December 1997, despite Tokyo's heavy interference and the deliberate phrasing of the answer choices supposedly biased in favor of base supporters, still showed that opposition (52.8%) outweighed support (45.3%) (Inoue 2007, 157–85). Nago mayor Higa Tetsuya nonetheless proceeded to "accept" the relocation and then resigned.

Protesters persisted, with ebbs and flows in turnout closely paralleling intermittent developments in the threatened change. By 2002, the revised construction plan called for a 2,000-meter runway on reclaimed land in waters off Henoko. Daily sit-ins at the aforementioned Tent Village began on April 19, 2004, in response to the Naha Defense Facilities Administration Bureau's move to begin a survey of the area. Protest turnout surged. Soon, officials began work to set up a scaffolding tower for drilling, and protesters took to the sea, at one point staging twenty-four-hour seaborne protests—a sit-in on the sea. The 2005 realignment plan then called for a "reclamation project centered on . . . Camp Schwab, with a 1,800-meter runway inshore from Henoko." When the authorities announced a boring survey in April 2005 in preparations for construction, opponents staged twenty-four-hour protests for forty consecutive days. The survey was canceled. Then, in the finalized 2006 agreement, the plan was revised yet again to include "dual V-shaped 1,800-meter runways stretching from . . . Camp Schwab" out to the sea (McCormack and Norimatsu 2012, 99–100). When the government began environmental assessments of the area in 2007, seaborne protests resumed in order to block the procedure. "I got a boat license—and I don't even have a driver's license!" said Tanaka Hiroyuki, a member of the Council Opposed to the Relocation of the Heliport (Heri kichi hantai kyōgikai) (Interview, September 11, 2016).

More than two decades of resilient opposition in this remote town is a puzzling development for policymakers in Tokyo and Washington, who meant the FRF project to be a burden-reducing measure for Okinawans. By moving MCAS Futenma from the densely populated city of Ginowan to the northern hamlet of Henoko, the allies sought to assuage local anger over the heavy U.S. presence and address operational needs at the same time. If they may be able to achieve the latter goal, the former goal remains as elusive as ever. If anything, the move gave activists new opportunities to highlight long-standing grievances associated with the overbearing U.S. presence—exactly the opposite of what the allies were aiming for.

For anti-base devotees flocking to Henoko's protest hut, the FRF project represents a quotidian disruption that threatens to "suffocat[e]" the ocean, the "source of life" for the people of Nago (Tanji 2006, 164). Many are against this new imposition, not the entire U.S. presence on the island. "We aren't saying that (Camp Schwab) should be shut down. We are only saying that we don't want an additional burden," says Nakaima Shinichiro, a Nago city official who oversees U.S. base-related issues (Interview, September 15, 2016). The semi-permanent nature of the proposed change—the U.S. military has said the new facilities will be used for 200 years to come, despite the Japanese government's PR efforts to portray it otherwise (McCormack and Norimatsu 2012, 96)—adds fuel to activist efforts to resist the change. Widespread apprehension about the change meant that even Nago's supposedly pro-base mayors, Kishimoto Tateo and Shimabukuro Yoshikazu, had to attach various conditions to their rather reluctant acceptance (*yōnin*), as opposed to support (*sansei*), of the relocation. One such condition stipulated that the FRF would have to be in use for only fifteen—not 200—years.

Much of the anti-FRF activism is aimed at delaying the proposed construction as long as possible. Looking back some two decades later, activists could not have been more successful at "slow[ing] the pace of base construction even if by inches or by minutes" (Yamajiro et al. 2018). With remarkable resilience and surprising optimism, base opponents—most of them elderly retirees devoting their free time to activism—have managed to keep the dreaded change perpetually at bay. The perennial threat, punctuated by occasional government offensives and activist counteroffensives, ensures that status disruptions surrounding Camp Schwab never quite fade into the background. In July 2014, some ten years after the Tent Village sit-ins began, opponents began separate protests at the main gate of Camp Schwab in response to Tokyo's move to begin a seabed boring survey. Along with the Tent Village in the vicinity, Camp Schwab's front gate became another scene of endless contention, resulting in a threefold surge in the annual protest turnout in Nago in 2014. The latest advancement came in December 2018, when land reclamation, another prerequisite for construction, finally began. The Japanese government, eager to establish the reclamation as a new normal, rushed to pour sand into the ocean—until, by the end of 2019, activists forced it to acknowledge that the discovery of the soft, unstable seabed would have to delay the project once again (*Asahi Shimbun* 2019). With no end in sight in this protracted tug-of-war, the window of opportunity for anti-FRF protesters remains wide open. And as a result, every day, rain or shine, without fail a group of people will come together and sit at the protest tent, looking out into the turquoise Henoko waters.

Few base towns match the level of intense contestation seen in Nago; Pyeongtaek was one of these, if only for several years. Home to Camp Humphreys, a U.S. Army base that has lived through a mega expansion associated with the LPP and the YRP (see chapter 2), the city saw a local anti-expansion campaign grow into a polarizing national debate in the mid-2000s.

For anti-base activists, Pyeongtaek is a "cursed" city that has faced the threat of base expansion twice. Each time, activists who organized opposition campaigns focused much of their effort on finding common ground with local residents. Status disruptions in the early 2000s had a precedent from the early 1990s, when the allies attempted to move Yongsan Garrison (but not the 2ID) to Pyeongtaek. Leftist activists, long disgruntled with the already imposing U.S. presence in the city, grabbed the chance to organize an anti-relocation campaign. "I simply thought that Yongsan Garrison shouldn't come to Pyeongtaek, a city already squeezed between two U.S. bases," says Kim Yong-han, a first-generation anti-base activist. He was referring to Camp Humphreys and Osan Air Base, the two American bases in southern and northern Pyeongtaek, respectively. He gathered six other like-minded Pyeongtaek residents, including a bookshop owner and another who ran a street food joint, and organized a group called the Citizens Association Opposing the Yongsan Base Relocation (Yongsan migungji Pyeongtaek ijeoneul gyeolsa bandaehaneun siminmoim) in 1990.

The travails of the group bespeak the difficulty of organizing for a supposedly radical cause in a place that never once overtly questioned the U.S. presence. The group, for example, got three phone calls on the day their office phone number was made public: one from a police officer who warned against a potential violation of the National Security Law, a Cold War relic once used to jail dissidents; another from a small business owner who had a death wish for activists who were allegedly ruining his business; and a journalist who wanted to write about this new, supposedly radical group. When they rented a place—a local wedding venue—to hold an inaugural event, the venue operators abruptly called off the event, claiming that they were receiving threats. When the group finally held the event, plainclothes police detectives showed up. Nonetheless, as the official membership grew from 7 to 150, the group went on to gather petitions, hold rallies and protest marches, and send protest letters to the U.S. military. They also ran newspaper ads that Kim now laughingly admits were hyperbolic: the influx of American troops, the ad claimed, was bound to spread "decadent culture and AIDS," among other unsavory things (Interview, July 3, 2016).

Given the toil Kim's group had to go through, it is unsurprising that the 1990 campaign was a lonely fight entirely driven by anti-base devotees. Even though Kim consciously refrained from making radical demands and focused instead on resisting the looming relocation, he was still routinely disparaged as a "commie" (*ppalgaengi*). His group spent a year organizing rallies where the only participants were fellow activists from an assortment of leftist groups. Later, when local residents who stood to lose their land established a separate grassroots group, they repeatedly rejected the activists' overtures for joint action. Pyeongtaek police officers, according to Kim, warned the residents' group against "allying with the commies." After one year of persistent courting on the part of the activists, the two groups ultimately joined efforts (Interview, July 3, 2016). By 1993, the government scrapped the relocation plan, citing local opposition and high costs. Planned land purchases in Pyeongtaek were suspended.

A decade later, when the threat of base expansion returned to the city, activists, including Kim, took it as a chance to end the long hiatus in local activism. Nineteen Pyeongtaek-based civic groups founded the Pyeongtaek Movement to Stop Base Expansion (Pyeongtaek daechaegwi) in 2001, as the allies began discussing potential realignment plans. In a parallel to the earlier movement, leftist activists tried, and repeatedly failed, to reach out to latent adherents. Activists say it took two years before residents of Paengseong, the rural town hosting Camp Humphreys, came to view relocation as a pressing issue. What pushed these farmers—most of them elderly and previously politically inactive—to mobilize was the newly menacing status change: a sharp spike in the size of the land demanded by the U.S., which jumped from 196 acres to 2,328 acres. Camp Humphreys, as a result, was going to triple in size, making it the largest U.S. military base overseas. This change, which made displacements a sudden reality, spurred the reluctant farmers into action, and the Paengseong Residents' Action Committee (Paengseong daechaegwi), a grassroots group, came about in July 2003 (Park 2010, 32–34). Even then, many were reluctant to resist what seemed to be a foregone conclusion. While the committee strove to be a Paengseong-wide group, villagers less affected by the expansion began to revoke their membership. Eventually, Daechuri and Doduri—the two most heavily affected villages in Paengseong, whose sense of loss was much more pronounced—became the two pillars of the residents' group (Park 2010, 35–53). These were the people who turned up every evening for candlelight vigils and stood next to leftist activists for the next 935 consecutive days.

Resisting status disruptions proved to be a race against time. As the government pushed ahead with land seizure after the parliament approved the revised LPP in December 2004, keeping open the window of opportunity associated with the expansion timeline became the primary mission of base opponents. The belated establishment in February 2005 of the Pan-National Solution Committee to Stop the Expansion of U.S. Bases in Pyeongtaek (KCPT; Pyeongtaeng migungji hwakjangjeoji beomgungmin daechaeg wiwonhoe), an umbrella coalition of 114 civic groups nationwide, was a desperate attempt on the part of leftist civic groups to turn the tide of the status transition. Its stated mission, from the very beginning, was to stop the land expropriation. Opponents—both diehard activists and local farmers—focused their efforts on delaying tactics. Individual activists, calling themselves "*jikimi*" (guardians), moved their residency to Daechuri and populated empty houses in town to prevent demolition. The KCPT held a series of large events that summoned thousands of leftist activists to Pyeongtaek. Local residents refused to take part in compensation negotiations with the government, repeatedly blocking defense ministry officials from entering the town and conducting land surveys (Park 2010, 70–73).

These delaying tactics did work, but not for long. By the end of 2006, the government announced that the original plan to complete the relocation by 2008 was no longer viable. The government blamed, among other things, "delays caused by the opposition from local residents and civic groups" (Y. Yoo 2006). Still, the postponement came at a time when the movement was dying out. Facing steady progress in the status transition, hard to undo once set in motion, more and more residents accepted government compensation and left. The violent standoff on May 4, 2006, which pitted some 1,000 activists against 11,500 police officers and 3,000 unarmed troops, ended in the forcible removal of opponents from their last holdout in Daechuri. By the fall of 2006, after the government began to demolish empty houses one by one, forty out of ninety-two households that had refused to budge—*jikimi* activists would climb up to the roof to stop the excavators—agreed to leave. While the daily candlelight vigils continued until March 2007, a sense of defeat prevailed. Some activists insisted that protests should continue, but local residents told them that it was time to stop (*Hankyoreh* 2010). The movement soon evaporated.

What has finally emerged from this $11 billion project is an "entire city . . . (built) from scratch" that is the size of downtown Washington, DC, complete with four schools, five churches, sports fields, a "super gym," a water park, and an eighteen-hole golf course (Fifield 2017). The construction, involving 655 new and revamped facilities both above and below the ground, is celebrated as an "engineering feat"—the "largest single activity in scope and scale" in any recent military construction (Satkowski 2014). Pyeongtaek activists and former Daechuri residents are not joining in the celebration; they continue to argue that the village could have remained intact if the 3,500-acre base had chosen not to build its golf course[1] (Interview with Kang Mi, June 11, 2016).

CFA Yokosuka (Yokosuka, Japan): Symbolic Disruption

How activists mobilized opposition against CFA Yokosuka, the largest U.S. naval base overseas, is a prime example of activist agency in generating—not just exploiting—status disruption. The disruption that this naval base went through was more symbolic than physical, something that only those who understand its potential implications would have noticed and cared about. Activists, however, presented this subtle but symbolic change as a disruption just as unsettling as the massive physical expansion that hit Nago and Pyeongtaek. As a result, they turned enough latent adherents against the change to achieve relatively broad-based mobilization, if only briefly.

Yokosuka, with its self-conscious identity as a naval port city, is probably the least likely candidate for high levels of anti-base contestation. As city officials made sure to remind me, it is a city known for cordial civil-military relations (Interview, October 5, 2016). In the place where American commodore Matthew Perry landed nearly 170 years ago and forced Japan to open up for trade, military port tours, where tourists on a cruise ship wave at the sight of American and Japanese warships, constitute one of the most popular tourist attractions today. Yokosuka Navy curry, a ubiquitous local specialty that took its inspiration from the British Royal Navy, is another indication of the close ties between the city population and the military. Indeed, multiple rounds of local government surveys show that support for the U.S. naval presence consistently outweighs opposition—except in 2008, which I turn to below. Unlike MCAS Futenma or Camp Schwab, the naval base does not invite much partisan debate either. Ozawa Ichirō, who once led the DPJ, commented in 2009 that the U.S. presence in Japan should be drastically reduced so that only the Seventh Fleet, headquartered at CFA Yokosuka, would remain. Given the DPJ's policy platform that called for a diminished U.S. footprint and greater independence from Washington, his remark indirectly highlights the perceived importance and the enduring nature of CFA Yokosuka, home to the only permanently forward-deployed American aircraft carrier outside the United States.

What is perhaps less known about the city, though, is the long-standing presence of anti-militarist activists, who proved their acumen when they mobilized even the friendliest of host communities against what seemed to be a merely symbolic status change. Activists mobilized preemptively in 2001 when they began to suspect that the U.S. military wanted to permanently homeport a nuclear-powered, as opposed to a conventionally powered, aircraft carrier. The USS *Kitty Hawk*, the last conventionally powered aircraft carrier in the U.S. Navy and at the time stationed in Yokosuka, was scheduled to be decommissioned by 2008 (Montgomery 2004). Despite repeated Japanese government denials, activists suspected that a construction project to expand a pier at the base, which resumed in 2003 after a long hiatus, was aimed at hosting a nuclear-powered aircraft carrier that would replace the USS *Kitty Hawk*. The opposition was not so much about the physical extension of the pier, but what it implied: a symbolic fortification, and fundamental transformation, of the U.S. naval presence.[2] Activists here like to refer to Japan's 1950 Former Naval Base Cities Conversion Law, which sought to convert four heavily militarized Japanese cities—Yokosuka and Sasebo, as well as Kure and Maizuru—into "port cities for peacetime industries" for "the ideal of peace-loving Japan" (Nishiyama 2014, 131). The nuclear transition at CFA Yokosuka, in that sense, could not have deviated farther from the vision of demilitarization (Nīkura 2016, 94). For Yokosuka's nuclear-wary pacifists, who would censure even brief visits by nuclear-powered warships, the rumored change represented a threat—and an opportunity for mobilization.

The rumored change, as activists predicted, became official policy in 2005. Civil society in this model host city, likening the deployment to the introduction of a nuclear reactor, rose up in full force. Long-standing pacifist groups, such as the Yokosuka Citizens' Movement for the Declaration of Denuclearization (Hikaku shimin sengen undō yokosuka) and the Yokosuka

Peace Squadron (Yokosuka heiwa sendan), resisted nuclear-powered aircraft carriers in the time-honored Japanese anti-nuclear tradition. New groups that sprung up demonstrate a direct link between status disruption and oppositional mobilization: The Miura Peninsula Liaison Council against the Deployment of the U.S. Nuclear-powered Aircraft Carrier (Genshiryoku kūbo no bokōka o soshisuru Miura-hantō renrakukai), the Kanagawa Action Committee to Stop the Homeporting of the Nuclear-Powered Aircraft Carrier (Genshiryoku kūbo no Yokosuka bokōka o tomeyou Kanagawa jikkō iinkai), and the Citizens' Coalition Concerned about the Homeporting Project of the Nuclear-Powered Carrier at Yokosuka (Genshiryoku kūbo Yokosuka bokōka o kangaeru shimin no kai).

Activists went on to carry out two city-wide petitions in 2007 and 2008 to demand a referendum on the nuclear question. The petition drive generated sizable support: the first round in February 2007 garnered 40,000 signatures, or one-tenth of the city's population, and the second round in May 2008 received 50,000 (Association for Referendum on the Homeporting of the Nuclear-Powered Aircraft Carrier 2015). Street polls conducted by activists showed 70 percent of the respondents opposed the deployment of a nuclear-powered aircraft carrier (Hanai 2006). Petition organizers were confident that public opinion was on their side; what they opposed, after all, was the nuclear transition, not the presence of CFA Yokosuka (Hanai 2006). The local government, however, snubbed the call for a referendum (see chapter 5). CFA Yokosuka's nuclear era began in September 2008 with the arrival of the USS *George Washington*, complete with its two nuclear reactors. Still, the year 2008 stands out as an odd one in this supposedly friendly base town: according to the city government's own survey in 2008, "opposition" to and reluctant "tolerance" of the U.S. presence (26.3% and 44.1%, respectively) far outweighed willing "support" (17.6%)—a clear deviation from other years, when support was much higher (Yokosuka City 2013). The anti-base campaign, in other words, succeeded in establishing the nuclear conversion as a significant status disruption, even in the absence of visible, physical changes to the base.

As the USS *George Washington* went on to call Yokosuka home for the next seven years, status disruption became the new normal. When the USS *Ronald Reagan* became the new occupant of the naval base in 2015, activists' attempts to resist the deployment, despite an uptick in protest turnout, made little difference. Although activist polls showed that only 13.7 percent of some 120,000 respondents in Yokosuka favored the deployment, such disapproval did not translate into the kind of relatively broad-based oppo-sition that the USS *George Washington* had temporarily faced (Association for Referendum on the Homeporting of the Nuclear-Powered Aircraft Carrier 2015). Today, protests continue in a manner typical of Japanese civil society: localized, low-profile, yet persistent. While some recurring events, such as the annual anti-base "festival" that activists continue to put together, contribute to the relatively high turnout in the city, a vast majority of anti-base events remain small—and thus practically invisible. Existing groups continue to organize regular protest events, although they attract few latent adherents. A female-only group, We Don't Need Nuclear-Powered Aircraft Carriers (Iranai genshiryoku kūbo), was established shortly before the USS *George Washington*'s arrival, and has since held protest events every Tuesday. When I joined the women in October 2016, they were meeting for the 366th time. The Yokosuka Citizens' Movement for the Declaration of Denuclearization, the mainstay of local activism, also continues its monthly rallies that date back to 1976. At one such event held at Yokosuka's Shioiri Station, which I attended, activists held up posters with antiwar, anti-base, and anti-Abe messages. One poster solicited a response: "Wave if you agree with us!" During the one-hour event, of all the passersby at the busy railway station, three smiled and waved.

MCAS Iwakuni (Iwakuni, Japan) and Camp Zama (Zama and Sagamihara, Japan): Punctuated Protests

Iwakuni, Zama, and Sagamihara, the three cities hosting MCAS Iwakuni and Camp Zama, respectively, were once quiet towns. Sporadic activism in Iwakuni lacked visibility, and Zama and Sagamihara seemed almost com-pletely devoid of anti-base activism. When these host cities found them-selves on the receiving end of the status disruption associated with the U.S. force redistribution, however, they mobilized. As these communities suddenly turned against the long-standing bases in their backyards, they threatened to become protest towns. Their headline-making dissent, however, came to an end as opponents—activists, latent adherents, and as we will see later in chapter 5, local political elites—failed to delay the transition.

Iwakuni got an unlucky draw in the realignment. To begin, it had to newly shoulder dozens of aircraft and several thousand American personnel from

NAF Atsugi as part of the relocation of a Navy carrier air wing—a response to constant complaints about the naval air base located in the greater Tokyo area. Similarly, in a measure designed to placate Okinawa, in 2014 Iwakuni came to host KC-130 refueling tankers, originally stationed at MCAS Futenma. The city was also the first overseas host for F-35B stealth fighters and has received regular visits from MV-22 Ospreys—the notorious aircraft widely detested for their questionable safety record—from Okinawa. These apparent burden-reducing measures in other base towns came at the cost of antagonizing Iwakuni. Japanese officials say the relocation of Carrier Air Wing Five (CVW-5) from Atsugi was based on geographic considerations. NAF Atsugi is landlocked, whereas MCAS Iwakuni faces the Seto Inland Sea; with the latter's offshore runway, aircraft fly over the water, instead of residential areas. Critics, however, worry that the concentration of aircraft—adding sixty-one jets from Atsugi to the already deployed sixty makes this marine airbase even larger in capacity than the colossal Kadena Air Base in Okinawa—is turning the city into "another Okinawa" (*The Mainichi* 2017). They also argue that MCAS Iwakuni's runway, relocated offshore in 2010 in consideration of noise and safety concerns, had the opposite effect by inviting the transfer of CVW-5 from NAF Atsugi. On-base construction went on for years to revamp more than 70 percent of the base to accommodate the aircraft, even to the annoyance of American troops themselves (Burke 2012).

For longtime activists looking to promote their cause, the proposed base fortification presented new opportunities. Prior to the threatened change, traditional leftist groups, such as the Yamaguchi Prefecture Executive Committee for the Abolition of the Security Treaty and the Removal of the Iwakuni Base (Anpo haiki Iwakuni kichi tekkyo Yamaguchi-ken jikkō iinkai), had staged sporadic, small-scale protests with little visibility. Their self-professed goals—ending the U.S.-Japan alliance and shutting down MCAS Iwakuni—found few audiences outside the narrow circles of anti-base devotees. With the looming realignment, however, activists could now talk about base issues with renewed salience. Activists preemptively organized themselves against base consolidation in the latter half of 2004, shortly before the planned relocation of Atsugi-based aircraft became official. And this time, they focused on disruptions to the normality established around MCAS Iwakuni, rather than the presence of the base itself. Protest turnout rose, culminating in a rally that drew 11,000 in December 2007—an unusually high number for this quiet, aging city of 136,000.

Many latent adherents, who did not particularly mind the base itself, still got behind the drive to resist its expansion. A 2006 poll, for example, showed that 70 percent of the respondents opposed the base consolidation, although 68 percent of them supported the U.S.-Japan security treaty that justifies the continuing American presence (*Asahi Shimbun* 2006). "Why are the aircraft coming to Iwakuni? What is burdensome (*meiwaku*) for Kanagawa is also burdensome for Iwakuni!" Tamura Jungen, a longtime city assemblyman and a base critic, summarized the local sentiment against the relocation (Interview, September 28, 2016). (NAF Atsugi is located in Kanagawa Prefecture, a part of the greater Tokyo region.) Many local activists echo that the new emphasis on status disruptions mobilized fellow Iwakuni residents. "Most people are okay with things staying the same, as we've coexisted with the U.S. military for a long, long time," says a former city council member. "What we don't like is the strengthening (*zōkyō*) of the base" (Interview, anonymous, September 27, 2016). The influx of Americans, expected to double the troop size to more than 10,000, also had special implications for the city as it struggled with a population decline. "When you think of the population ratio between American personnel and Iwakuni residents, it is nearing one to ten, which is a bit overwhelming," said another former city council member, whose family home in Iwakuni's Yokoyama neighborhood is surrounded by empty, abandoned houses—a hallmark of Japan's shrinking population (Interview, anonymous, September 27, 2016). Base town residents, in other words, interpreted expected losses associated with base expansion in relative, rather than absolute, terms.

New anti-base groups that sprung up at the time attest to the mobilizing effect of the threatened status disruption. In November 2005, local housewives established a group called the Citizens' Association Opposing Relocation of the Carrier Air Wing and Nighttime Landing Practice (Iwakuni eno kūbo kansaiki butai to NLP iten hantai no shimin no kai). In early 2006, two new groups—the Association for the Referendum's Success (Jūmin tōhyō o seikōsaseru kai) and the Association against Acceptance of U.S. Carrier-borne Aircraft (Amerika kūbo kansaiki ukeire hantai ni "maru" o suru kai)— emerged to support a city-wide referendum, led by a mayor we will turn to in chapter 5. "I suspect that (Tokyo) believed that there would never be any opposition in Iwakuni, since it's Iwakuni," Ōkawa Kiyoshi, a pastor who took part in the anti-expansion campaign, says of the quiescence that had prevailed in Iwakuni's subnational base politics. For once, the usually "meek" (*otonashii*) people of Iwakuni, in Ōkawa's own description, were ready to prove Tokyo wrong (Interview, September 30, 2016). The referendum, held in March 2006, overwhelmingly rejected the relocation.

The non-binding referendum nonetheless failed to influence the allies' decision. Protests continued, but so did preparations for the realignment. As status transition progressed, opponents launched another campaign. The Association to Defend Atagoyama (Atagoyama o mamoru kai), founded in 2008, opposes the construction of U.S. military housing on Mt. Atago, a mountain housing a shrine that the local community treasures. Since August 2010, the group has held regular protests at the Atagoyama site—the neighborhood surrounding the site is festooned with yellow ribbons carrying anti-base messages—on every 1st, 11th, and 21st of the month. The housing project, dating back to 1998, initially began as an unusually ambitious urban development plan for the city of Iwakuni and Yamaguchi Prefecture. Local authorities targeted residents with a promise to build a new housing complex—a "dream town" (yume no maitaun) that would accommodate thousands (Asia-Wide Campaign Japan 2015). With less-than-enthusiastic responses from locals, coupled with the fortification of MCAS Iwakuni, however, the city and the prefecture called off the plan in 2007. In a total about-face, the defense ministry abruptly came into the picture, purchased the land, and said it would instead build housing units and various facilities for U.S. troops—those poised to arrive in Iwakuni as a result of the relocation of aircraft from NAF Atsugi.

Locals who willingly sold their land without intending to see it go to the U.S. military, as well as those who oppose MCAS Iwakuni, felt deceived. "The landowners were repeatedly told: 'Please sell your land for the development of eastern Yamaguchi,'" Okamura Hiroshi, who leads Atagoyama protests, recalls. "It makes no sense that our land will now become a site for U.S. military housing" (Interview, October 1, 2016). Tokyo is acting "as if it can do whatever it wants to do in Iwakuni," opponents said at a rally I attended in October 2016. Once again, however, they were unable to turn the tide. After the government acquired land ownership in 2012 and made military housing construction an inevitable outcome, protest turnout halved. Some sued the government, but to no avail. In the meantime, as fate would have it, they lost one member in a fatal car accident involving an American service member. Some thirty residents I met in the fall of 2016 were some of the last-remaining opponents, and they were losing the race against time. The only consolation for them, they told me, was that the size of the housing project has been reduced—"probably because we made some noise."

In Zama and Sagamihara, the two cities jointly hosting Camp Zama, a brief renaissance of anti-base activism in the mid-2000s similarly coincided with abrupt disruptions to the status quo. The history of the base as the Imperial Japanese Army Academy, or "Japan's version of West Point" (Robson 2020), as well as its current status as the U.S. Army Japan Headquarters, has earned Camp Zama a unique reputation as an "elite" base—something locals do seem to prefer over bases with combat troops. Coupled with this relatively benign reputation is the lack of immediate sources of everyday grievances. "It is a very quiet base, at least on the surface," Kaneko Tokio, a Sagamihara native and a longtime city councilman, says of the general local perception of Camp Zama. "There wasn't much of an opposition movement to speak of" (Interview, October 10, 2016). Indeed, the number of complaints about noise, a frequent source of local grievances in other host communities, averages around a dozen per year. The base generates so few protests that when it received twenty-one complaints about helicopter noise in one day, an all-time high, it made headlines (Kusumoto 2005). If anything, golf balls accidentally hit out of an eighteen-hole golf course on the base constitutes the majority of local complaints. Activists diligently keep a record of the number of golf balls found outside the fence, but stray golf balls—47 in 2007, 143 in 2008, and 21 in 2009—were still nothing compared to aircraft crashing onto a local college campus, as Ginowan residents witnessed, or stray ammunition rounds, a fixture of life in Pocheon.

When base opponents ended the relative calm in this activist wasteland, they did so by exploiting status disruption: in line with the U.S. force realignment plans, the I Corps, a U.S. Army corps based in Fort Lewis, Washington, was to relocate half a world away to Camp Zama. As in the case of Yokosuka, the threatened change was more symbolic than physical. Camp Zama, for example, was not going to triple in size as Camp Humphreys did—although reports at one point suggested that there would be several hundred new American troops, and that the base might double in size (Johnson 2004). Given the absence of obvious physical changes, activists warned instead that the relocation would radically transform what Camp Zama symbolized. The I Corps oversaw some 40,000 troops at the time, some of them operating in the Middle East (Johnson 2004); as its oversight stretched to this conflict-ridden region, the relocation could potentially push the limits of Japan's post–World War II constraints on the use of force (Pempel 2007, 117). Activists argued that the relocation, officially promoted as an effort to enhance allied interoperability, would further reinforce base functions (*kichi kinō no kyōka*) and implicate Japan in America's military adventures. In base officials' own words, Camp Zama was about to go "from administrative to operational" (Little 2007).

Beginning with an "emergency" rally by activists in the greater Kanagawa Prefecture area in August 2004, activist communities mobilized against this unlikely target. By 2005, several local groups arose, such as From Bus Stop to Base Stop (Basu sutoppu kara kichi sutoppu no kai) and the Association against the I Corps Relocation to Camp Zama (Kyanpu Zama e no Amerika rikugun daiichi gundan no ichū o kangeishinai kai). The former group began weekly sit-ins at Camp Zama every Wednesday, as well as monthly protests every third Saturday. Kanagawa-wide anti-base groups, such as the Kanagawa Peace Movement Center (Kanagawa heiwa undō sentā) and the Prefectural Joint Struggle Committee for Base Removal (Kichi tekkyo o mezasu kenō kyōtō kaigi), frequently joined forces. Protests that drew thousands, a rare feat for Camp Zama, regularly took place in 2005 and continued into early 2006. Protesters shared one simple message: "I Corps headquarters, stay out!" Activists seized on this rare moment of fluidity to newly press for their longstanding agenda. In Sagamihara, which also hosts Sagami General Depot, a U.S. army facility, activists made renewed calls for its return (*Mainichi Shimbun* 2005).

Efforts to delay the relocation, however, were not as successful as those in Nago and, to a lesser degree, Pyeongtaek. With virtually no physical change to the base, activists could not resort to the kind of physical delaying tactics—sit-ins aimed at blocking construction work, for example—that activists in Nago and Pyeongtaek could opt for. Relocation quietly took place in December 2007, and the window of opportunity closed. Base officials declined to reveal the exact number of soldiers that were added, except that the numbers were "in double digits, not triple digits" (Little 2007). The two-digit number was much smaller than the feared number of 300. Larger rallies came to an end, and since 2008, only a handful of anti-base events have managed to attract a crowd larger than 100.

As the post-relocation normal set in, the movement transformed itself into regular gatherings of a small group of highly dedicated individuals—a recurring pattern in Japan's localized anti-base activism. Members of From Bus Stop to Base Stop continue to hold weekly sit-ins, which date back to November 2005, as well as monthly marches every third Saturday, which began in April 2006. I joined them one Saturday afternoon in June 2017. To those who view these small acts of resistance as a quixotic quest, activists have this to say: "If we keep quiet, everyone will assume that we are content with the way things are." Silence, they told me, is akin to endorsement. The characterization of the I Corps relocation as "the most politically effective approach to strategic transformation" (Calder 2007, 246)—the reason being that base functions were redistributed among already existing bases, and not offloaded onto an entirely new base—belies the local frictions it touched off even in the quietest of the host towns.

Bases on the Move, Movements in Decline

In other base towns, meanwhile, activists have welcomed base reductions and relocations. Many first-generation anti-base activists in Seoul, Uijeongbu, Dongducheon, and Daegu saw base contraction as a meaningful alleviation of local grievances—a mission accomplished. As these cities quickly embraced the post-disruption normality, activism declined. Even in Uijeongbu, where locals lighted the fuse for nationwide protests some twenty years ago over a fatal accident involving two American G.I.s, activist-organized events commemorating the victims of the accident have drawn fewer and fewer people each passing year. Despite what the stylized image of angry protesters in news would have us believe, the kind of large-scale mobilization and sustained passion that we occasionally witness in places like Nago is not representative of everyday life in base towns.

Yongsan Garrison (Seoul, Korea), Camp Red Cloud (Uijeongbu, Korea), and Camp Casey (Dongducheon, Korea): Packing Up and Leaving

For activists who once flocked to Yongsan Garrison, Camp Red Cloud, and Camp Casey with pickets in hand, the scheduled relocations of these bases generated hopes that they could finally bid farewell to these long-standing fixtures of local life. Even better, the relocations came with a deadline, which seemed unmovable at the time. The fixed schedule associated with the physical relocations created concrete local expectations of a new normal, and activists demobilized as a result. This de-escalation, as I show below, contrasts with the enduring dissent in Ginowan, Yamato, and Ayase, the other supposed beneficiaries of base reduction.

If anyone were to guess which American base faces the fiercest opposition in Korea, Yongsan Garrison, a sprawling base of 630 acres in central Seoul, might very well be the first guess. As the most visible, and the most visceral, symbol of the U.S. presence in Korea, the base irked enough national political elites that there was a bipartisan consensus for its relocation as far back as the 1980s. The decline in protest activities since the 2004 YRP, however, shows how activists interpreted base contraction in the form of base relocation as something of a mission accomplished.

Anti–Yongsan Garrison activism in the late 1990s and into the early 2000s centered on the call for the return of the base site to Korea. Consciously refraining from the politically charged demand for a full troop withdrawal and base closures, activists, many of them leftist-nationalist in their orientation (see chapter 4), argued that the land on which U.S. bases stood should be returned. In 2001, some thirty civic organizations organized a coalition called the Campaign for the Return of the Yongsan Base (Yongsan migungiji banhwan undongbonbu). The coalition, which held monthly rallies near the base, had many allies at the time. The Association of Anti-American Women (Banmi yeoseonghoe) separately held weekly protests on Wednesdays, and the Joint Convention for Reclaiming Yongsan Base (Uri ttang yongsan migungiji doechatgi silcheondan yeonseokoeui) joined forces with the coalition every fourth Wednesday (Im 2001). The National Campaign for the Eradication of Crimes by U.S. Troops in Korea (Juhan migun beomjoe geunjeol undong bonbu) also packed the protest calendar with their weekly rallies. For this brief period, the district of Yongsan looked like a favorite hangout of anti-base activists.

The campaign came to an end after the announcement of the YRP, which stated that Yongsan Garrison would relocate, if not close, by 2008. Although activists were internally divided between those who were happy to see the base move to Pyeongtaek and those who rejected such NIMBY sentiments, the movement as a whole quickly dwindled (Interview with Lee Hyun Choul, July 8, 2016). The relocation, after all, addressed the long-standing activist demand, even if in an incomplete form. A clear expiry date for Yongsan's physical presence in Seoul—few expected the actual relocation would take another decade—further took the steam out of the movement. "Those who focused on Yongsan turned their attention to other places," said Kim Yong-han, who led the coalition movement of the early 2000s. "The relocation meant that there was no longer a target to fight against" (Interview, July 3, 2016). Both protest frequency and turnout saw a sharp drop in 2004.

Soon, debates over Yongsan Garrison began to center on the state-led plan to turn it into a park—a transformation from an off-limits zone to a decisively public space. Such disparate groups as anti-base groups, bureaucrats, landscape designers, and real estate developers began vying to influence the post-conversion Yongsan. While their visions for an ideal future for Yongsan widely diverged, they were predicated on the shared belief—the new normal—that the base was poised to leave.

Moving north of Seoul, in Uijeongbu, the calm surrounding Camp Red Cloud, home to the 2ID headquarters until its relocation to Pyeongtaek in 2018, is a far cry from the fury it once generated. Although few seem to remember it today, the largest nationwide protests against the U.S. military in Korea's history began with local gatherings in front of Camp Red Cloud in the early summer of 2002. The news that two fourteen-year-old girls on their way to a birthday party were crushed and killed by a U.S. mine-clearing vehicle from the 2ID—the same news that would go on to arouse national anger—was initially just local news that received scant attention. The very first protest over what the U.S. military calls the Yangju Highway Incident—Koreans call it the Hyosun-Misun incident (Hyosuni Miseoni sageon) instead, after the two girls' names, with more emotional undertones—took place at the gate of Camp Red Cloud. To the surprise of Uijeongbu-based activists who anticipated a small turnout, some 180 students from the nearby Uijeongbu Girls' High School, clad in school uniforms with tears in their eyes, came running to join the protest that day (C. J. Yoo 2002; Interview, anonymous, July 12, 2016). By the end of the year, Camp Red Cloud saw at least 114 more protests, punctuated by Molotov cocktails, egg throwing, and fence-cutting attempts. "Anti-Americanism Sweeps Korea," news headlines screamed (Demick 2002). Alarmed, the U.S. military replaced wire fences with concrete walls at five of its bases in Uijeongbu, including Camp Red Cloud.

As it turned out, it probably did not have to. Despite American officials' fears that they were never "going to recover from" the political fallout from the tragedy (Kirk 2002), protests in this northern Korean city subsided after the initially localized anger engulfed the rest of the country and, from 2003 onward, became few and far between. The city's return to quiescence coincided with the planned relocation of major U.S. bases in the city: Camp Red Cloud, Camp Stanley, and Camp Jackson.[3] The relocation, initially planned for 2008, marked the end of an era, and the movement against bases on the move became increasingly untenable. Uijeongbu activists, like their peers in Yongsan, redirected their attention to the less politically charged issues of environmental remediation, base conversion, and redevelopment (Interview, anonymous, July 12, 2016). Changes in the composition of local civil society correspond to both status disruption and the general decline in activism. For example, the Uijeongbu chapter of the Citizens' Committee to Reclaim U.S. Base Land, established in 1996, disbanded. The People's Solidarity for Participatory Democracy in Northern Gyeonggi (Gyeonggibukbu chamyeoyeondae), another group that worked on base issues, left Uijeongbu and settled in the neighboring city of Yangju. A separate group called the Uijeongbu Citizens' Alliance for a Peaceful City without U.S. Bases (Migungiji eomneun pyeonghwadosi mandeulgi Uijeongbu simin yeondae), founded in 2003 after the stormy protests of 2002, changed its name in 2007 to the Citizens' Campaign for Camp Falling Water Conversion (Hollingwoteo jeonmyeon gongwonhwareul wihan simin undongbonbu). The renaming reflected the evolution of the anti-base agenda in the city: from contestation of U.S. bases to the redevelopment of the returned base sites.

Dongducheon activists, once pioneers of activism against U.S. military prostitution, shared this anticipation of post-relocation normality. Camp Casey, another pillar of the 2ID eleven miles south of the DMZ, was scheduled to move to Pyeongtaek by 2008.[4] The poorest city in Gyeonggi Province, where a slew of American military installations occupy some 42 percent of the land, was eager to move on to a future without bases. The scheduled removal of Camp Casey, which stood in the middle of the city, brought a sense of closure even to the most devoted activists in town. "We lost the drive since the bases were supposed to leave . . . there was a sense of relief that the fight was over," says a former member of the Dongducheon Citizens' Association (Dongducheon siminyeondae). "We also got tired . . . we were getting older, had children to take care of, and had to get jobs," another former activist says (Interviews, anonymous, July 11, 2016). According to Kim Tae-jung of My Sister's Place (Durebang), an advocacy group for female camptown workers based in Uijeongbu and Dongducheon, the planned departure of the bases meant that the city could afford to devise many ambitious redevelopment plans, thereby transforming the nature of base issues (Interview, August 26, 2016). It was in this context that activists in Dongducheon, Uijeongbu, and Seoul demobilized—as those in Pyeongtaek mobilized.

Camp Walker (Daegu, Korea): Small Change, Big Influence

Activists in the southwestern city of Daegu also demobilized, but not because bases moved elsewhere. They did so even as the city, which hosts three major U.S. Army bases, came to be designated one of the two "enduring hubs" for the USFK. The new label attached to the Daegu enclave, which consists of Camps Walker, Henry, and George,[5] should have been an ominous development for base opponents; it suggests that the bases here, along with the ones in another hub in Pyeongtaek, are likely to stay indefinitely (Lostumbo et al. 2013, 242). What is more, for a city of 2.5 million people, the characterization of the two hubs as something that took intrusive bases "away from large urban centers" (Pettyjohn 2012, 90) made little sense. Nonetheless, unlike in Pyeongtaek, where a mega expansion of Camp Humphreys precipitated a militant counter-response, Daegu, as a logistics hub, experienced no overt physical transformation. Also, unlike in Yokosuka, where activists seized on symbolic changes to CFA Yokosuka, no such attempts were made in Daegu. If anything, local opponents of Camp Walker, a key pillar of U.S. Army Garrison Daegu, demobilized as a result of the planned removal of a seemingly inconsequential facility: a seventeen-acre heliport.

This relatively negligible status change pales in comparison with, say, the partial return of Okinawa's colossal Northern Training Area, where 10,000 acres of the 19,300-acre site have been returned in yet another attempt to assuage the disgruntled Okinawans. Similarly, the large-scale relocation of Yongsan Garrison and the 2ID to Pyeongtaek dwarfs the retrieval of a small site. And yet, the return of the H-805 Heliport at Camp Walker, a long-standing source of local grievances, proved to be a stabilizer that easily offset the potentially significant political implications of Daegu's reinforced status as a southern military hub. Indeed, while a handful of activists occasionally stop by Camp Walker to denounce what they call imperialist U.S. military strategy, few protest noise pollution.

This was not always the case. According to a 2001 survey by Bae Jong-jin, a first-generation anti-base activist and a longtime resident of Bongdeok-dong, a Daegu neighborhood bordering Camp Walker, a majority of local residents surveyed complained of stress, poor hearing, and difficulties in conversing and watching television due to helicopter noise (Interview, July 11, 2016). Cha Tae-bong, a septuagenarian grocer from Daemyeong-dong, another neighborhood standing next to the army base, takes pride in the fact that he led local protests in the 1990s. Cha keeps a journal that is half a log of everyday noise levels and half an outlet for his ruminations as a "subject of a small and weak nation," as he repeatedly calls himself. Even the fireworks celebrating the Fourth of July meant debris landing on his roof and just some more noise. Cha wrote to everyone he possibly could: presidents ranging from Kim Young-sam to Lee Myung-bak (he claims he once got in trouble for sending a letter to Chun Doo-hwan, Korea's last military strongman), a series of top American base officials in Daegu, the Korean defense ministry's U.S. Base Relocation Office, the Joint Chiefs of Staff, the Anti-Corruption and Civil Rights Commission, and the Daegu Supreme Prosecutors' Office. The list goes on. "At this moment I'd like to say that I'll do my best whatever I can within my authority allowed to help out our neighborhood's problem," went the vaguely worded response, dated May 1995, from the Commander's Office in Daegu (a Korean translation was attached). Responses from Korean officials were similarly non-committal. Frustrated, Cha teamed up with his neighbors and younger Daegu activists to organize multiple rounds of protests in the 1990s, getting himself arrested at least once for attempting to enter the base.

For people like him, the removal of the heliport came as a relief. Once the allies began discussing the heliport issue in 1995, residents were quick to establish expectations for the new normal. In 2002, the heliport agenda became part of the LPP, and in 2009, the SOFA Joint Committee agreed to the return of the site. Although the negotiations took nearly two decades to finally materialize, locals nonetheless welcomed the progress. An entry from his diary, dated May 7, 2016, refers to the bulldozing of the wall surrounding Camp Walker in preparation for the return of the heliport site: "It pains me to think of my neighbors who passed away before they got to see this." Cha went from a troublemaker to a recipient of a "Certificate of Appreciation" from the U.S. military in Daegu. "We appreciate the sacrifices made by the residents in their support of the defense of this great nation," the certificate said (*Maeil Shinmun* 2020), although Cha would be the first person to tell you that he was never given any alternative. Still, for the aging, politically conservative residents of Daemyeong-dong, who never demanded a wholesale withdrawal of American troops, the return of the site is a cause for celebration. A group of residents I spoke to as we stood before the partially destroyed wall of Camp Walker were not anticipating something grandiose. Their wish for the bright new future of the heliport site? "A big grocery store, maybe."

Interpreting Quotidian Disruptions

We now turn to a curious anomaly in status disruption. Contrary to the dominant patterns of status expansion and protest mobilization we saw re-peatedly in other base towns, base expansion at Kunsan Air Base and Osan Air Base (and to a lesser degree, Camp Mujuk) proceeded smoothly without provoking any discernable response on the part of local residents. Activist efforts to exploit status quo changes as an opportunity for mobilization—a recipe for mobilization success in many other host communities—bore little fruit. Of these communities, the quiescence surrounding Osan Air Base in northern Pyeongtaek in particular invites comparisons with the intense con-testation of Camp Humphreys in southern Pyeongtaek. Differing levels of mobilization corresponded to the relative perception of threat on the part of latent adherents: when compared with the mega-expansion at Camp Humphreys, changes at Osan Air Base seemed like something local residents could stomach. When latent adherents were unwilling to contest the status changes, there was not much activists could do. By contrast, in the perpetual protest towns of Ginowan, Ayase, and Yamato, activists have not let status contraction—or changes that herald a reduced U.S. presence, which has led to demobilization in other communities—take the steam out of protests. Instead, base opponents perceive the base reductions in their towns as a mere reshuffling, rather than an alleviation, of grievances.

Kunsan Air Base (Gunsan, Korea), Osan Air Base (Pyeongtaek, Korea), and Camp Mujuk (Pohang, Korea): Embracing Disruption

Despite activists' hopes and efforts to the contrary, residents in Gunsan, the northern half of Pyeongtaek, and Pohang embraced status disruptions—even sizable ones in the first two cases—that U.S. force redistributions entailed. The muted responses in the three communities highlight how locals interpret the threat of disruption. While professional activists invariably attempted to organize an opposition movement based on perceived losses (i.e., those re-lated to base expansion), latent adherents' responses depended on a relative, rather than an absolute, perception of loss.

The expansion of Kunsan Air Base, home to the Eighth Fighter Wing (the "Wolf Pack") in the southwestern port city of Gunsan, was a surprisingly

anticlimactic affair. And it proved to be so despite the potential for conflict: land seizures and potential displacements reminiscent of Pyeongtaek's
battle against Camp Humphreys. Indeed, activist communities flamboy-
antly warned against "the second Pyeongtaek crisis," as the air base was
slated to host two Army helicopter battalions and new munitions storage
facilities. The allies, for their part, feared anti-base "hard-liners" in this city
(Slavin and Hwang 2007), home to the longest-running anti-base rallies in
Korea. Nonetheless, the expansion of the "last warrior base in the Air Force"
(Houlihan 2007) did not provoke the kind of dramatic resistance seen in
Pyeongtaek and Nago. Quite the contrary: local activists who attempted to
launch an anti-expansion campaign were left feeling, in their own words,
"disappointed and demoralized" (Interview with Kim Pan-tei, June 15,
2016). Land expropriation progressed smoothly. By 2007, the defense ministry, virtually unopposed, was well on its way to clearing 315 acres of land
(Slavin and Hwang 2007).

This rather puzzling outcome—the lack of response to the physical, sizable
expansion—had to do with the failure on the part of activists to persuade latent adherents into action. Although professional activists in the city sought
to organize a joint campaign with local residents against base expansion, the
response from the residents most affected by the status disruption, including
those subjected to displacements, were lukewarm at best. For many of the
644 households affected by the expansion, the looming status change was not
damaging enough to risk confrontation with the highest authorities in Seoul
and Washington. While three separate residents' associations sprung up between 2005 and 2006 in response to land expropriation in Okseo County,
a rural town bordering the base, their demands differed from those of the
activists (Yun 2007). Although residents did stage several joint protests with
leftist civic groups in Gunsan (only after much behind-the-scene courting
from the latter), the agenda slowly shifted from absolute opposition, as favored by local career activists, to greater monetary compensation, as preferred by Okseo residents. At a series of protests in early 2008, residents
called for higher compensation, not the repeal of the expansion decision.
Some of them, in the words of a Korean government official, were even "really
thankful for being able to sell their lands that no one wanted." The constant
clattering from the nearby air base, after all, made the land "commercially
undesirable" (Slavin and Hwang 2007).

The acquiescence of Okseo contrasts with the militancy of Paengseong,
where a group of elderly farmers turned into unlikely squatters. If anything,

residents of Haje, a village in Okseo, had been seeking collective relocation since as early as 1999 due to base-related grievances: noise, water pollution, and fears of potential accidents involving munitions storage facilities on the base. Residents even wrote petition letters to the defense ministry and the now-defunct Ombudsman of Korea, a government agency that people could direct their grievances to (*Jeonbuk Domin Ilbo* 2004). Base expansion, in this sense, provided a chance to actually relocate and receive government compensation for doing what they had already hoped to do. When locals embraced base expansion, there was no way activists could turn Gunsan into another Pyeongtaek. Instead, activists took up the role of silent advocates, helping the residents negotiate compensation (Interview with Goo Jung-suh, June 13, 2016). Not every locality, after all, wants to become an anti-base battleground.

Similar dynamics at Osan Air Base, the Seventh Air Force headquarters some twelve miles north of Camp Humphreys, attest to the importance of the relative—as opposed to absolute—attribution of threat on the part of local residents. Activists protested both bases, the two targets of the mega-expansion, but the subsequent trajectories of these like-minded campaigns widely diverged. Again, the potential for conflict was there. Although Camp Humphreys in southern Pyeongtaek dominates the spotlight as the most contested base in Korea's history, initial resistance to the 2ID's relocation came from northern Pyeongtaek, home to Osan Air Base. Activists in Songtan, the area surrounding the air base, began organizing as early as 2001 against the proposed base expansion. At the time, the size of the land to be expropriated in Songtan—408 acres—was twice that of Paengseong, a village adjoining Camp Humphreys. This brought a sense of urgency to the former community but left the latter relatively unperturbed. In an attempt to resist land seizures, in 2002 activists launched what they called the Buy One Pyeong Movement (*ttang hanpyeong sagi undong*) in Geumgakri, a rural village slated for land expropriation.[6] A local farmer offered 2,000 square meters (or 605 *pyeong* in Korean measurements) of his land in Geumgakri for people to purchase—one *pyeong* per person. Each one of the 605 participants paid 50,000 won ($45) to own a piece of what they named the "field of peace."

The feared loss of land, and the accompanying sense of injustice, however, began to diminish in Songtan after the revised LPP drastically increased the size of the land to be expropriated in Paengseong by more than tenfold.

Suddenly, the land confiscation in Songtan seemed to pale in comparison. Locals went from talking alarmingly about the huge land grab in northern Pyeongtaek to downplaying its scale; it was no longer a "whopping" 408 acres, but "only" 408 acres, which seemed insignificant when compared to 2,328 acres that southern Pyeongtaek residents were going to have to give away. Camp Humphreys, newly facing a threefold expansion in "the largest construction and transformation project in the U.S. Department of Defense's history" (U.S. Army Garrison Humphreys 2018), emerged as the new activist cause célèbre. Pyeongtaek activists who focused their initial efforts on Osan Air Base began to redirect their attention to Camp Humphreys. "The fighting spirit was gone," says Lee Cheol-hyeong, a longtime Pyeongtaek activist. "500,000 *pyeong* (408 acres) of land is still a lot of land, but somehow it ceased to be an issue" (Interview, June 18, 2016). In a development that paralleled the case of Gunsan, noise pollution, a typical source of local grievances, further dampened the campaign against the air base, home to the Seventh Air Force and the 51st Fighter Wing. Local residents, having suffered decades of noise pollution, increasingly favored the option of government-funded relocation over an uphill battle against Seoul and Washington. By the end of August 2005, the defense ministry acquired 94 percent of the area adjacent to the air base—when the number stood at 58.4 percent in Paeongseong (Park 2010, 97). The "field of peace" was gone.[7]

Camp Mujuk, the only U.S. Marine base in Korea in the southeastern port city of Pohang, similarly emerged unscathed from the base realignment. An increase in the land granted to the U.S. military as part of the LPP— an additional 82 acres—hardly raised an eyebrow in a city where the heavy Korean Marine presence dwarfs the small American presence. A dozen local civic groups, including the Pohang chapters of the Korea Federation for Environmental Movements and the Korea Youth Corps, did establish a coalition to oppose the land grant, a decision made without local input. Their activity, however, was limited to issuing written statements and sending questionnaires to local political elites and the defense ministry (*Kyongbuk Ilbo* 2002). Unlike in Pyeongtaek and Gunsan, where local residents faced displacements, the land grab here did not involve any reported instance of government land seizures that affected local people. The new land grant was simply too trivial to even become an issue, much less unite activists and latent adherents, in this quiet town already on the periphery of anti-base activism.

MCAS Futenma (Ginowan, Japan) and NAF Atsugi (Ayase and Yamato, Japan): Reshuffling Grievances

Sometimes, status disruption at one base is directly intertwined with that of another. Activists, locally based and yet nationally networked, know how to connect the dots. Policymakers' attempts to address old grievances at one base, therefore, risk provoking new grievances at another—a pattern repeatedly seen in the tumultuous process of U.S. base repositioning. In one such case, the FRF construction at Camp Schwab in Nago is meant to alleviate the well-publicized grievances in Ginowan, home to MCAS Futenma. Similarly, the relocation of troops and aircraft from NAF Atsugi to MCAS Iwakuni means that the alleviation at the former base comes at the cost of fortification at the latter base. Nonetheless, contestation surrounding MCAS Futenma and NAF Atsugi—the two supposed beneficiaries of the realignment—persisted, as activists viewed the realignment as a mere redistribution of grievances.

Popular resistance to the offloading of the base burden from MCAS Futenma onto Camp Schwab offers an important caveat that status contraction does not always guarantee protest demobilization. Given the familiar cliché to describe the former base as the "most dangerous base in the world," anti-Futenma activists, one may assume, might be happy to see it move elsewhere. Quite the contrary—MCAS Futenma, standing in the middle of Ginowan, is an all-you-can-eat buffet of protests. Protests of all flavors happen every week throughout the entire year. Activists kick off the protest scene each year with the "new year car protest" (*shinshun jidōsha demo*) in early January. In a tradition dating back to 1984, opponents drive along the base's 7.5-mile-long fences and call for its immediate return. Every May since 1978, hundreds, and sometimes thousands, of people from and outside Okinawa march through the island in a three-day "peace march," where they unfailingly make a stop at Futenma. Other groups—such as the Meeting of Kamados (Kamadu-gwa no tsudoi), a women-only group, and students and faculty of Okinawa International University, the site of a U.S. helicopter crash in 2004—have regularly staged their own rallies. The deployment in 2012 of MV-22 Ospreys, widely detested for its questionable safety record, has only added to the protest calendar. Every Monday evening, a group with a self-explanatory mission—the Association for Gospel Singing at the Futenma Base Gate (Futenma kichi gēto-mae de gosuperu o utau kai)—indeed gathers and sings. Every morning Monday through Friday, Futenma's Nodake gate and Ōyama gate see returning picketers who hold up anti-base signs and chant slogans as base personnel drive into the gate for work. Every Friday evening, more picketers show up to protest.

As base opponents in Ginowan and Nago remain united in their resistance to the reshuffling of grievances within Okinawa, however, the perennial impasse in the scheduled relocation puts activists in a catch-22 situation. As opponents in Nago continue to block the construction of the Futenma replacement facility, their counterparts in Ginowan also continue their protests because MCAS Futenma, the very subject of contestation, remains indefinitely in place—precisely as a result of base opponents' successful campaign against its relocation within Okinawa and the authorities' refusal to move it off the island. At one anti-Futenma protest I attended in September 2016, participants heckled truck drivers carrying materials for construction work at the base. "Why would Futenma need construction work, when it is supposed to be closed within a few years?" Akamine Kazunobu, a Ginowan resident, said of the on-base construction (Interview, September 21, 2016). The U.S. military, for its part, explains that it needs to improve the old, outdated base, especially to better accommodate the Ospreys (Ashton 2015)—the very impetus for the spike in protests in Ginowan. Critics of anti-base activists also like to point out that the 2004 military helicopter crash at Okinawa International University, a university neighboring Futenma, would not have happened if the relocation had proceeded as originally planned (Interview with Robert D. Eldridge, June 12, 2017). In the face of the intransigence of the allies, a successful NIABY (Not in Anyone's Backyard) campaign that has delayed the FRF construction indefinitely has inadvertently allowed Futenma to stay indefinitely—and even to invite the menacing Ospreys.

Activists remain similarly unappeased in Yamato and Ayase, the two cities hosting NAF Atsugi. The largest U.S. naval air base in the Pacific—its presence was so imposing that hundreds of residents left the surrounding communities in the 1960s (Kanagawa Prefectural Government 2007, 110)—has undergone major changes as part of the U.S. military realignment: the aforementioned relocation, completed as of 2018, of Carrier Air Wing 5 from NAF Atsugi to MCAS Iwakuni. Noise pollution has always been a primary source of grievances against the naval air base, which has seen a vibrant anti-noise campaign dating back to the 1970s. The relocation of the fighter-jet squadrons, accompanied by a reduction of key base functions and a decrease in troop numbers, was supposed to address these long-running grievances in the two host cities. Residents were hopeful, for example, that property prices would finally go up (Chugoku Shimbun 2008).

Just like anti-Futenma devotees, however, anti-Atsugi activists do not perceive the status reduction as progress. Instead, the staunchest critics call this apparent burden-reducing measure "deception." "We are worried that the relocation to Iwakuni might actually double the noise level at Atsugi," says Kaneko Tokio, a Sagamihara city council member who leads the noise pollution lawsuit against this former kamikaze base. The reasoning is that aircraft based at MCAS Iwakuni will still make stops at NAF Atsugi for fuel before and after training in Gunma Prefecture, actually increasing the number of stops routinely made at Atsugi (Interview, October 10, 2016). Furthermore, this apparent attempt at noise reduction ignores the elephant in the room: CFA Yokosuka, whose military functions are closely intertwined with those of NAF Atsugi. Most jets flying to the latter are carrier-based aircraft originating from the former; as long as the Seventh Fleet calls Yokosuka home, NAF Atsugi is bound to generate the same grievances. Indeed, the very first anti-Atsugi noise pollution lawsuit in 1976 was triggered by the increase in noise levels associated with the deployment of an aircraft carrier to Yokosuka.

Anti-Atsugi activists, therefore, continue their opposition despite the ostensibly favorable status change. The Alliance for Prevention of Explosive Noise at Atsugi Base (Atsugi kichi bakuon bōshi kiseidōmei), established in 1960, has led multiple rounds of noise pollution lawsuits and won compensation from Tokyo, if not from Washington, each time. The latest round, filed in 2017, involves 8,879 plaintiffs—the highest-ever number for noise pollution lawsuits here. The Yamato Citizens' Liaison Committee for Protection of Peace and Life (Heiwa to kurashi o mamoru Yamato shimin renrakukai) and the Kanagawa chapter of the Japan Peace Committee (Nihon heiwa iinkai), a nationwide organization affiliated with the JCP, have held a protest march every third Sunday of each month since January 1981. Such routinized protests, however, have become increasingly predictable over time. High contestation, in this sense, coexists with low visibility.

Conclusion

Activist efforts to seize on status quo disruption have led to some of the largest anti-base movements in the world. In towns hardest hit by base expansion, where latent adherents joined activists in protesting an unwelcome intrusion into their everyday life, their joint action evolved into major episodes of peacetime challenges to U.S. military bases.

These disquieting disruptions show how some of the basing policies meant as strategic moves, or even as conciliatory gestures to local host populations, have ended up becoming major headaches for the allies. The relocation of the 2ID to Pyeongtaek, the nuclear transition in Yokosuka, and the military fortification in Zama and Sagamihara were not politically motivated. The relocation of MCAS Futenma from Ginowan to Nago, as well as the relocation of aircraft from NAF Atsugi to MCAS Iwakuni, were supposed to address local grievances. And yet, what the allies meant to be a solution of some sort—to a wartime force posture that seemed increasingly outdated in Korea, and explosive local anger over a rape case in Okinawa—opened up a whole new can of worms instead, heavily politicizing policy, complicating implementation, and alienating every single party to the debate. In Ginowan, MCAS Futenma still stands firm, regularly inviting some of the biggest antibase protests in Okinawa. Even as protests eventually subsided in places like Pyeongtaek, Yokosuka, and Iwakuni, the contested transition process was not the smooth one that the allies had probably hoped for. Too often, policy implementation—the shuffling and reshuffling of American personnel and the machinery of war—comes at the cost of antagonizing the localities involved.

As we have repeatedly seen, resisting these disruptions is a battle against time: it is not so much about reversing the decisions that impose the disruptions on local communities as it is about delaying their execution. Given the temporally limited nature of the window of opportunity, base opponents focus their efforts on keeping that window open as long as possible—thereby keeping the eventual status transition at bay for as long as possible. As we have seen, Nago opponents have succeeded most spectacularly on this front, repeatedly blocking government attempts to jump-start the ever-elusive FRF construction. At the time of writing, the daily sit-in at Henoko's Tent Village is well past the 6,000-day mark. While the authorities did make headway, with some 30 percent of the land reclamation completed by the end of 2021, activists continue their attempts to slow down the status transition. In addition to the discovery of the soft seabed, activists have also argued that the soil the Japanese government is procuring for the reclamation may contain the remains of the war dead—both Japanese and American soldiers who died in the Battle of Okinawa (Burke and Kusumoto 2021). All these efforts have pushed Tokyo to concede that the FRF construction will take another decade—until 2032, nearly thirty-six years after the Futenma relocation plan surfaced. In the meantime, Nago remains very much a protest town.

Still, Nago is a clear outlier. Despite the potentially explosive mobilizing power of status disruptions, they have been eventually executed in almost all places. Successful movements may be able to extend the clock, but such delaying tactics are often capable of doing only that: delaying, not undoing. Not all base town residents think that delaying is worth all the efforts of resisting a decision imposed by the highest authorities in Washington. When latent adherents remain unresponsive to activists' overtures, even major disruptions cannot lead to broad-based mobilization. Despite the threat of land expropriation, and despite professional activists' best efforts, latent adherents in Gunsan and northern Pyeongtaek chose to embrace, rather than fight, the disruptions. Some assumed the futility of any resistance, and others saw that the loss of land, in comparative terms, as not significant enough to warrant costly organizing efforts. In mobilizing against status quo changes, perhaps the biggest challenge for activists is to persuade latent adherents that the transition they are fighting against is not a foregone conclusion.

4

Framing Bases

On September 9, 2012, tens of thousands of protesters thronged a seaside park in Ginowan, a central Okinawan city home to a base that had become a perennial irritant in the U.S.-Japan alliance: MCAS Futenma. In what organizers claimed was the largest protest since the end of the U.S. occupation of the island in 1972, participants were united in their condemnation of the looming deployment of MV-22 Osprey aircraft—or "the most dangerous aircraft in the world." Accusing the aircraft of having a questionable safety record—the tiltrotor aircraft crashed in Morocco and Florida earlier that year, earning it the ominous moniker "widowmaker"—protesters held up signs in bright red and yellow that read, in English, "Osprey DANGER." "It cannot be considered normal to live under conditions in which an Osprey may fall from the sky at any moment," a speaker told the crowd (Spitzer 2012). It was not the first or the last such gathering that the deployment touched off. A countless number of anti-Osprey protests ensued in the following weeks and months in Okinawa, with a unanimous focus on safety threats. Some Ginowan residents began showing up at Futenma's Nodake gate and Ōyama gate every morning, with their anti-Osprey messages on display for anyone entering and exiting the embattled base. Fellow Okinawans driving by would occasionally wave and honk in support.

As protests raged in Okinawa, base opponents elsewhere in Japan were closely following the development, fearing that the deeply unpopular aircraft might make stops at U.S. military bases in their own communities. Indeed, the expression "Okinawaization of the mainland" (*hondo no Okinawa-ka*) began to gain currency among mainland base opponents (*Akahata* 2014). As if to lend credence to their apprehensions, the aircraft did pay an unexpected visit to Sasebo, a mainland port city that is home to CFA Sasebo, on March 23, 2015. Some sixty activists, most of them members of a local labor union, immediately organized a protest rally. This event, however, had a noticeably different take on the nature of the problem: the U.S. tiltrotor was condemned as a "threat to the citizens who yearn for peace," rather than as a threat to everyday safety (*Nishinippon Shimbun* 2015). To these seasoned activists in

Base Towns. Claudia Junghyun Kim, Oxford University Press. © Oxford University Press 2023.
DOI: 10.1093/oso/9780197665275.003.0004

Sasebo, the Ospreys were not too different from, say, the USS *Enterprise*, the nuclear-powered aircraft carrier whose port call they so vehemently opposed in the 1960s: they all represented American militarism, a menace to the ostensibly peace-loving people of Japan.

Why do we see these drastically different rhetorical responses to U.S. bases, and how do these differences factor into mobilization? In this chapter, I show how activists assign meaning to their anti-base causes—nationalistic, ideological, and pragmatic—with varying mobilization success. Although U.S. military bases are an embodiment of international security, anti-base protest discourses often draw on local experiences and pragmatic, everyday grievances associated with the American presence. In doing so, anti-base activists go directly against the tendency of many other locally grounded social movement actors to globalize their grievances (Gordon and Jasper 1996; Bob 2005; Tsutsui 2017). This unusual rhetorical parochialism is partially a necessity for activists pursuing supposedly radical goals; by helping them ward off accusations of ulterior political motives, pragmatic frames facilitate impression management and appeal better to latent adherents. At the same time, rhetorical pragmatism also allows the broad anti-base cause to be tailored to specific local grievances. This primacy of the local in anti-base framing, however, poses a dilemma: as pragmatism prevails, activists and the authorities increasingly squabble over technicalities, precluding the possibility of asking more fundamental questions about the American military presence. Activists' conscious decision to subordinate their maximalist aspirations to mundane local grievances, in this sense, ultimately thwarts the ambition that got them involved in activism in the first place. The rhetorical safe haven that pragmatic framing provides, in the end, may be a rhetorical trap.

High Pragmatism, High Contestation

The high-intensity activism we see in protest towns is in part a rhetorical feat. Protest organizers in these communities know how to maximize their broader appeal, opting for grassroots resonance over abstract principles. In Nago and Pyeongtaek, for example, protest discourses about protecting local ways of life struck a chord with local residents, who have a deep attachment to the sea and the land, respectively. In Ginowan, Ayase, and Yamato, a never-ending supply of daily grievances easily lend themselves to resonant pragmatic rhetoric. MCAF Futenma, with its reputation—albeit factually incorrect—as the "most dangerous base in the world," and NAF Atsugi, where noise pollution lawsuits began as early as 1976, give base opponents little incentive to deviate from their pragmatic focus on aircraft accidents and noise pollution. Given the predominance of rhetorical pragmatism across these protest towns, much of the literature that distinguishes Okinawa from the Japanese mainland—with the implicit assumption that Okinawa is uniquely pacifist—does not align with the on-the-ground discursive practices of anti-base activists.

excellent point.

Camp Schwab (Nago, Japan) and Camp Humphreys (Pyeongtaek, Korea): Protecting Local Ways of Life

The high contestation at Camp Schwab and Camp Humphreys is buttressed by activists' rhetorical efforts to draw attention to the intrusion of the bases into local life. Base opponents frame their activism as a way to preserve local ways of life, which center on the pristine nature of Henoko and the fertile farmland of Pyeongtaek, respectively. For activists deeply committed to pacifist principles and leftist-nationalist ideals, this deliberate pragmatism requires making a conscious rhetorical choice.

Even in Okinawa, a place many consider to be a pacifist icon, activists direct people's attention to practical grievances grounded in their life experiences. The alleged threat that the FRF construction poses to Henoko's nature and its inhabitants, and the fear that it will "annihilate a way of life" in this quiet fishing town (Dudden 2014, 181), has both unified anti-base activists in Okinawa and elevated the movement to a transnational cause (Spencer 2003, 129–30; C. J. Kim 2021). Opponents flooding into this secluded hamlet—Nago natives, as well as legions of sympathizers hailing from other parts of Okinawa and occasional visitors from the mainland—have highlighted the tangible threats of environmental degradation associated with the FRF project. The central claim is that construction will destroy the coral reefs that provide habitat for the dugong, an endangered marine mammal designated as a natural monument in Japan. Befitting the ecological focus, the elusive mammal has become a popular movement symbol. A number of groups bear its name, such as Dugong Network Okinawa, Dugong Protection Fund Committee, and Save the Dugong Foundation (Taylor 2010, 275–76).

Cartoon images of the dugong appear on all sorts of protest leaflets, posters, and T-shirts (Inoue 2007, 176–77).

Protest rhetoric juxtaposes military bases and the local environment, with the former as a threat to the latter: "The situation is urgent: there is a reckless, ongoing attempt to build a base in the precious ocean where dugongs live" (*Ryukyu Shimpo* 2001). "Protect the ocean, the habitat for the dugong" (*Jugon no umi o mamore*) is a ubiquitous slogan. When Caroline Kennedy, as U.S. ambassador to Tokyo, visited Okinawa in 2014, she faced a loud cry from some 200 activists: "Don't kill the dugong!" (*Ryukyu Shimpo* 2014). The ecological focus, with its universal appeal, drew in global actors. A transnational group of activists took the issue to a U.S. court in 2003, which resulted in a landmark lawsuit dubbed *Dugong v. Rumsfeld*. In this symbolic suit, activists claimed that the FRF construction violated the U.S. National Historic Preservation Act by failing to protect this precious marine mammal. Prominent international environmental groups, such as Greenpeace, have made similar pleas to stop the construction and preserve marine biodiversity (Tanji 2008; C. J. Kim 2021). In 2018, Okinawa's biodiversity featured as a major agenda item at a global anti-base activist conference in Dublin that I attended.

Activists are mindful of their empirical credibility. The Japanese government's environmental assessment, for example, became a subject of intense scrutiny. In a 2007 statement repudiating the government's proposed assessment plan, Okinawan NGOs and like-minded lawmakers criticized the proposal for "lack[ing] research on existing studies on the dugongs, seaweed beds, and coral reefs," and "fail[ing] to mention the type of aircraft to be used and how it will be operated" (*Ryukyu Shimpo* 2007). Domestic legal battles—a suit against the environmental assessment and a separate suit against a landfill, a prerequisite for the FRF construction—similarly appeal to concerns about noise pollution and marine biodiversity. More recently, opponents have managed to marshal even more scientific arguments against the FRF. They have pointed to the geological weakness of the seafloor, as well as the presence of an active fault line found in the area (*Ryukyu Shimpo* 2017)—yet more attempts to resort to technical expertise to back up their opposition. Tokyo has conceded that the soft seabed would indeed have to be strengthened, further pushing back the target completion date by another decade. Both supporters and opponents of the construction, in this sense, operate within the same discursive framework dominated by rhetorical pragmatism.

In Pyeongtaek, Korea, the predominance of pragmatic framing at the height of the contestation over the threefold expansion of Camp Humphreys further highlights the primacy of the local in anti-base organizing. Even as the anti-expansion campaign evolved into a national leftist-nationalist coalition movement, many activists pursuing pan-Korean ideals—that is, activists who condemn the U.S. military for allegedly obstructing national reunification—mostly prioritized pragmatic, locally grounded grievances in order to maximize the movement's resonance (Yeo 2006). Vulnerable to the frequent charge that they are politically motivated agitators manipulating locals, activists knew that the public face of the campaign had to be local farmers who stood to lose their farmland. For this reason, both Pyeongtaek-based civic groups and the KCPT, an umbrella coalition of leftist-nationalist activists nationwide, put the villagers and their immediate grievances on center stage.

The very physical nature of the American military primacy—the bases must stand on foreign soil, after all—means that the base conflict often centers on the question of the land. Indeed, the villagers who joined hands with the leftist activists had experienced displacements twice before: during the Imperial Japanese military's base construction in 1942, and then the U.S. expansion of the base, called K-6 at the time, in 1952. The second expansion came in the middle of the Korean War, and locals, left with little recourse, were forced to vacate their homes. As evictees struggled to survive, they managed to turn salty mud flats into arable land, from which the famous Pyeongtaek rice began to be grown (Park 2010). Now, they were being asked to let go of that land for the third time. In a village called Daechuri, literally "Great Farm Village," the pragmatic emphasis on farming and farmland was bound to resonate.

Although some leftist-nationalist activists stubbornly invoked American hegemony and the divided Korean peninsula, most managed to subordinate their pan-Korean ideals to latent adherents' attachment to the soil they tilled. In the first protest event held by the KCPT, participants shouted the following slogans: "We cannot grant the land cultivated with our blood and sweat!" "We oppose the base expansion decision made without villagers' input!" (H. Choi 2005). The frequently heard KCPT slogan "Let's farm again this year" epitomizes the careful considerations put into this locally resonant frame (Yeo 2006, 48). Various signs put up in the area—"Our land will forever remain farmland," "(Our) rice is the best!," and "I want to cultivate my own land" (Park 2010)—reinforced the movement's pivot to the local. When activists took the matter to the Constitutional Court, their central claim was that the expansion violated the residents' right to a livelihood (Park 2010, 292). In a further attempt at impression management, the KCPT refrained from violence. After the first round of what activists called the Grand Peace March turned into a violent collision with riot police, the KCPT had to make sure that its subsequent marches proceeded peacefully (C. J. Kim 2017, 315).

If activists' rhetoric required a conscious choice, villagers naturally leaned toward pragmatic rhetoric as they drew from their life experiences to highlight the perceived injustice of base expansion. At the inaugural meeting in 2003 of the Paengseong Residents' Action Committee, a residents' association, a member gave a speech: "Those of us who have suffered from noise, tremors, and pollution caused by the base, and those of us who stand to lose our land and are forced to leave our hometown today . . . we need to collectively solve our problems" (Park 2010, 32). When they held an impromptu candlelight vigil in September 2004 to protest the arrest of the village head for obstructing a public hearing on the relocation, the event had to be held at 8 P.M., after everybody had returned from a day's work at rice paddy fields—the very fields set to be expropriated for base expansion. Participants, many of them too shy to speak into the microphone, nonetheless made some startling statements that day: "I will defend my land until the end. . . . If I die, I die here" (Park 2010, 48–52). As they continued to hold vigils, they chose a peculiar venue: a greenhouse. Village-led protests continued to evoke the images of aggrieved farmers and their attachment to the Pyeongtaek land. In one such event in January 2006, farmers led an eleven-day tour of the country in farm tractors, which bore banners reading: "We want to continue cultivating our land next year." In March 2006, protesters plowed their rice fields to signal their resolve to continue farming (*Hankyoreh* 2006). These unlikely activists—elderly farmers with no prior political socialization—were among the last-remaining group of squatters who defied eviction.

MCAS Futenma (Ginowan, Japan) and NAF Atsugi (Ayase and Yamato, Japan): Shared Everyday Grievances

Despite the scholarly tendency to treat U.S. military bases in Okinawa as something that defies comparison with bases elsewhere, activists across Japan resort to similar rhetorical strategies and adopt similar tactics, both institutional and disruptive, to challenge them. Local opposition against MCAS

Futenma and NAF Atsugi revolves around immediately recognizable—and immensely predictable—grievances associated with air operations: noise pollution and aviation accidents. Nowhere in their discourses does one find allegations of some imperialist ruse. Okinawa, despite its unique historical experiences and global reputation as an anti-base icon, shares more common traits with other host communities than what much of the literature, which treats Okinawa as sui generis, may suggest.

At MCAS Futenma, perhaps the most embattled U.S. Marine base in the world, activists' emphasis on instantly recognizable grievances guarantees a steady flow of protesters. Activist-organized protest events between 2000 and 2015 show that aircraft accidents and the deployment of the MV-22 Osprey tiltrotor aircraft, both closely related to everyday safety concerns, are the most frequent points of contention. This particular category of base-related grievances has cumulative effects, as old and new accidents form coherent narratives of everyday victimization. The crash in 2004 of a U.S. Marine helicopter on the campus of a local university bordering MCAS Futenma, for example, has led to regular commemorative events ever since—initially every month, and later every year. "We cannot predict when aircraft will fall on us from Okinawa's sky," participants said on the fifth anniversary of the crash (*Ryukyu Shimpo* 2009b). Critics do not view the 2004 crash as an isolated event; instead, they link it to a series of similar accidents, such as the crash of an F-100 on Okinawa's Miyamori Elementary School in 1959 that killed eighteen and injured more than 200. The deployment of the Ospreys in 2012 added fuel to the fire. The "accident-prone" Ospreys can cause "a catastrophic accident . . . on this densely populated island," protesters argued (Tritten 2012). Japanese policemen reciting the safety precautions against street protests were instantly met with a rebuke: "Ospreys are more dangerous!" (*Ryukyu Shimpo* 2012). Indeed, in addition to the well-known cases of crashes, the aircraft had an emergency landing in North Carolina just a day before a large anti-Osprey rally in September 2012. This "breathlessly reported" accident, according to *Time* magazine, "likely . . . swelled" the protest turnout (Spitzer 2012).

These repeated accidents, while unfortunate and often tragic, add legitimacy to the opposition and further incentivize the use of pragmatic spin. According to activists, protest turnout "typically unimaginable a decade ago" became a reality due to—or, more ironically, thanks to—the "timing" of the accidents prior to its controversial deployment to Okinawa. "Even within Okinawa, people tend to respond differently (to base issues) depending on where they live," activists explain. Residents of the Okinawan capital of Naha, where fewer American facilities stand today, would often shrug off base-related grievances. The best response activists could generate from Naha residents was that of bystanders: "Well, that's tough." Things changed when the Ospreys came. "Those living in southern Okinawa, who never raised their voice, began to do so" (Interview, anonymous, October 12, 2016). Practical concerns were galvanizing enough that even then-governor Nakaima Hirokazu and Ginowan mayor Sakima Atsushi—both supporters of Futenma's relocation within Okinawa, which in the peculiar context of Okinawan base politics makes them "pro-base"—were against the Ospreys' deployment.

In mainland Japan, challengers to NAF Atsugi share this pragmatic focus. Contrary to the popular perception that base opposition in Japan is spatially confined to Okinawa, activists in Ayase and Yamato retain consistently high mobilization levels, if with much lower visibility. A long-standing fixture of local protests is monthly anti-base marches dating back to 1981. The marches invariably condemn "explosive noise" (*bakuon*) and reference monthly statistics on noise complaints filed in the two host cities. "If one person makes an official complaint about the noise, you can assume that there are hundreds who think there is a noise problem," says Kaneko Tokio, a city councilman and a longtime anti-Atsugi activist (Interview, October 10, 2016). Just like at Futenma, the storyline of everyday grievances merges with memories of tragedies. Activists, for example, routinely talk about "living as a human being" and "enjoying family dinner, watching television, and forgetting the irritability and headaches" (Association for the Prevention of Noise at Atsugi Base 2001). The 1964 crash of a U.S. F-8U Crusader, which killed five civilians in Yamato, is repeatedly invoked: "Stop falling on us!" (*mō ochinaide*) (Atsugi Residents Association to Eliminate Explosive Noise and Oppose Homeporting of the Aircraft Carrier 2015).

Noise pollution, a perennial nuisance in many base towns, unites activists throughout Japan. The iconic slogan for anti-noise protests is distinctively pragmatic and immediately relatable: "Bring back the quiet nights." In challenging this tangible, measurable problem that "destroys our living conditions" (*Ryukyu Shimpo* 2009a), Futenma, Atsugi, Kadena, Yokota, and Iwakuni activists have resorted to the most institutionalized form of contention: lawsuits. In addition to bringing together those already committed to the anti-base causes, these lawsuits, led by groups such as the Plaintiffs' Group for the Futenma Noise Pollution Litigation (Futenma bakuon soshōdan), have managed to bring on board those who are otherwise indifferent to base issues. The practical benefits of the suit—plaintiffs always win compensation, however meager in the eyes of the activists—are enticing enough that those who are not necessarily against the U.S. presence itself do not mind joining hands with those seeking the eventual closure of the base. Whatever intention participants may have, organizers see lawsuits as a "means of anti-base activism," and a relatively effective one at that, as far as broadening the potential constituent base is concerned (Interview with Takahashi Toshio, September 3, 2016; Taira Shinchi, September 21, 2016). This pragmatic approach, backed by institutional means of contention, is a far cry from the direct action approach some of these activists once took; in a particularly tense moment in 1969, they staged a three-day sit-in on the Atsugi airfield in the midst of burning tires. The 300-strong tire-burning protest managed to stop flights for three days, but not for longer (Interview with Kaneko Tokio, October 10, 2016). Eventually, lawsuits emerged as a pragmatic alternative that was more palatable to target audiences.

Pragmatism, in other words, runs through protest towns as a driving force for broad-based mobilization. Mobilization in this context is a by-product not of the distinct Okinawan identity or the ubiquitous pacifist ideology, but of common everyday grievances. Activists from Okinawa and the mainland, for example, travel to Tokyo every year for what they call *seifu kōshō*, or negotiations with the government. With lawyers in tow, they officially complain to government officials—not about Okinawa's unique misfortune, but about the common problems that unite communities hosting major U.S. air facilities. I joined Kadena, Yokota, and Atsugi activists in their annual meeting in 2017 at the land ministry and the environment ministry. They debated noise pollution issues, citing such technical terms as WECPNL and LDEN—two different measures of noise pollution, with different implications for noise claims and corresponding compensation levels. Practical challenges, activists across Japan have learned, prompt government responses.

High Dogmatism, Low Contestation

For every contested base that dominates the headlines, there is a quiet one that does not invite the locals' attention. In places that lack immediately recognizable grievances, activists organizing sporadic protests tend to employ broader, absolutist frames that simply fall flat. Their unabashedly ideological and nationalistic rhetoric ensures that their already small following remains just that—small. As we shall see, Gotemba residents do not share the vision for a pacifist utopia promoted by anti-Camp Fuji activists. Similarly, despite activists' rhetorical efforts to the contrary, Pohang and Jinhae residents exhibit little nationalistic aversion to the seemingly inconspicuous U.S. presence. This presents a dilemma for those leading anti-base opposition. On the one hand, rhetorical pragmatism, with its focus on sleep disturbances, broken windows, and oil leaks, precludes the radical changes that motivates activists in the first place. On the other hand, maximalist rhetoric, while radical and subversive, remains detached from the local experiences that motivate latent adherents.

Camp Fuji (Gotemba, Japan): Internationalist Ideals

The city of Gotemba, home to both the iconic Mt. Fuji and Camp Fuji, a U.S. Marine base that sits at the foot of the volcano, was once on the alert against American encroachment: schoolgirls in the immediate postwar era wore pants, instead of skirts, as school uniforms in ominous anticipation of the influx of U.S. troops. In the 1950s and 1960s, hundreds of local women resisted U.S. artillery shelling at the northern slope of Mt. Fuji, with human excrement among their chosen protest tactics (Apter 1984, 79). In 1965, in opposition to the U.S. military's use of land for the practice firing of "Little John" rockets, hundreds of local farmers staged a sit-in in the target area and burned tires in protest (Trumbull 1965). Today, however, the American presence in the area generates little such apprehension and opposition. Overshadowed by the Japan Ground Self-Defense Force, which controls the 34,000-acre East Fuji training field jointly used by the United States, the relatively small U.S. Marine presence seems to be an afterthought.

What contributes to the apathy are the internationalist anti-militarist ideals that local activists, divided over their disparate partisan affiliations with the JCP and the SDP, continue to evoke. Sporadic protests make broad, radical demands, such as the repeal of the U.S.-Japan alliance and the withdrawal of U.S. forces—not just from Japan, but also from the rest of Asia. A protest statement in 2003 by three local civic groups, for example, listed all three demands as they decried the Iraq War (Shizuoka Citizens' Action for Peace and Human Rights 2003). While activists constantly point to Mt.

Fuji as a UNESCO World Heritage site, their attempt to juxtapose the beautiful mountain with ugly militarism lacks empirical support. A common argument goes along the lines of: "Mt. Fuji's status as a UNESCO heritage site cannot coexist with its status as a military base" (Social Democratic Party of Shizuoka 2012). The frequently used slogan "Don't shoot Mt. Fuji" (*Fuji o utsu na*) is an anti-militarist call to stop the military training itself, and not a jab at the environmental destruction it may or may not entail. The slogan, after all, is often accompanied by other, ideologically minded ones: "Don't shoot the masses of Asia" (*Ajia minshū o utsu na*) and "U.S. forces, go home" (*Beigun wa kokyō e kaere*) (Jinken Heiwa Hamamatsu 2013).

Noise pollution associated with military training, which many other base opponents would frame as a pragmatic, everyday concern, becomes another source of anti-militarist opposition for Gotemba activists. While training produces noise, Camp Fuji and the adjacent training areas are located far enough from residential areas that they receive relatively few complaints. Driving through the vast area surrounding the American and Japanese installations here feels like touring a never-ending field in the middle of nowhere. As a result, anti-Fuji rhetoric lacks the immediacy and concreteness that characterize pragmatic framing seen elsewhere. For example, protests here against what are commonly known as "104 exercises," live-fire training that relocated from Okinawa to East Fuji as part of the 1996 SACO agreement (see chapter 2), are noticeably different in tone from those that used to take place in Okinawa. In Okinawa, shooting exercises over Prefectural Route 104, accompanied by an ominous sign "warn[ing] drivers to be careful of overhead projectiles" (Mitchell 2016), used to provoke an outcry over safety concerns. By contrast, Fuji activists condemn the 104 training as "training to invade Asia" (Shizuoka Citizens' Action for Peace and Human Rights 2004) that will "lea[d] to the massacre of citizens in Asia and other parts of the world" (*Shizuoka Shimbun* 2011). Mt. Fuji, they argue, should be a site of peace, not war.

If we were to set aside the question of resonance, activists have good reasons for this expansive rhetoric. "Troops train here and then go to Iraq, Afghanistan, and Syria," says Suzui Takao of the Shizuoka Peace Movement Center. "This is a site of war; you just don't get to see the enemy" (Interview, October 13, 2016). Still, absolutist rhetoric, if well-reasoned and true to the activists' conviction, does little to mitigate the isolation many feel in Gotemba, a city deemed to be an inhospitable place for activists waging peace. "It requires courage" to be an anti-base activist here, a Shizuoka native says, as people associate the heavy military presence—both Japanese and American—with economic benefits and a welcome influx of population (Interview, anonymous, October 13, 2016). Even those who could well have been the most disgruntled with the U.S. presence—local farmers whose access to land is restricted by the allies' joint use of the immense East Fuji maneuver area—remain largely satisfied with the way things are. Farmers of the region have fought to retain their access to the communal land in the area, which they have depended on for their livelihood since Japan's early modern Edo period, and as a result, have rights to enter the training field today. As negotiations over their access rights became routinized, local groups, such as the East Fuji Maneuver Area Farmers' Reconstruction Federation (Higashi-fuji enshūjō chiiki nōmin saiken renmei), have become interest groups that get to have a say in how the allies use the maneuver area. From the perspective of anti-base activists, this unique arrangement keeps latent adherents, as "powerful" stakeholders of the land, happy enough (Interviews with Watanabe Kiichi, October 12, 2016; Suzui Takao, October 13, 2016). After all, the farmers who fiercely contested the U.S. military in the 1950s and 1960s in the area were motivated by threats to their access rights—something much more concrete than universal pacifism or American militarism—although their activism did converge later with the then-thriving leftist movement (Apter 1984).

Tellingly, it was only when activists adjusted their rhetorical focus that they saw a slight increase in public receptivity. As the Ospreys—anathema to Japanese anti-base activists nationwide—began making trips all the way from Okinawa to Camp Fuji, activists adopted a pragmatic critique of the accident-prone aircraft. To the activists' surprise, local people who would "never" show up at typical anti-base protests joined anti-Osprey events—although their number still remained "overwhelmingly small" (Interview with Suzui Takao, October 13, 2016). Even the aforementioned farmers' federation, a group that seems to have found peace with the American use of the training area, joined the chorus of opposition. Activists also began to adopt a more pragmatic form of contention by joining a network of mainland activists, called the Eastern Japan Liaison Committee (Higashi-nihon renrakukai), to monitor the Ospreys' flight routes and training patterns so that they could make safety complaints to the authorities. Identifying the routes requires some detective work; activists typically compile Osprey-related noise complaints in various municipalities and connect their locations with a line on a map. Still, traditional ideological frames cast a long shadow over how activists assign meaning to the menacing aircraft: in addition to pointing out immediate safety concerns, Camp Fuji activists argue that the deployment assists the American "invasion of Asia" and "the U.S. Marine's use of Japan to prepare for global war" ("Don't Shoot Mt. Fuji" Executive Committee 2012).

Camp Mujuk (Pohang, Korea) and CFA Chinhae (Jinhae/ Changwon, Korea): Nationalist Hangover

Substitute absolutist pacifism with unyielding ethnic nationalism, and we see protest framing at Camp Mujuk and CFA Chinhae. Despite their strategic importance as the only American Marine and naval bases in Korea, respectively, the two bases get little attention even from the most committed activists in the country. Instead, they invite sporadic protests from traditional leftist-nationalist groups that stubbornly invoke pan-Korean nationalism despite its declining appeal to the Korean public. Joint U.S.-Korea military training, such as the annual Key Resolve exercises, is a common source of contention. Not coincidentally, these drills are Pyongyang's greatest pet peeve; its threatened withdrawal from the Nuclear Non-proliferation Treaty in 1993, for example, was partially provoked by the resumption of the temporarily suspended "Team Spirit" exercises (Cumings 1997, 474–75).

Leftist-nationalist activists are both the organizers of and the only participants in these small-sized protests, where they cling to familiar anti-American slogans with virtually no reference to pragmatic grievances. Their critique of military training, for example, does not stem from the supposedly universal anti-militarism that anti-Fuji activists share; instead, it has to do with the ever-elusive goal of national unification. Military exercises heighten tensions on the Korean peninsula and agitate North Korea, activists argue, and should therefore be suspended. One of the biggest protests against Camp Mujuk, a small Marine base tucked away in the southeastern port city of Pohang, took place in 2015, when members of the National Action against War (Jeonjaengbandae pyeonghwasilhyeon gungminhaengdong) condemned the allies' joint drills as an "offensive" war game designed to ultimately "occupy" North Korea (Jeon 2015). The small U.S. naval presence in the southeastern harbor city of Jinhae—typically just ninety personnel (Lostumbo et al. 2013, 28)—also attracts similarly anti-American, pro-unification civic groups. Spearheads of Unification (Tongil seonbongdae), a group of unionized workers from the Korean Confederation of Trade Unions, makes an occasional stop at the installation to protest joint military exercises. When activists condemned the USS *Los Angeles*, a nuclear-powered submarine that visited Jinhae in 2005, they linked the issue to the peculiar situation of the Korean peninsula: the denuclearization principle the two Koreas committed to in 1992. Subsequent visits by other U.S. nuclear-powered warships to Jinhae have since attracted little attention from activist groups. As I show below, these obsessive references to North Korea at CFA Chinhae stand in sharp contrast to Japanese activists' equally stubborn references to universal anti-nuclear ideals at CFA Yokosuka and CFA Sasebo. Nuclear sensibilities of Korea and Japan, after all, are uneven—the atomic bombing that practically ended the colonization of the former gave the latter a national narrative that portrays itself as a war victim.

Rhetorical Outliers

We now turn to two types of rhetorical anomalies. First, Yokosuka emerges as a deviant case in which exclusively pacifist framing has driven the relatively broad-based opposition against CFA Yokosuka's nuclear turn (see chapter 3). Yokosuka's unique status as the only overseas homeport for America's nuclear-powered aircraft carriers enables activists to tap into Japan's cultural antipathy against nuclear weapons, although the visibility of the local activism has declined after the nuclear transition. The case of Sasebo, home to another U.S. naval base, attests to the uniqueness of the case of Yokosuka; in the absence of an external shock like the one that briefly rejuvenated activism in Yokosuka, Sasebo activists' staunch pacifism finds little resonance outside the most devoted circles of activists. Second, the two U.S. air bases in Gunsan and northern Pyeongtaek have proven to be an anti-base activist's nightmare. Activists have not only failed to exploit status disruptions, as we saw the previous chapter, but they also struggle to turn their rhetorical emphasis on practical grievances—and there is a never-ending supply of these at air bases—into a rallying point.

CFA Yokosuka (Yokosuka, Japan): Pacifist Perseverance

The relative success that Yokosuka activists achieved in mobilizing the local population against the deployment of a nuclear-powered aircraft carrier

(see chapter 3) defies the prevalence of rhetorical pragmatism in other protest towns. The abiding relevance of anti-nuclear principles among activist
communities here has to do with the fact that Yokosuka is a naval port city.
As Yokosuka activists regularly witnessed the arrival of American nuclear-
powered warships, or worse, warships suspected of carrying nuclear
weapons, they naturally opted for protest rhetoric that played into Japanese
people's "nuclear allergy"—their postwar aversion, rooted in the trauma of
Hiroshima and Nagasaki, to nuclear weapons. This aversion is well known.
Policymakers knew, for example, that dispatching the USS *Harry S. Truman*
to Yokosuka in place of the USS *George Washington* would be an unsavory
choice, given Truman's involvement in the atomic bombings (Halloran
2005). Some warned against "historical sensitivities . . . develop[ing] political traction" in Yokosuka, advocating instead for Guam as a destination for
American sailors (Erickson and Mikolay 2012, 82).

Their apprehensions proved true when Yokosuka activists turned against
the deployment of the USS *George Washington*, a nuclear-powered aircraft carrier. The activists' opposition stemmed from their rejection of the
militarized use of nuclear power. A protest event held shortly before its deployment, for example, featured local members of the National Confederation
of Trade Unions (Zenroren) and JCP officials, who called the deployment a
"flagrant defiance against Yokosuka citizens and the people of Japan, the only
atomic-bombed country" (*Akahata* 2008). When the aircraft carrier docked
at the Yokosuka base, leftist activists, some of them staging a seaborne protest aboard small boats, greeted it with a chant: "We won't make Yokosuka
the base for a war" (Hongo 2008). While activists do speak of dangers associated with the use of nuclear energy, especially after the 2011 Fukushima
nuclear disaster, their opposition is more about the potential danger that lies
somewhere ahead if things somehow go wrong, instead of tangible, visible
risks one can measure now. "America says that the nuclear-powered aircraft
carrier has never had an accident, but that is safety dogma, like the nuclear
power plants in Japan," protestors said in a rally in 2015, likening the warship
to a nuclear reactor (Slavin and Kusumoto 2013). Yokosuka activists have
relied on this absolutist anti-militarist rhetoric for so long that they fail to
switch gears even when they can. When the infamous Ospreys made a brief
stop here in October 2014—which would have easily invited pragmatically
framed opposition in other localities, as we have seen in Okinawa and, to a
lesser extent, Gotemba—activists instead condemned the visit as a "concentration of weapons directly related to war efforts" (Tanaka 2014).

Comparably strong pacifist rhetoric used by activists in Sasebo has not generated the same level of community involvement. Unlike CFA Yokosuka, CFA Sasebo did not go through the same kind of destabilizing status quo disruption. Home to the Navy's only permanently forward-deployed amphibious squadron, this relatively unobtrusive naval base—as one observer notes, "you have to look for it in this small city" (Cumings 2009, 409–10)—does not provoke the strong emotions and intense grievances seen elsewhere. Given the relative calm surrounding the base, and given the nature of naval bases where nuclear-powered warships lend themselves to anti-nuclear framing, activists here regularly invoke universalist pacifism. And it once worked pretty well—in the 1960s, the heyday of Japan's leftist activism. In 1968 alone, leftist activists in Sasebo and the rest of Japan managed to create a PR disaster for the U.S. military on two occasions. One followed a militant reception that awaited a port call by the USS *Enterprise*, the Navy's first nuclear-powered aircraft carrier. A "symbol of involvement in Vietnam and nuclear weapons," the warship's visit to Sasebo touched off violent resistance on the part of radical student groups and peace activists. Another coincided with a visit by the USS *Swordfish*, a nuclear-powered submarine, which provoked widespread suspicions of radioactive contamination at the Sasebo harbor (Tetsuo 2008, 56–57).

The once-explosive anti-nuclear cause is now little more than a mundane slogan. Today, long-standing anti-base groups and like-minded labor unionists carry on the pacifist tradition in the city, but with declining visibility. When the nuclear-powered aircraft carrier USS *Abraham Lincoln* sailed to Sasebo in August 2002, for example, activists from the Nagasaki Peace Movement Center (Nagasaki-ken heiwa undō sentā) denounced the visit as a "militarized use of the port" and a violation of Japan's non-nuclear principle banning introduction of nuclear weapons. The seemingly long-obsolete non-nuclear tenet is very much alive in activist chants: "Abide by the non-nuclear principles!" (*Mainichi Shimbun* 2002). But this continued emphasis on nuclear aversion no longer attracts national—and even local—attention, especially in the absence of the kind of high-profile status disruption that Yokosuka went through. Although local trade unions continue to supply warm bodies to protests, organizers lament declining interest even among the unionized workers (Interview with Yamaguchi Harayoshi, September 26, 2016). Similarly, the Sasebo Citizens' Association (Jūkyū-nichi Sasebo shimin no kai), which has staged street rallies on the 19th of every month since February 19, 1968, exactly a month after the *Enterprise* arrived in Sasebo, has seen its membership dwindle over time. The group's monthly rally has been reduced to a low-key march through a busy shopping mall near the naval base, attended by a handful of people each time.

For these devotees, CFA Sasebo, or any other military base for that matter, represents a tool of war. A longtime participant in the monthly march asks a rhetorical question: "Is it nice that our town proliferates as a result of killing people?" (Interview with Miyano Yumiko, September 23, 2016). Inaction on the part of host communities, these activists believe, equals tacit approval of violence and destruction—if not in Sasebo, then in other far-flung corners of the world where American troops wage battles. And by not opposing militarism, the reasoning goes, base town dwellers are not just victims by virtue of having to live alongside bases and all that entails, but are potential perpetrators by virtue of condoning the violence they produce. "The problem is not the harm inflicted on us by the base (*higai*), but the harm we allow to be inflicted on others (*kagai*) because of the use of the base," a Sasebo-based pastor and activist explains (Interview with Fukazawa Shō, September 23, 2016).

These earnest pleas and far-reaching insights, however, do not fly well in the city, where base-community relations remain largely amicable. The 2011 earthquake and tsunami, which galvanized the already nuclear-averse activists, did little to stir latent adherents to action. Much to the activists' dismay, the Fukushima nuclear meltdown in 2011 proved to be far from a boon for the anti-base cause. If anything, American troops, alongside their SDF partners, emerged as heroes in disaster relief missions—as "Operation Tomodachi" (*tomodachi* means friends) tried to convey in not-so-subtle terms—and anti-base activists ended up looking completely out of touch. Members of the Sasebo District Labor Union Congress (Sasebo chiku rōdō kumiai kaigi), for example, faced hostility from locals when they decided to press ahead with rallies against port visits by nuclear-powered warships, which were becoming more frequent as a result of the widely celebrated relief operation. Locals remonstrated with the unionists, whom they increasingly saw as hopeless peaceniks: "Are you telling our benefactors (*onjin*) to leave?" "Can't you at least be thankful this time?" Activists stubbornly stood their ground. Aircraft carriers, they argued, are still an "apparatus designed to kill people" (*Nishinippon Shimbun* 2011).

Kunsan Air Base (Gunsan, Korea) and Osan Air Base (Northern Pyeongtaek, Korea): Making Peace with Movement Foes

We now turn to the opposite case: protest rhetoric that highlights everyday local grievances but nonetheless finds little resonance. Gunsan's status as a quiet town belies the fact that the city is home to the longest-running anti-base rallies in Korea. The initial catalyst for activism against Kunsan Air Base, dating back to 1997, was a rather technical matter: a fivefold increase in the fees the U.S. military demanded for the commercial use of its runway by Korean aircraft (Moon 2012, 110–11). Conforming to the pragmatic origin of collective action, the protests that have ensued revolved around such pragmatic issues as noise and water contamination (Baek 2001), even though initial protest organizers—including Father Moon Jeong-hyun, an activist priest who embodies the unique historical marriage of pro-democracy, pro-unification, and anti-base activism—were nationalistically motivated.

This rhetorical pragmatism represents a conscious gap between what activists believe and what they choose to say. In highlighting immediate local grievances, activists refrain from preaching their belief that such negative externalities are "mere byproducts" of the American presence, and that focusing on them therefore does not "get to the essence of the problem" (Interview, Kim Pan-tei, June 15, 2016). Instead, activists in the area have conducted probes into water quality and noise levels to show that local complaints can be empirically proven. When residents faced displacements due to base expansion, activists demanded property rights for the affected individuals, rather than an end to the U.S. presence (J. Kim 2007). They have also offered legal consultations for those who wish to file complaints. Some of these efforts have been successful. Father Moon, for example, claims that he was later thanked by Korean military officials who were negotiating the runway fees at the time, because his activism—which, in its earliest phases, involved egg-throwing, "Yankee go home" slogans, and a letter from the U.S. military notifying him of a lifetime ban at U.S. bases—helped them negotiate better (*OhmyNews* 2019). An activist-led noise pollution lawsuit in 2004 awarded 1,878 residents living near the base some 3.29 billion won ($2.8 million) in compensation (Green Korea United 2004). In 2011, activists celebrated a court finding that noise from Kunsan Air Base caused the death of 400 rabbits at local farms.

Protest turnout, however, continued to decline. What began as a weekly protest at the main gate of the air base turned into a monthly event in 2008 due to dwindling participation, even in the face of the base's expansion (see chapter 3). Successful lawsuits led to compensation, but not higher protest turnout. Deep-rooted skepticism toward leftist activists—in Okseo, a small township abutting the air base, it does not help that many activists are not Gunsan natives—limits their mobilization potency. Several episodes illustrate the challenges activists face in warding off suspicions and winning over latent adherents. When Father Moon began protesting runway fees, bar owners from the "American Town," an entertainment district some four miles away from the air base, took chartered buses to visit—and condemn—Moon (*OhmyNews* 2019). In 2001, when the routine protests at the air base were still a weekly event, activists were forced to move their Friday protests to Wednesdays; they had to placate angry shopkeepers nearby, who accused them of driving away American customers precisely when the sales were picking up at the beginning of the weekend. Once, restaurant owners physically confronted activists who were holding a press conference over the alleged use of Agent Orange at Kunsan Air Base in 1968; one particularly disgruntled restaurateur, claiming that the activists were depriving him of his "right to a livelihood," chose to pour a bucket of beef bone broth on them (G. Kim 2011). In 2016, when Gunsan was being discussed as one of the potential candidate sites to host the controversial U.S. THAAD (Terminal High Altitude Area Defense) anti-ballistic missile defense system, activists chose to feature the names of various political parties—the ones that opposed the deployment—on their protest banners, deliberately creating the impression that the parties co-sponsored the anti-THAAD campaign. "People will see civic group names and think we're just doing what we've always been doing," Kim Pan-tei, a longtime Gunsan activist, explains. "If they see party names, they will think that the issue is serious enough to get political parties involved" (Interview, June 15, 2016).

Even the occasional latent adherents who seek to take matters into their own hands face various hurdles. Ha Un-ki, a car repair shop owner, organized a handful of protest events between 2006 and 2012, bringing together up to 150 local residents each time. Oil leaks found near the air base since 2003, which angered local farmers, provided a rare occasion in which latent adherents took to the streets, both with and without career activists. (In 2005, when the U.S. military offered 500,000 won [$440] in apparent compensation for a leak, local farmers and activists wrapped eggs with the 10,000-won bills and threw them back into the base.) However, for a non-career activist like Ha, who had not organized any formal civic group, activism proved to be particularly costly. He had to field constant questions from the local police about his ties with activist groups. Police dialed up other elderly participants, insinuating that they should not participate in protests. There were rumors that Korean Air Force officials—the 38th Fighter Group of the Korean Air Force shares Kunsan Air Base—publicly complained about him. Ha lost both American and Korean customers. "I gave up . . . it's impossible to fight the U.S. military," Ha says (Interview, June 14, 2016).

Nonetheless, Gunsan activists remain on the alert for opportunities to relate the U.S. presence to the everyday life of the approximately 4,000 residents of Okseo. When I accompanied a longtime local activist on a tour of Okseo, we ran into a local restaurant owner, who, upon spotting him, immediately began complaining about aircraft noise. Goo gave her advice he always gives: call the city hall to lodge complaints, and keep a record of when the jets take off and when the noise levels peak. The localized, routinized form of anti-base activism also continues, despite internal concerns about the lack of mobilization capacity and movement vibrancy. On June 15, 2016, I joined activists at the main gate of Kunsan Air Base for their 576th rally. A large placard hung on the closed gate made pragmatically minded pleas: "End nighttime training! Find solutions to oil leaks and pollution! End Korea-U.S. military training!" The thirty-minute protest—attended by ten people, all of them familiar faces to one another, and closely watched by policemen and base personnel—was repeatedly interrupted by aircraft noise. It represented business as usual for both the activists and the onlookers.

Opponents of Osan Air Base face a similarly hostile environment. In Songtan, the area surrounding the air base, a hypothetical protest demanding its closure—due to, say, its embodiment of militarism—would attract ten anti-base devotees and 100 angry counter-protesters. Some 500 small and midsize businesses operate in the Shinjang-dong shopping district outside the main gate of the airbase, including 350 shops, forty clubs, and at least eighteen hotels (Pyeongtaek City 2015). While bad blood between activists and shopkeepers is not uncommon, it is much more pronounced here than, say, in Seoul's Itaewon, near Yongsan Garrison. "This is a place where shopkeepers would come out with LPG cylinders to stop us from protesting," Lee Cheol-hyeong, a Pyeongtaek activist, says of the unusual protest equipment that counter-protesters threaten to set alight (Interview, June 18, 2016). Other tactics on the part of the shopkeepers include playing loud music and having Russian "bar girls" dance next to protesters—or those who "ruin our business." Local economic elites are in favor of the U.S. presence, and their family members, as they go on to become city council and district council members, ensure the continued quiescence. Despite noise pollution being an enduring source of grievances, the economic dependence, as well as the relatively favorable local perception of airmen as ostensibly "better-educated and better-behaved" than Army soldiers, makes this community a particularly unaccommodating place for anti-base activists. Indeed, a 2006 survey shows 40 percent of the 300 respondents living in the vicinity of Osan Air Base said they "like" or "very much like" American troops in Korea—a contrast to the 19 percent of those living near Camp Humphreys who expressed the same sentiment (D. S. Kim et al. 2006).

This hostility directed at anti-base activists acts as an external constraint on their protest framing, and as a result, major protest events in the area take on decisively pragmatic tones. The first wave of anti-base mobilization, as we saw in the previous chapter, centered on land expropriation. When the second wave of protests came in 2013, activists forged an alliance with the most unlikely challengers of the U.S. military: local shopkeepers and owners of "juicy bars"—or establishments where women, mostly from the Philippines and Russia, sell drinks to U.S. servicemen. These business owners, usually the most adamant supporters of the base, were disgruntled with the "off-limits" policy that bans American servicemen from entering certain establishments or areas over concerns of safety, prostitution, and violence. While the U.S. military says the ban contributes to military discipline, bar owners claim that it is often unfairly enforced. According to them, a brawl among service members, or service members secretly bringing in their own liquor bottles into a local establishment, can still get these businesses blacklisted. Business owners can appeal their cases at the Armed Forces Disciplinary Control Board, but they have likened the experience to a "military trial" (E. Kim 2012). Many were already aggrieved about a highly publicized incident in 2012 where U.S. military police officers on routine patrol handcuffed three Korean civilians, including a local shopkeeper, over a parking dispute.

The growing disgruntlement led to an exceptional case in which business owners turned to Pyeongtaek activists—the very activists that they, in their most confrontational moments, threw feces at (Interview with Kang Mi, June 11, 2016). For more than a month in the summer of 2013, business owners and activists staged joint rallies demanding an end to the policy, at one point prompting the authorities to designate the entire area off-limits. They portrayed the policy as an arbitrarily enforced rule that threatened business owners' livelihoods (Hong 2016)—a virtual "death sentence" (Hwang 2013). Although protests tapered off due to internal disagreements among shopkeepers about their goals, this period remains the only instance of even fleeting, if ironic, solidarity between the most fervent pro-base actors and the most devoted anti-base actors. Activists took the opportunity to reflect on whether they had ever really "tried to help and connect with the locals." And in their renewed efforts to find common ground with latent adherents, activists say they are aided by rhetorical pragmatism—without which they will remain "a small group of weirdos . . . alienated from the rest of the community" (Interview, Lee Cheol-hyeong, June 18, 2016).

A Pragmatic Turn

[handwritten margin note: examining the changes is only possible by examining data over time]

Where one activist sees a pragmatic challenge, another sees an ideological anathema. We finally turn to the last set of base towns that have seen competing visions of dogmatism and pragmatism. Opponents of Yongsan Garrison and Yokota Air Base have learned that a rhetorical shift—from absolutist to pragmatic—helps increase the movement resonance. Perhaps the most dramatic pragmatic turn happened in Pocheon, home to Rodriguez Live Fire Complex. Latent adherents who have evolved into reluctant protesters go to great lengths to present themselves as "innocent" activists seeking to improve their living conditions. Their refusal to join hands with leftist-nationalist activists has been one way to prove their innocence, which shields them from potential accusations of ulterior political motives.

Yongsan Garrison (Seoul, Korea) and Yokota Air Base (Western Tokyo, Japan): Competing Visions

Activists challenging Yongsan Garrison and Yokota Air Base[1] have resorted to a unique mix of pragmatic and alternative framing strategies: protests targeting the former exhibit a pronounced nationalistic element, whereas those against the latter feature a substantial ideological component. Over time, however, activists have increasingly opted for rhetorical pragmatism.

Nationalistic anger at Yongsan has faded as a rhetorical tool of activism, and renewed pragmatism at Yokota has brought in new movement adherents.

Perhaps counterintuitively for a base with such a high national profile, two major campaigns against Seoul's Yongsan Garrison in the early 2000s indicate early activist efforts to highlight pragmatic grievances and eschew nationalistic rhetoric. The first campaign was an environmentally minded one, and the second campaign involved weekly anti-crime rallies. They both sought to rewrite the SOFA, rather than demand the immediate withdrawal of the troops or termination of the alliance. Notably, even as Yongsan Garrison remained a favorite picket location for Korean leftist-nationalists, there was not a single mention of North Korea—a marker of nationalistic anti-base rhetoric—in these campaigns.

The high-profile challenge against Yongsan Garrison in 2000 began when Seoul-based Green Korea United exposed a base employee's dumping of formaldehyde into Seoul's Han River. Soon, the campaign evolved into what the *New York Times* described as "a major embarrassment for the U.S. command . . . with implications for agreements governing the 37,000 U.S. troops" in Korea (Kirk 2000). Environmental activists framed the dumping—it allegedly involved 480 bottles of formaldehyde, each containing 16 ounces of the toxic chemical—as a careless act that threatened the health of ten million Seoulites, who depended on the Han River as a source of drinking water (Green Korea United 2000). Protests that ensued focused primarily on the legal implications of the disposal and demanded a SOFA revision and an official pledge to prevent recurrences (*Maeil Business Newspaper* 2000). Lee Hyun-choul, a former activist who unveiled the case to the public, notes how the pragmatic focus exerted a new kind of pressure on the otherwise unresponsive U.S. military—even as nationalistically minded activists, in an internal frame dispute, criticized the environmentalists for not echoing the familiar "Yankee go home" slogan. "The U.S. military was accustomed to typical anti-American protests, but was quite at a loss when it came to environmental challenges," he recalls. Unable to dismiss protesters as a handful of radicals, the U.S. military issued its first-ever public apology since the Korean War (*Los Angeles Times* 2000). Washington was also prodded into adding an environmental clause to the SOFA some thirty-five years after the agreement was signed—a "nice, not so costly political gesture that anyone could agree with," in Lee's words (Interview, July 8, 2016). The episode became so ingrained in public memory that popular Korean filmmaker Bong

Joon-ho's 2006 blockbuster, *The Host*, opens with a fictionalized account of the dumping, which then creates a mutated monster that wreaks havoc on Seoul.

Weekly protests by the National Campaign for the Eradication of Crimes by U.S. Troops in Korea, a group established in 1993 and disbanded in 2018, similarly questioned the legal foundation of the U.S. military presence. Activists, including those motivated by their nationalist convictions, sought to go beyond the traditional, nationalistic interpretation of G.I. crimes—the 1992 murder of Yun Geum-i, a camptown prostitute, was once decried as the death of "our nation's daughter" (Schober 2016, 62–84)—and focus instead on the legal status of U.S. troops (Moon 2012, 131–32). Over time, the National Campaign evolved into an NGO that presented itself as data-driven rather than emotion-driven. It regularly collected crime statistics and documented cases, with its website serving as a database (Interview with Park Kyung-soo, August 23, 2016). Even at the height of the national fury over the Yangju Highway Incident in 2002 (see chapter 3), the group acknowledged that U.S. servicemen in Korea committed fewer crimes than their host state counterparts. Their stated goal was not to drive out the Americans in uniform, but to raise public awareness on the issue of criminal jurisdiction (Y. Choi 2008, 71).

Still, these pragmatists coexisted with leftist-nationalists who embody the unique confluence of pro-democracy, pro-unification, and anti-American sentiments. Various anti-American groups, including the Association of Anti-American Women and the Campaign for the Return of Yongsan Base, flocked to Yongsan in the early 2000s. The former group branded itself as a "sovereign association of women . . . seeking unification with North Korea," likening "anti-American struggles" to anti-Japanese colonial struggles (M. Lee 2001). The latter similarly emphasized national pride in its justification for anti-Yongsan activism: "The U.S. Yongsan base, which tramples on our nation's pride and sovereignty, is undeniably a place of humiliation" (Campaign for the Return of Yongsan Base 2001). Protesters sang songs titled "Listen, Yankee"—probably an homage to the 1960 book of the same title, by the sociologist C. Wright Mills, on Cuban revolutionaries—and "Our wish is unification" (M. Kim 2001). Activists frequently condemned the U.S. military's "hegemonic" and "hostile" policy against North Korea, whose "deterrence capabilities," they argued, "only amount to a means of self-defense." "Our nation (*uri minjok*) will prevail over foreign forces (*oese*)," Han Sang-ryeol, a prominent unification activist, called for Korean ethnic unity at a rally in 2003 (Song 2003). In 2004, the blatantly named Yankee Expulsion Campaign began its short lifespan in Yongsan. Reverend Kang Hee-nam, formerly a leader of the Pan-Korea Fatherland Reunification League (Beomminryeon), was at the helm of this fringe group. Kang was also behind a controversial movement to remove the statue of Douglas MacArthur, whom he blamed for Korea's national division.

Provoking nationalistic resentment against the base occupying the heart of the capital was an easy mobilization tool—but only insofar as traditional leftist-nationalist groups were concerned. For all the symbolism of Yongsan Garrison, it is telling that the only anti-Yongsan campaign that won widespread public support was a decisively environmental, rather than nationalistic, one. The counternarratives of the U.S. as an imperialist impediment to inter-Korean reconciliation would have found more resonance in the 1980s. They are now mostly a distant memory in Yongsan.

Moving from Korea's capital to Japan's, activists contesting Yokota Air Base, the U.S. Forces Japan headquarters in western Tokyo, also alternate between dogmatism and pragmatism. Pacifists contesting the air base can simply tap into their existing support base. The Nishitama Association for the Removal of Yokota Base (Yokota kichi no tekkyo o motomeru nishitama no kai), which has organized monthly sit-in protests in the city of Fussa every third Sunday since 2009, stands out as the most active group. In articulating its stated goal of closing down the base, the group often evokes anti-militarist ideals. When activists began monthly sit-ins in 2009, for example, they declared that the Japanese Constitution's war-renouncing Article 9—the institutional bedrock of Japan's postwar pacifism—does not align with the U.S. military presence (Nishitama Association for the Removal of Yokota Base 2009). The group's newsletter is fittingly titled "Peace to the world; we do not need a base of war" (*sekai ni heiwa o sensō no kichi wa iranai*). The distinctive pacifist spin coincides with the perception that Yokota, albeit a target of the first-ever noise pollution lawsuit against U.S. military bases in Japan, is quieter than other air bases. Yokota mainly houses freighters, which are quieter than the fighter jets deployed at other bases (Interview with Fukumoto Michio, October 11, 2016).

By 2012, however, activists made a noticeable rhetorical shift, bringing with it an uptick in protest turnout. With the growing apprehensions about the potential deployment of the CV-22 Osprey—the Air Force variant of the Marine Corps MV-22 Osprey—at Yokota, routine protests took on a more urgent, pragmatic tone. "The fact remains that the Ospreys, whether they are operated by the Marine Corps or the Air Force, are still dangerous," activists said as they cited the aircraft's controversial safety record (Nishitama Association for the Removal of Yokota Base 2012). Following the official decision in 2015 to deploy them at Yokota—five were officially deployed in October 2018—hardly any protest by the Nishitama Association went by without mentioning the notorious aircraft and the accompanying safety concerns. To back up their pragmatic concerns, activists have turned to annual statistics comparing the flight times and the number of accidents involving the Ospreys. They have also compared the accident rates of the Ospreys to those of the more familiar C-130 cargo planes to demonstrate the comparative risk. Their analyses led to a simple prescription: "Stop the flights!" (Nishitama Association for the Removal of Yokota Base 2015).

Rodriguez Live Fire Complex (Pocheon, Korea): Pragmatism as a Fixation

If local residents in some base towns are reluctant to follow the lead of activists, those in Pocheon, home to the Rodriguez Live Fire Complex, go one step further: they ward off all overtures from activists and instead take matters into their own hands. As elderly local farmers transitioned from silent onlookers to voluntary human shields against shooting practices, the 3,390-acre firing range just twelve miles south of the Demilitarized Zone rapidly grew into what USFK officials came to identify as the latest flashpoint in base politics.

The fact that mobilization came only after six long decades of silence, however, shows that the absolute magnitude of grievances is no automatic guarantee of contestation. The four rural townships surrounding this mammoth live-fire range—"the range is like an egg yolk and the villages are like egg whites," residents tell me, so there is no escaping it—have lived with ear-splitting noise and errant shells since the Korean War concluded with an armistice. For the U.S. military, which fought to end the war decades ago, live-fire training constitutes "the gold standard for war fighting readiness" (Sisk 2020); for residents, however, it is almost as if the Cold War battles have never quite ended. A series of headlines from *Stars and Stripes*, an American military newspaper, captures the essence of local experiences here: "Training Suspended at Firing Range in Korea after Missile Goes Astray" (Robson

2015); "Protesters Call for End of Errant Shells at South Korean Range" (Slavin 2015); "South Koreans Complain about Stray Rounds, Noise from Live-Fire Range" (Fichtl and Chang 2017); and "US Commander Apologizes for Stray Ammunition Rounds in South Korea" (Gamel 2018). Add routine forest fires—Mt. Bulmu, which has become an unlikely protest spot among desperate locals, is literally a shooting target—and tremors disrupting class-room activities, and the picture is now complete. Even so, this is an improve-ment from the old days when locals who made a living off of selling empty shells repeatedly fell victim to accidental explosions caused by unexploded shells in the mix.

And yet, none of the diehard anti-American activists who would come and go managed to persuade the locals to join a campaign against this obtrusive base. On the contrary, locals found occasional outbursts of anti-American activism off-putting. One particularly high-profile event in 2003 involving the Korea Federation of General Student Councils (Hanchongnyeon), an anti-American student group that succeeded Jeondaehyeop in 1993 (see chapter 2), only served to further alienate local residents here. In August 2003, Hanchongnyeon activists descended on the Rodriguez range, climbed onto an American tank, and with the Korean national flag wrapped around their shoulders, set fire to the Stars and Stripes as American soldiers, taken aback, tried to wrestle it from them (K. Kim 2003). "It's been 50 years since we were liberated from Japan. However, it's just verbal liberation. We've been under [the] U.S. in the same manner," an angry student statement read (Giordono and Choe 2003). While this dramatic stand-off excited the stu-dent group's already dwindling core support base, the public was unsym-pathetic to what was seen as a random, seemingly misplaced eruption of anti-American nationalism. In fact, the incident contributed to the ultimate demise of this once-thriving but increasingly stigmatized organization, ruled illegal in a 1998 Supreme Court decision for engaging in activities allegedly benefiting North Korea (*ijeokaengwi*)—a violation of Korea's controversial National Security Law, a Cold War relic.[2]

More than a decade later, when a rash of near-miss accidents involving stray bullets finally pushed local residents to their limits, they were deter-mined to build a strictly local movement grounded in pragmatic, everyday grievances. "There has been no compensation for either the live fire training that goes on for 320 days a year, or misfiring accidents that repeatedly occur," the Youngpyeong-Seungjin Firing Range Task Force (Yeongpyeong-Seungjin sagyeokjang daechaegwiwonhoe), an association of locals from the four badly affected townships of Changsu, Yeongjung, Idong, and Yeongbuk, said in their inaugural statement. "We have lived in constant fear, and students' educational rights have been infringed upon" (S. Kim 2014). In one of the first major protest events that followed yet another accident involving a stray shell, more than 1,000 people—a staggering number given the previous lack of any grassroots mobilization—gathered at the range in April 2015. Some of these gray-haired protesters brought with them the calves they grow at local farms—a sign of protest against miscarriages caused by the daily din of war. "We have long endured the noise, forest fires, and dust, but we cannot live on with the constant fear that bullets may fall on our heads at any moment," the Task Force said (Kyeong 2015). At particularly tense moments, locals have climbed the nearby Mt. Bulmu, since acting as voluntary human shields has proved to be the only way to actually suspend the exercises—even if it means the intensity of the training may double the very following day. Protest slogans implored: "You try and live here once," and "Death on the doorstep" (Go 2017).

This overwhelmingly pragmatic emphasis reflects the demography and political orientations of the host community. The familiar mantra of national security—that opposing U.S. bases is unpatriotic because the U.S. presence deters North Korea and thereby bolsters national security—continues to prevail. According to a 2015 poll, some 75 percent of the 500 elderly residents living in the most affected areas said that the firing range itself is "necessary" in some form or fashion. Of these respondents, 8.4 percent considered it the price that has to be paid for the sake of national security, 13.8 percent supported its existence as long as it moved elsewhere, and 53 percent were actually willing to put up with the trouble in exchange for adequate compensation (Y. Choi 2016). Even when the anti-Rodriguez movement began in earnest in 2015, some felt the need to ask: "But what if North Korea invades us?" (Gwon 2015) Added to the national security rationale are the decisively quotidian concerns the residents share. These reluctant activists, in their own words, are more concerned about the land contamination affecting the prices of local farm produce than, say, American grand strategy. After all, this is a place where the number of protest participants goes down during the busy farming season.

In guarding the pragmatic, grassroots nature of their activism, local base opponents have chosen to reject any involvement of "outside forces" (*oebu seryeok*)—or those who they fear may adulterate the supposed purity of the movement. "People there reject even the notion of being associated with (outside) civic groups," explains Cho Seung-hyun, a Seoul-based activist, with a tinge of frustration in his voice (Interview, June 1, 2016). In what appears to be something of a fixation, local organizers also take pains to avoid appearing anti-American. They once suspended protests, citing the escalation in tensions with North Korea (J. Lee 2015)—even as the same rationale allowed the U.S. military to resume training (after it had been temporarily suspended due to local protests) and produce the same dreadful noise that pushed them to mobilize in the first place (Nam 2016). Local activists are aware of the trade-off. By rejecting offers from third-party supporters, they know that Pocheon's ordeals will not be advertised in the way that Pyeongtaek's struggle was. At the same time, they do not have to worry about "depending on" and "being controlled by" outside activists. Most important, they get to live up to the idealized image of "pure" grassroots activists and use it as leverage. Indeed, the organizers of the Pan-Citizen Committee against the Pocheon Firing Range (Pocheonsi gun gwallyeonsiseol beomsimin daechaegwiwonhoe), the successor to the Task Force, maintain that the movement's legitimacy comes from its pragmatism (Interview with Lee Gil-yeon, July 13, 2016). At Rodriguez today, the tall, sturdy walls built around the range after the 2003 student raid stand as a reminder to the residents protesting today—that they should not let their everyday struggles get buried under clunky anti-American slogans.

Conclusion

Even as these base towns grab international headlines, much of the activist rhetoric remains locally grounded. High-intensity activism in protest towns has been buttressed by the resonant frame of everyday grievances. For the diehard nationalists in Korea and the staunchest defenders of pacifism in Japan, this deliberate parochialism constitutes a conscious strategy. As activists subordinate their more radical ambitions to the rather quotidian concerns of base town residents, they adhere to the primacy of the local.

By contrast, in many quiet towns, activists have largely defied the primacy of the local by exclusively invoking internationalist anti-militarist ideals. They have done so at their peril. In some ways, the lack of the resonance of the anti-base agenda in some of these quiet towns speaks to a larger political phenomenon in Korea and Japan: the weakening appeal of the Old Left and its pursuit of increasingly anachronistic ethnic nationalism in Korea and increasingly infeasible absolutist pacifism in Japan. Mass protests in the two countries in recent years became possible only when an otherwise non-politicized public voluntarily participated in collective action. Korea's 2008 protests against U.S. beef imports, for example, were marked by horizontal associations of eclectic individuals who refused to follow instructions from traditional leftist groups (Cho 2009). Impeachment protests against Park Geun-hye in 2016–2017 saw similar dynamics, with a limited role played by leftist civic groups. In Japan, the brief revival of anti-nuclear activism following the 2011 Fukushima disaster similarly featured those with no ties to political organizations (Oguma 2016). Traditional anti-base activism as waged by the Old Left simply lacks broad appeal today, especially at the subnational level.

Rhetorical pragmatism, however, is a mixed bag. On the one hand, it forces the authorities to pay attention to, and sometimes even attempt to address, local grievances. In the cases of MCAS Futenma and NAF Atsugi, the allies have sought to relocate the base or some of the core base functions elsewhere to appease locals. Similarly, if it were not for the pragmatically oriented opposition to the Ospreys in Okinawa, former deputy secretary of state Richard Armitage would not have felt the need to complain that this "third-order" issue was making "the tail wag the dog" (*Kyodo News via Japan Times* 2012). Base opponents continue to win compensation in noise pollution lawsuits. An environmental clause has been added to the SOFA. On the other hand, parochial framing limits the discursive boundaries of anti-base activism to technical, procedural matters, and invites only incremental achievements. Plaintiffs of noise lawsuits may receive compensation, but the sources of noise pollution, such as nighttime flights, remain unaddressed. Ginowan schools may get soundproofed windows installed, but the Ospreys continue to take off and land outside their windows.

At times, the need to couch anti-base opposition in the pragmatic language of everyday grievances seems to amount to self-censorship. When even the most active participants of protests feel the need to downplay their involvement—two female base opponents I met in Iwakuni refused to describe themselves as activists, as the word carries with it certain political connotations at which Japanese society looks askance—it comes as no surprise that they care about moderating the supposedly radical anti-base cause. Perhaps they find no better option: if pragmatic rhetorical strategies inadvertently preserve power relations by failing to raise more fundamental questions, expansive ideological rhetoric seems to fail at building a localized movement to begin with. Activists, in this sense, face a dilemma not just in their adherence to, but also in their defiance of, rhetorical pragmatism: pragmatism is no recipe for radical changes; but without pragmatism, one cannot even begin to build a movement in the first place.

5

Governing Bases

It did not take long before I realized Iwakuni was a base town. The day
I landed in this seemingly nondescript city—September 27, 2016—happened
to fall on the anniversary of the crash of an American bomber in Iwakuni's
Yokoyama district, near the famous Kintai Bridge, three months into the
Korean War. Coincidentally, the place where I was staying stood next to
the site of the tragedy, where the blaze from the crash burned down several
family houses sixty-six years prior. Three civilians perished. This misfortune,
locals told me, is long forgotten. The city, after all, has seen American aircraft
take off from Iwakuni on their missions to Korea, Vietnam, Afghanistan, and
Iraq—and the city has thrived as a result. Tokyo began funneling money into
Iwakuni as early as 1966 to ensure that Iwakuni remains what it is: a base
town. The "base money" (*kichi manē*) brought many things to the city: new
street lamps were among the first batch of sweeteners (*Chugoku Shimbun*
2020). Some five decades later, as MCAS Iwakuni continues to stand where it
has always been, there are some newer signs that remind the people here that
being a base town pays off. During my visit, I saw a new, all-glass city office
building, a shiny new airport, and new sports and leisure facilities that were
being constructed—all of which owe their existence to the subsidies Iwakuni
received from Tokyo in return for hosting the base. Iwakuni residents, I was
told, were happy with them.

It is no surprise, then, that local elites here would not want to risk losing
this steady supply of money, which reportedly accounts for 9 percent of the
city's budget—and that if anyone dared to go against the tide, they would
be in trouble. This is precisely what happened to Ihara Katsusuke, who, as
the mayor of Iwakuni, became an unlikely veto player in the business-as-
usual base politics in the mid-2000s. After his vocal opposition to the fortification of MCAS Iwakuni made international headlines, he soon found
himself "bullied," "harassed," and ultimately "crushed," in the words of local
base opponents. The sleek city hall building that stands out in the monot-
onous city landscape was a reward from Tokyo, but this latest inducement
came only after Tokyo punished Ihara for his dissent by suspending subsidies

Base Towns. Claudia Junghyun Kim, Oxford University Press. © Oxford University Press 2023.
DOI: 10.1093/oso/9780197665275.003.0005

earmarked for its construction until he caved in. With Ihara's defeat in the subsequent election, Iwakuni's rare moment as the front line of anti-base activism in the Japanese mainland ended. Quiescence has returned to the city, which remains as much a base town as ever.

What does the story of Iwakuni's dependence on base money and the mayor's failed opposition tell us about local political elites governing base towns? How does Iwakuni's experience compare with other localities, where local elites keep base issues at bay? Did the mayor have anything in common with other local heads who have also made their names as anti-base advocates? In this chapter, I shed light on the role of local elite allies as occasional veto players in base politics. As elite involvement legitimates a potentially thorny anti-base stance in the eyes of the latent adherents, activists routinely court local elite support. Elites, for their part, get to play a role as a champion of local interests, looking after a marginalized locality onto which U.S. military bases have been loaded. Their motivations, however, vary; they range from enthusiasts who fully embrace the movement to opportunists who appropriate the movement. Both types come with consequences. Elite anti-base enthusiasts, with their staunch opposition to what the authorities deem a matter of national and international security, risk inviting retaliation from the central government. The ensuing local-central conflict can ultimately alienate latent adherents—the very people activists sought to win over by seeking local elite support in the first place. Elite opportunists, on the other hand, tame and appropriate the movement in a way that only serves their own instrumental interests. Unlike much of the literature that treats elite allies as an automatic political opening, support from local political elites is not always a boon for anti-base movements in the long run.

Local Elites as Allies and Foes

Activists hope that local political elites will do what they cannot: hold local referenda, create administrative hurdles to base construction, and articulate their grievances in negotiations with the state. For this reason, even as architects of high-intensity activism, activists in protest towns still court local elite support. In some of the fiercest base towns, base opponents have managed to ally with local political elites at different points in time. Elites, for their part, range from enthusiasts to opportunists. In Nago, where every mayoral election centers on the inevitable question of whether one supports the

FRF construction or not, activists found a loyal movement ally in Inamine Susumu. Widely supported by anti-base constituents, the mayor became a movement enthusiast and an unlikely veto player in interstate base politics—until his wholehearted support invited Tokyo's retaliation and made Nago residents wary of the city's uncertain future. In Pyeongtaek, activists actively sought—and then severed—ties with local elites, who wanted to tame the movement and use it as political leverage in negotiations with the central government. In Yokosuka, activists successfully took advantage of a looming election as a chance to pressure mayoral candidates, only to see the new mayor go from ally to foe. In both Pyeongtaek and Yokosuka, single-issue activists demanded that elites represent their uncompromising goals, whereas elites preferred compromises. The elusiveness of elite support in protest towns, where the high salience of base issues gives local elites more incentives to get involved, shows the difficulty facing social movements with supposedly radical goals in winning political representation—even at the local level.

Camp Schwab (Nago, Japan): Small-Town Mayor, Global Influence

Even in the most active protest towns, activists court elite support to further legitimate their cause. And sometimes, such efforts pay off handsomely. Inamine Susumu, who served as Nago's mayor from 2010 to 2018, embodies the potentially explosive influence of local government dissent not just on subnational base politics but also on high-level alliance politics. Inamine, with his election pledge to never allow a new base in any form, "whether on land or sea" (*umi ni mo riku ni mo*), was the first Nago mayor to unequivocally and invariably embrace the movement against the FRF construction in Henoko (see chapter 3). His election victory in 2010, widely seen as an affirmation of Nago people's popular rejection of the already long-delayed project, was a big boost for local opponents who finally gained an ally after more than a decade of wishy-washiness on the part of the city leadership. This small-town election carried with it political implications on an international scale. The *New York Times*, for example, predicted that Inamine's win may "widen a diplomatic rift" between the allies and even lead to calls to reduce U.S. troops in Japan (Fackler 2010). When Inamine won re-election in 2014, the newspaper called it an "embarrassing blow" to Washington and Tokyo (Fackler 2014).

Okinawa's base opponents enjoyed a series of electoral victories at the time, which newly empowered the movement. Inamine's mayoral career began shortly after Hatoyama Yukio of the Democratic Party of Japan took office in 2009 and became the first prime minister to explicitly defy the allies' pursuit of the FRF by pledging to move MCAS Futenma out of Okinawa. There were expectations that Inamine's win, which came on the heels of Hatoyama's victory, might just be "the final nail in the coffin of the base-building plan" (Penn 2013). Hatoyama's ambitious bid ultimately ended in failure, however, partially because no other localities volunteered to host Futenma and partially because he faced adamant opposition—not to mention consistent rebuke and ridicule—from the foreign policy and security establishments in Washington and Tokyo (McCormack and Norimatsu 2012; Interview, Hatoyama Yukio, June 19, 2017). Still, the prime minister's high-profile support for Okinawa's anti-base cause, while it lasted, provided Inamine and local anti-base constituents with unprecedented visibility and legitimacy. In Okinawa, electoral rebellion continued. In the November 2014 gubernatorial election, the "All Okinawa" coalition, which sought to prioritize Okinawan identity over political differences between the left and the right, led to Onaga Takeshi's win. The defeat of Nakaima Hirokazu, the incumbent governor at the time, was attributed to his backpedaling on his promise to resist the FRF construction and his permitting the landfill, a prerequisite for the construction. A series of LDP setbacks in the December 2014 general elections was further evidence, at least from the perspective of base opponents, of a popular mandate against the Henoko project.

The mayor and anti-base activists were practically indistinguishable in rhetoric and action to such a degree that international media described Inamine as a movement "spokesman" (Penn 2013). The annual "peace march" across Okinawa, a tradition that began in 1978 to protest the continuing U.S. military presence on the island, regularly featured Inamine, who would give an impassioned speech against the allies' basing policy. He also appeared at the aforementioned "new year car protest" against Futenma, where he would call for the closure—not just relocation—of the embattled base. In a sign of local-central conflict, his political rhetoric frequently targeted Tokyo. At an anti-base event in August 2014, the mayor, wearing a "cape decorated with multicolored dugong," averred that Okinawa was "under attack" by

Tokyo (Mitchell 2014). He joined protesters who encircled the Diet in Tokyo in February 2016, accusing the state of "ignor[ing] democracy and local autonomy" (*Kyodo News* 2016). When daily sit-in protests in Henoko reached the 5,000th day in December 2017, he stood with protesters in a show of solidarity (Yamajiro et al. 2018). He moved ordinary Nago citizens into action. A guitarist, who "used to be non-political" but is now a regular face at the Henoko protest hut, became a Nago city council member in 2014 with the sole purpose of "protecting and supporting Inamine" (Interview, Ōshiro Shōken, September 11, 2016).

Just as base opponents adopted various delaying tactics to slow down the status transition (see chapters 3 and 4), the mayor took full advantage of his administrative power to do the same. For example, he threatened to reject requests to use a fishing port for transportation of construction materials and refused to grant permission for fuel tanks. "(The central government) will need approval, consensus, or consultation with the mayor. . . . I will not cooperate," he told foreign journalists shortly after his reelection in 2014 (Yoshida 2014). Continuing pressure from the central government reinforced the image of his dissent as a struggle for local autonomy and further galvanized his supporters. "Even as the central government manages to move ahead with the (construction) plan, our bond (*kizuna*) with Inamine and Onaga will remain unwavering," Ōshiro Satoru, the secretary-general of Okinawa Peace Movement Center, said of the then-incumbent mayor and governor (Interview, September 9, 2016).

With high-level contestation backing Inamine's dissent, the central government intensified its not-so-subtle damage control strategy: dangling economic assistance as a carrot. According to Itokazu Keiko, a member of the House of Councilors and an Okinawan native, the government tries to forcibly spoon-feed the localities, telling them to "eat it, just eat it!" (Interview, September 19, 2016). As *The Economist* (2007) once commented on this carrot-and-stick approach, "[i]f it is not nibbled, out will come the big stick." Northern Districts Development (*Hokubu shinkō jigyō*) funds, part of the Okinawa Development Budget (*Okinawa shinkō yosan*) handled by the Cabinet Office, date back to 1999 when Okinawan governor Inamine Keiichi and Nago mayor Kishimoto Tateo greenlighted the FRF. Under the program, the state doled out 100 billion yen ($940 million) to Okinawa's northern municipalities, including Nago, over ten years between fiscal years 2000 and 2010. The program has since been extended to 2021. When subsidies for U.S. base relocation were separately introduced in the fiscal year of 2007, Nago received 1.8 billion yen ($17 million) in 2008 and 2009, only to see the flow of aid stop with Inamine's 2010 election win. Nago city officials and Henoko protesters seemed to shrug off this thinly veiled retaliation. As city officials put it: "The state said, 'We won't give you money.' We said, 'Oh, is that so?'" (Interview with Nakaima Shinichiro and Koichiro Nakazato, September 15, 2016). The Okinawa-wide development budget, typically around 300 billion yen ($2.9 billion) a year, similarly declined after Onaga took office in 2014. Still, even as Tokyo flaunted "offers of largesse" right before the mayoral election in 2014 in the form of massive public works projects, Inamine went on to win his second term (Fackler 2014).

If the local-central confrontation in Nago invigorated anti-base opposition, it also provoked fears about the city's uncertain future as a renegade town: could this small town continue to disobey Tokyo? In a pattern that we will see repeated in Iwakuni, the Japanese government is skilled at instilling and cultivating such fears, which pressure latent adherents into questioning the viability of local opposition. In a crucial mayoral election in 2018, Inamine ran against Toguchi Taketoyo, a former Nago assemblyman backed by Abe Shinzō, his LDP, and its formerly neutral coalition partner Komeito. The tried-and-proven LDP strategy of evading divisive issues, and thus blocking them from entering the realm of electoral contentions, was in play. Conservative heavyweights, such as Chief Cabinet Secretary Suga Yoshihide and LDP Secretary-General Nikai Toshihiro, descended on Nago to promise economic prosperity, all the while deflecting the obvious Henoko question. Koizumi Shinjirō, a rising star of the LDP, attracted a huge crowd anxiously awaiting his opinion on the FRF construction, but he only harped on about garbage sorting and local beer (Kirishima 2018). Inamine, whom Toguchi blamed for a "lost [eight] years" of apparent "stagnation" (Yamajiro et al. 2018), was narrowly defeated. Base realignment subsidies, suspended during Inamine's tenure, immediately resumed. His loss was so deeply tied to base opponents in the city that one activist noted: "There is no denying that a deep concern (exists) over how the electoral defeat . . . will affect" the direction of the anti-FRF movement. Another activist wondered: "How is it that we failed to carry Inamine to victory?" (Yamajiro et al. 2018). As trucks carried construction materials into Camp Schwab, protests continued at its gate—with Inamine among the crowd of protesters (*Okinawa Times* 2018).

Camp Humphreys (Pyeongtaek, Korea) and CFA Yokosuka (Yokosuka, Japan): Fleeting Alliances

The close ties we saw between Inamine and local base opponents remain an anomaly, rather than the norm. In Pyeongtaek and Yokosuka, local political elites, even as they saw the two bases in their electoral districts evolve into protest hotspots, responded to activist overtures with what was at best brief, weak support. While activists remained perpetually disgruntled with the absence of strong, sustained support, they did seek to take advantage of what little leverage they could generate from elite involvement. Activist efforts were nonetheless limited, however, as their maximalist demands clashed with local elites' preference for compromises.

Pyeongtaek-based activists, seeking greater legitimacy for their apparently radical anti-relocation agenda, proactively courted elite endorsement in the earliest phases of the movement. Activists' overtures to local political elites began as early as 2003. As national attention on the large-scale relocation of U.S. forces to Pyeongtaek mounted, and as early opinion polls indicated public opposition, elites responded to the overtures. In fact, the elite rhetoric during this brief period was rather strong for local politicians in Korea, whose first instinct is to stay away from high-level alliance politics. On multiple occasions, the mayor, city council members, and two lawmakers representing Pyeongtaek expressed their "absolute" and "unconditional" opposition to the relocation. The two lawmakers, one from the liberal ruling party and the other from the conservative opposition, submitted a joint resolution to the parliament in July 2003: "We are absolutely opposed to the unilateral (relocation) decision, which will have a crucial impact on the lives of local people in the affected areas" (Gi-su Kim 2005, 63–64). Members of the Pyeongtaek city council and the Gyeonggi provincial council joined activist-held protests during this brief period of elite-activist alliance. Pyeongtaek mayor Kim Sun-ki also agreed to an activist proposal to establish a joint committee with local base opponents and met with the defense minister to register his opposition.

Once activists and the local elites got together, however, the two sides soon discovered their differences. Activists had maximalist goals: an absolute opposition to the relocation in any form. Their elected representatives, on the other hand, only partially opposed the relocation: while they unequivocally rejected the relocation of the 2ID, they were willing to tolerate, if not enthusiastically support, the relocation of Yongsan Garrison. Even as Mayor Kim rebuffed the popular claim that Yongsan Garrison should leave Seoul because it hurts national pride—his response was "Who doesn't have pride?"—he never defied what had long been a national policy goal, now newly articulated as the YRP (Gi-su Kim 2005, 87). The two lawmakers representing Pyeongtaek at the national assembly also partially opposed the relocation. While they endorsed the Yongsan relocation, they argued that moving the 2ID south of the capital would end its status as a "tripwire"—the idea that U.S. forces near the border with North Korea act as a deterrent—and thereby undermine national security (Gi-su Kim 2005, 295–97).

Continued interactions between activists and local political elites only served to highlight a growing gulf between the absolutist-minded activists and the compromise-prone elites. Activists accused local elites of using the security rationale as a mere political cover; the underlying sentiment behind their partial opposition, according to activists, was that Yongsan Garrison was an "elite" base, whereas the 2ID had a "bad image" due to its association with "crimes" (Y. Kim 2005). Calling the watered-down partial opposition a tacit approval, the activists ended up leaving the joint committee that the mayor had set up (Gi-su Kim 2005, 78). Once the two sides confirmed the unbridgeable gap, they went their own ways. "From the beginning, the city assumed that the relocation would take place, and focused on extracting economic benefits out of the deal," says Kim Yong-han, an activist behind the boycott, who later went on to run, unsuccessfully, for mayor himself (Interview, July 3, 2016). Frustration on the part of the activists is palpable in a September 2003 statement: "(The city) should stop fidgeting over what the central government and the U.S. may think, and should mobilize citizen power and lead a fight . . . those in charge of the Pyeongtaek administration must do their duty" (Pyeongtaek Movement to Stop Base Expansion and Paengseong Residents' Action Committee 2003). By mid-2004, Song Myung-ho, who replaced Kim as mayor, stated that the relocation "is not a matter to be decided by the local government" (Gi-su Kim 2005, 130). Later, the city responded to the large-scale land expropriation and the eviction of local farmers with a vague statement expressing "regret" (Gi-su Kim 2005, 142).

Adding to the reluctance on the part of local elites to comment on national security issues were Seoul's promises of economic prosperity. Activists allege that local elites stopped protesting the 2ID relocation after the central government unveiled plans to introduce a special economic assistance bill designed to appease Pyeongtaek. Activists, arguing that the law was aimed at rendering the relocation irreversible, raided—and broke off, to the great embarrassment of the authorities involved—a public hearing on the special bill (R. Park 2010, 48–50). Mutual hostility prevailed between civic groups and local elites. The animosity ran so deep that a protest event in December 2005 included a symbolic funeral where activists set fire to a bier carrying the names of the following parties: the Roh Moo-hyun administration, the defense ministry, George W. Bush, as well as Pyeongtaek's mayor and the city council (S. Park 2005). For protesters, local representatives, who went from allies to foes, were just as culpable as the state. Nonetheless, the special law, introduced in December 2004 and to be in effect between 2006 and 2026, proved to be lucrative. It has poured nearly 19 trillion won ($17 billion) into Pyeongtaek (Ministry of the Interior and Safety 2020), and a host of benefits that came with the bill ended up attracting such business giants as Samsung and LG to this port city. As a result, Pyeongtaek, now home to large Samsung semiconductor factories the size of sixteen soccer fields, has even seen steep population growth in an otherwise rapidly aging society: from 370,000 when the mayor stood against the relocation to 560,000 in 2021. Daechuri is now a distant memory.

Similar overtures and eventual frustrations characterized the relationship between Yokosuka activists and their local representatives in the run-up to the deployment of the USS *George Washington*, a nuclear-powered aircraft carrier (see chapters 3 and 4). Yokosuka at least partially owes its unparalleled status as the sole overseas homeport of U.S. aircraft carriers to its local political elites. The city's strategic importance—the American presence here validates U.S. extended deterrence guarantees to Japan (Tetsuo 2008)—dates back to 1973, when mayor Nagano Masayoshi and the sharply divided city council reluctantly upheld the deployment of the USS *Midway*. The local understanding at the time was that the *Midway*, the first aircraft carrier to be forward-deployed in Japan, was going to stay for only a few years—which, over time, proved to be little more than wishful thinking. The nuclear transition of the mid-2000s presented another rare chance for the city to do something about its status as a permanent base town. The city of Yokosuka, after all, declared itself "nuclear-free" in 1984, if only because of popular pressure (T. Takahara 1987).

When civic groups mobilized against the deployment of the USS *George Washington*, they considered Mayor Kabaya Ryōichi a likely ally. Kabaya, after all, came to office in June 2005 following an election that Japan's liberal *Asahi Shimbun* predicted "could have ramifications for" the

U.S.-Japan alliance and U.S. extended nuclear deterrence (*Asahi Shimbun* 2005). As activists successfully raised public awareness of the impending nuclear transition, his electoral fortunes at least partially depended on whether he endorsed or rejected the deployment. With other mayoral candidates vowing their strong opposition, Kabaya, despite the backing of then–prime minister Koizumi Junichiro, was forced to brand himself as an opponent of the nuclear turn. During his campaign, he presented himself as a more level-headed candidate: the two other candidates, leaning farther left, were calling for the closure of the naval base and an end to the deployment of any type of aircraft carriers, nuclear-powered or otherwise (*Asahi Shimbun* 2005). After Kabaya won the election, civic groups pressured him to keep his election promises, sending him an anti-nuclear petition with some 324,000 signatures. In response, the mayor formally asked Tokyo's foreign ministry officials, and later the U.S. ambassador to Japan, to respect the will of Yokosuka citizens (*Mainichi Shimbun* 2005b). He also partially complied with a request from civic groups to stop an on-base construction project, by granting his permission only on the condition that the construction would not be used to accommodate nuclear-powered vessels (*Mainichi Shimbun* 2005c).

The feared transition nonetheless took place, with the announcement in October 2005 of the deployment of the USS *George Washington*. The foreign minister simply announced the decision in a perfunctory phone call to the mayor that lasted for less than a minute (*Asahi Shimbun* 2006). The mayor called the move a "betrayal," and the city council echoed him, citing local sentiments and safety concerns (*Chūnichi Shimbun* 2005). Base opponents in the city welcomed this continued opposition and pressed for more; they demanded a bigger opposition movement where the city government and civic groups would come together "as one body" (*ittai*) (*Mainichi Shimbun* 2005e). Kabaya publicly pledged to do what was possible within his means to stop the proposed transition from taking place, and officially asked the U.S. ambassador and the Japanese foreign minister to reconsider the plan. Considering the fact that Kabaya's predecessor, Sawada Hideo, refrained from even using the word "nuclear" in his ostensible opposition to a nuclear-powered aircraft carrier—instead, he expressed support for the continued use of a conventionally powered aircraft carrier (*Mainichi Shimbun* 2005a)—Kabaya's rhetoric presented at least a modicum of progress for activists. A news report at the time grouped activists and the mayor together in the broad anti-base camp, noting how the deployment decision came as a "shock" to all of them (*Mainichi Shimbun* 2005d).

This budding solidarity, however, was short-lived. By June 2006, Kabaya "accepted" the deployment, saying that his defiance had "hit a thick wall." "There is no legal basis for my opposition," the mayor claimed, because the deployment of a nuclear-powered aircraft carrier had become an established fact. The reversal, as we will see in the cases of Iwakuni, Zama, and Sagamihara, had to do with state pressure exerted on dissenting localities. The central government ramped up pressure on Yokosuka before its annual budget request, as it wanted to include a budget for boring surveys at the port and prevent any further delays that "may hurt the credibility of the Japan-U.S. alliance" (*Tokyo Shimbun* 2006b). The mayor, given the local administrative rights guaranteed under the port and harbor law (Ishimaru 2007, 55), could have opted to withhold permission for boring surveys. He chose not to do so. The surrender was immediately celebrated by J. Thomas Schieffer, the U.S. ambassador to Japan, who pledged to "continue to listen and seriously consider the views of local residents and political leaders regarding this deployment." He claimed the U.S. military "tried very hard to accommodate" Kabaya's request, but that "detailed study" proved the inevitability of the deployment of the USS *George Washington* (Duong 2006). Despite the pleasantries, however, the authorities probably considered the mayor's acquiescence a foregone conclusion. When even the fiercest critics of U.S. overseas basing call the Seventh Fleet "the only truly indispensable" U.S. forces in Asia, with its continued presence at CFA Yokosuka as "a primary American policy objective" (C. Johnson 1996), it is difficult to imagine policymakers paying serious heed to what a local mayor has to say.

In the eyes of local civic groups, Kabaya went from an ally to a betrayer. Now left on their own, activists denounced the mayor's short-lived dissent as a tepid, pro forma opposition never meant to be a serious challenge—in other words, "a mere campaign tactic" (Hanai 2006). One prominent anti-base group, led by a local lawyer who later ran unsuccessfully for mayor himself, considered a recall campaign against the mayor. While the anti-deployment movement was a still a relative success that brought latent adherents on board, the very lack of local elite allies severely limited its efficacy. Although activists generated broad support for a city-wide anti-base referendum in

2007 and 2008, local political elites refused to hold the referendum. "Foreign affairs, constitutionally, are handled by the state," Kabaya said, dismissing the idea of a referendum as something "unfamiliar" (*najimanai*) and therefore inappropriate. His administrative authority over the Yokosuka harbor, the mayor argued, could not influence such matters as the deployment of a nuclear-powered aircraft carrier (*Mainichi Shimbun* 2007a). To this day, activists deplore the mayor's refusal to acknowledge the petition, which rendered their efforts practically futile. Commenting on the attitudinal differences observed across base towns, a Yokosuka activist says that variations in the intensity of anti-base opposition "exist not just in local civil society but also in the local administration" (Interview with Nīkura Yasuo, October 4, 2016). Yokosuka's city government, according to local activists, "presumes" the inevitability of the continuing U.S. presence (Interview with Nīkura Hiroshi, October 7, 2016).

Bringing Unruly Mayors into Line

We now turn to local political elites in other, less contentious base towns who rose to fame by initiating—not simply following—anti-base activism. Rare dissent on the part of the mayors of Iwakuni, Zama, Sagamihara, and Dongducheon raised the profile of anti-base causes and gave activists some much-needed legitimacy. What sets them apart from the outlier case of Nago, however, is the duration and the nature of the mayoral dissent. In Iwakuni, Sagamihara, and Zama, local elites quickly caved to pressure from the central government. Iwakuni, in particular, became a target of overt retaliation from the central government, which eventually dissuaded many latent adherents from participating in what the authorities presented as a futile quest to resist the U.S. military. In Dongducheon, meanwhile, local elites readily suspended their showy and ultimately opportunistic opposition the moment their instrumental needs—extracting money from the central government—were met. In all three cases, monetary interests prevailed in how the central government controlled their local counterparts, although Tokyo and Seoul took distinctive approaches: Japan punished dissenting localities by withdrawing material benefits, whereas Korea rewarded them by conceding to their demands for monetary compensation. Quiescence, it seems, can be bought off.

MCAS Iwakuni (Iwakuni, Japan) and Camp Zama (Zama and Sagamihara, Japan): Dissent and Punishment

Rare moments of resistance against MCAS Iwakuni and Camp Zama coincided with equally rare moments of local elite dissent. In both cases, local representatives positioned themselves as champions of their constituents vis-à-vis the overbearing central government. While the ensuing local-central conflict elevated base issues to a larger question of local autonomy and democracy, it also reminded many base town residents that dissent may only result in retribution—and that opposition, after all, might be futile. Once base issues were excluded from political arenas, quiescence returned to these towns.

In Iwakuni, Mayor Ihara Katsusuke, a soft-spoken former labor ministry bureaucrat, emerged as an unusual ally of the anti-expansion movement. The mayoral dissent began after the announcement, made without any local input, that a U.S. Navy carrier air wing from NAF Atsugi was coming to MCAS Iwakuni (see chapter 3). Although the mayor was not against the base itself, he objected to the way Tokyo treated local consent to its fortification as a foregone conclusion. In a move that quickly politicized the base realignment, Ihara called a referendum on the relocation in 2006, urging Iwakuni citizens to "let the nation know what we really want" (*Daily Yomiuri* 2006). This unusual bid—even more unusual for a city that had relied on base-related government subsidies since the 1960s—was immediately met with cynicism. The Iwakuni City Council, local businessmen, and the powerful conservative media, whose coverage of the referendum ranged from "openly skeptical" to "slightly hostile" (Johnston 2006), contended that a small municipality cannot shape the direction of national security matters. "Iwakuni should not cause any more confusion by uselessly confronting the government," Japan's largest conservative daily lectured Ihara in an editorial (*Yomiuri Shimbun* 2006).

On the side of the mayor was an assortment of local groups, including traditional anti-base activists and members of the local parent-teacher association. Like-minded activists from the greater Yamaguchi Prefecture and the Chūgoku region flocked to Iwakuni in a show of solidarity. Some 10,000 leaflets were distributed in support of the referendum, the first of its kind outside Okinawa. "Let's go vote," urged banners displayed at Iwakuni's railway stations (*Mainichi Shimbun* 2006a). Many Iwakuni natives living elsewhere in Japan traveled back home just to cast a ballot. The referendum, held on

March 12, 2006, was a success for Ihara and his supporters: with a 58.68 percent turnout, itself an achievement given the conservative boycott, some 87 percent of the voters rejected the air wing transfer. Ihara, linking the local referendum to the question of local autonomy, announced that the "democratic process has worked" (Johnston 2006). He subsequently won reelection in a landslide victory in April 2006, which many saw as a reaffirmation of the people's will (*min'i*) against the relocation.

Then Tokyo struck back, turning what was a mundane administrative issue into a political controversy with international implications. The central government, which had pledged 3.5 billion yen ($32 million) in subsidies to help replace the decrepit city hall, abruptly suspended its plan even as the new building was already under construction—the official reason being that Ihara opposed the military relocation. (Ironically, the construction itself was made possible with state subsidies Iwakuni received in return for accepting air tankers from MCAS Futenma, a decision made by Ihara's predecessor.) Iwakuni also suddenly found itself ineligible for government-provided base realignment subsidies that were doled out to all other compliant municipalities. Tokyo's overt show of state power over a small-town mayor lacked any semblance of subtlety. The withdrawal of the state subsidies "was an inconceivable way of handling issues between the state and a locality—a betrayal of trust, and a breach of promise," says Ihara, recalling that he was never once invited to the negotiating table as an equal (Interview, September 28, 2016). Activists were further galvanized by the widening central-local rift. A protest leaflet from January 2007 features caricatures of Ihara and the then prime minister, Abe Shinzō; in one cartoon image, the somber-faced Ihara is depicted as a defender of "citizen safety" (*shimin no anzen*) against the mean-looking Abe, who is trying to shove aircraft onto Iwakuni. In another image, citizen supporters are seen cheering for Ihara, holding slogans reading "Listen to citizen voices!" and "We won't be deceived!"

As Ihara faced increasing pressure to cave in, the central-local elite fissure continued to serve as a rallying point, culminating in an 11,000-strong rally in December 2007. A feat for a small, conservative city like Iwakuni, the event was described as an opportunity to vent anger against the state's harsh treatment (*kuni no shiuchi*) of the mayor, and, by extension, his anti-base backers. Participants denounced both Tokyo and Iwakuni's pro-base, anti-Ihara city councilmen for exerting undue pressure on the mayor. "We won't be defeated by the move to recall Mayor Ihara, who is fighting for citizen safety against the pressure from the state and the prefecture," the protest statement read (Jūmin tōhyō o chikara ni suru kai 2007). Activists also organized a fundraising campaign as Ihara scrambled to find alternative sources of money to finance the stalled construction of the city office. By July 2007, Iwakuni citizens donated a total of 6.36 million yen ($58,000) to the city (*Asahi Shimbun* 2007a), and at the aforementioned rally in December 2007, participants raised an additional 1.3 million yen ($11,800) on the spot. When the rally organizers delivered the money to Ihara, they said they were seeking to "protect local autonomy and democracy" (*Mainichi Shimbun* 2007b). For these anti-base constituents, the central-local confrontation posed renewed questions about the quality of democracy in Japan. "Money and power stifled citizens' voices," says Ōkawa Kiyoshi, a local pastor who supported Ihara. "Japan is not a democracy" (Interview, September 30, 2016).

While state pressure rallied Ihara's anti-base supporters, the rest of the city began to worry about the potential fallout from the continuing confrontation. "The people got anxious," Ihara recalls. "Even the people who might have agreed with me in principle began to fear that Iwakuni might get crushed [by Tokyo]" (Interview, September 28, 2016). The City Council turned increasingly hostile to Ihara, pressuring him to accept the relocation and receive state subsidies. The council repeatedly struck down the supplementary budget bills proposed by the mayor, which he intended to use to help fund the construction without state subsidies (*Asahi Shimbun* 2007a). The beleaguered Ihara soon voluntarily resigned, with the intention of making the subsequent election a vote of confidence for him and his anti-base dissent. For this nondescript city, the mayoral election in February 2008 was an unusual one: it was not only a "political test" for Tokyo, but also a test of "whether base realignment as a whole will move forward" (Johnston 2008).

In the end, Ihara was narrowly defeated by Fukuda Yoshihiko, a pro-base LDP member of the House of Representatives. A politician that Agence France-Presse described as having "parachuted in from Tokyo" (Campion 2008), Fukuda portrayed the relocation as a foregone conclusion and tried to discredit and disunite base opposition. He threatened that Iwakuni might go bankrupt if the confrontation with Tokyo continued. Iwakuni could well become "another Yūbari," he warned, referring to a former mining town in Hokkaido reeling from bankruptcy and a rapid population exodus (*Akahata* 2008a).[1] Smear tactics targeting Ihara included allegations that he was a "communist." The fearmongering worked. The subsidy freeze ended immediately after Fukuda's win. Ihara supporters use the word "bullying" (*ijime*) to describe the state behavior at the time. Tokyo's message, they argue, was clear: "If you oppose bases, you'll become like Ihara." Ihara, for his part, is now leading an aptly named local political party: Grassroots (Kusanone).

While activists in the city continue their opposition, Ihara's setback was just as much of a setback for them. The perceived legitimacy of the anti-base position rested on the referendum outcome and Ihara's subsequent re-election. The mayor's defeat now seemed to point in the opposite direction. Mayoral elections in the city have since consolidated Iwakuni's pro-base stance at the local elite level. In 2016, Himeno Atsuko ran against Fukuda with a decisively anti-base slogan: "Independence or dependence? Iwakuni is capable of independence" (*jiritsu ka, izon ka. Iwakuni wa jiritsu dekiru*). Fukuda scored an easy win. Today, local anti-base activism is less visible, with no viable chance of a popular movement in sight. The city assembly continues to be dominated by pro-base conservatives. In the Diet, Kishi Nobuo, Abe's brother, continues to represent the Yamaguchi Second District, the electoral district in which Iwakuni is situated. (In 2020, he became Japan's defense minister.)

And money has continued to roll in. Base realignment subsidies for 2008–2022 are expected to total more than 20 billion yen ($195 million) (*The Mainichi* 2017). In addition to the current city office, Iwakuni Kintaikyo Airport, which opened in 2012 as a joint civilian-military airport in return for accepting the relocation, is another shiny new reminder to Iwakuni residents that supporting American military bases pays off. Yet another perk includes free school lunches provided at Iwakuni's elementary and junior high schools. All these measures nudge—or coerce—localities into accepting their life alongside American bases. "The current mayor says *irasshai, irasshai* (welcome, welcome) to the U.S. military, and most people are content with the money flowing in," Tamura Jungen, one of the few anti-base city councilmen, laments (Interview, September 28, 2016). Today, a small group called the Iwakuni Citizens' Association to Carry on the Referendum's Achievements (Jūmin tōhyō no seika o ikasu Iwakuni shimin no kai) seeks to commemorate, and hopefully revive, the spirit of 2006. "We believe that the true will of the people resembles magma, unignited beneath the surface but still there," says Ōkawa Kiyoshi, the group's leader (Interview, September 30, 2016). The underlying anti-base sentiment that he believes exists, however, finds no political representation in the face of strong pro-base local-central elite unity.

Local-central elite conflict surrounding another spell of mayoral dissent in Zama and Sagamihara mirrors Iwakuni's experience. When activists mobilized against the relocation of the I Corps headquarters to Camp Zama (see chapter 3), they had the full backing of the mayors of the two host cities: Hoshino Katsuji of Zama and Ogawa Isao of Sagamihara. These adjoining cities with a combined population of nearly 750,000 have long called for more efficient urban planning, which they say would require the "reorganization (*seiri*), reduction (*shukushō*), and return (*henkan*)" of Camp Zama. Although this stated principle may have been little more than rhetoric, the fortification of Camp Zama, which indicated a significantly consolidated and prolonged U.S. presence, was something neither city celebrated. The mayors, after all, had no say in the relocation decision.

The two mayors moved preemptively, declaring the proposed relocation "unacceptable," paying a rare visit to the foreign and defense ministries in protest, and submitting written opposition to the U.S. embassy in Tokyo (*Mainichi Shimbun* 2004). Both cities passed resolutions rejecting the relocation. "Koizumi-san, what are you thinking? You said we cannot overly burden Okinawa," Ogawa said in a media interview, asking prime minister Koizumi Junichiro why it was then okay to "burden" Zama and Sagamihara instead (T. Johnson 2004). It was the first time base opponents here had gained prominent elite allies since 1972, when the mayor of Sagamihara lent his support to citizens engaged in a "tank struggle" (*sensha tōsō*)—a 100-day-long anti-Vietnam War protest that sought to block the passage of American tanks sent from Vietnam to the Sagami General Depot for repairs.

Activists savored the uncommon chance to have local elites validate their seemingly radical agenda. "The city governments . . . have already jointly expressed their absolute opposition," protesters said at their first rally against the relocation in August 2004. "With this emergency gathering as a starting point, we, in association with the city governments, shall fight to deter the relocation" (Kaneko 2004). Hoshino went on to bring together the city government, the city assembly, and civic groups in a new task force dubbed the Liaison Council of Zama City against the Relocation (Zama-shi kichi henkan sokushin tō shimin renraku kyōgikai). The group placed hundreds of banners, posters, and stickers carrying anti-relocation messages on city-owned buildings, bulletin boards, and vehicles (Kamoi 2005). The Council began collecting signatures for an anti-relocation petition, and by May 2005, it gathered 60,000 signatures from nearly half the city's population. By August, the Liaison Council of Sagamihara City on the Return of U.S. Bases (Sagamihara-shi beigunkichi henkan sokushin tō shimin kyōgikai), a similar network led by Ogawa, collected 210,000 signatures from one third of

Sagamihara's residents. The council also distributed some 130,000 postcards, divided into two types—one to be sent to State Secretary Condoleezza Rice and Defense Secretary Donald Rumsfeld, and the other to be sent to their Japanese counterparts. "No other municipality comes close to what we did," Kaneko Tokio, a Sagamihara city councilman, proudly notes (Interview, October 10, 2016).

The mayors adopted unusually flamboyant rhetoric. Hoshino, a self-described conservative, famously remarked that he would still oppose the relocation "even if a missile were to strike" him. (According to anti-Zama activists, this statement was probably an homage to the former Sagamihara mayor behind the 1972 tank struggle; he pledged at the time that he would remain opposed to U.S. military bases even if he were to be "run over by a tank.") Hoshino also told foreign minister Aso Taro that he may "think about" accepting the relocation if the city receives one trillion yen ($9.8 billion) in return—just another form of rebuke (*Tokyo Shimbun* 2006a). The Sagamihara liaison council led a high-profile protest event in November 2005, where some 3,200 participants formed a human chain to encircle Camp Zama (*Mainichi Shimbun* 2005f). From Bus Stop to Base Stop, a local group that holds regular anti-Zama sit-ins and marches, adopted the Sagamihara mayor's remark as its movement slogan: "If we keep quiet, we will still be a base town in 100 years" (*damatte itara hyakunen saki mo kichi no machi*). The slogan, beautifully embroidered on a large fabric protest banner, is an unmistakable sight at monthly anti-Zama marches that continue to date.

Despite the backing of anti-base devotees, however, the two mayors became increasingly aware of their limited ability to turn the tide. Shortly before the allies announced the finalized realignment plans in May 2006, the city governments hinted at the inevitability of the looming relocation. Instead, they began to focus more on practical demands such as partial land returns and state subsidies—or what they called "nuisance fees" (*meiwakuryō*) (*Mainichi Shimbun* 2006b). Around the same time, the Sagamihara city government, which also hosts the Sagami General Depot and the Sagamihara Housing Area, began to respond more favorably to government overtures. Ogawa, for example, expressed his intention to endorse the relocation on the condition that parts of the U.S. Army depot be returned to the city free of charge.[2] The depot has had its fair share of contesters, with the Sagami Depot Watchdogs (Sagami hokyūshō kanshidan) monitoring every little movement at the installation; a partial retrieval of the site was going to address at least some of the discontent in the city. Extending the Odakyū Tama railway line to Sagamihara Station has also been an urban planning goal for the city, long impeded by the presence of the depot (K. Takahara 2005).

Hoshino managed to drag his feet longer, only to face retaliation from Tokyo—the same kind of punishment bestowed on Ihara. Zama was excluded from the list of municipalities eligible for realignment subsidies, although Sagamihara, in a typical carrot-and-stick approach, made the list just in time and received 156 million yen ($1.46 million) (*Asahi Shimbun* 2007b). Despite continuing opposition on the part of the Zama government, the eventual relocation of I Corps took place at the end of 2007. By July 2008, Hoshino suspended what had become a futile opposition. The subsidies soon followed. A large banner that had hung on the Zama city hall for nearly four years, reading "(We) oppose the U.S. I Corps relocation to Camp Zama," came down at the request of the defense ministry (*Akahata* 2008b). In a mayoral election in September 2008, Endo Mikio, a pro-base candidate who had previously headed the Zama Chamber of Commerce, beat Kamoi Yoko, an anti-base rival backed by the JCP. "With the new mayor, the stance of the city completely changed. . . . Zama is now in 'big welcome' (*dai kangei*) mode" when it comes to U.S. bases, Kaneko notes (Interview, October 10, 2016). With this leadership change, Camp Zama ceased to be on the local political agenda.

Camp Casey (Dongducheon, Korea): Elite Preemption and Government Concessions

If local elite dissent in Nago, Iwakuni, Zama, and Sagamihara amplified the voices of their anti-base constituents, elite initiatives in Dongducheon, home to Camp Casey, appropriated the anti-base cause. Sizable protest mobilization in 2004 and 2014 would have been unlikely without elite initiation, especially as traditional anti-base groups in this northern city demobilized in the early 2000s (see chapter 3). Elite preemption here, however, narrowed the realm of possibilities for what local governments can do when their interests clash with the U.S. presence. As local elites made their instrumental demands a quid pro quo for the continued American presence, traditional anti-base groups with maximalist goals stood by.

Top-down anti-base mobilization in Dongducheon, the poorest city in Gyeonggi Province just eleven miles south of the Demilitarized Zone, might puzzle observers. The city saw two waves of local government-led protests in the 2000s, first against the planned relocation of the 2ID to Pyeongtaek, and then against its retention. These seemingly contradictory responses—wanting the Americans to stay, and then complaining that they stayed for too long—should be interpreted in the context of the city government's fixation on linking the U.S. military presence to the sluggish local economy and leveraging it to extract economic gains. The U.S. presence, for most host communities, is a double-edged sword: a source of income, but also a cause of economic dependency and a hurdle to urban planning. In Dongducheon, where U.S. bases occupy 42.5 percent of the land that many believe could be put to more profitable use, the economic dilemma runs particularly deep. The first wave of city-led protests of 2003–2004 called for monetary compensation for the 2ID's sudden relocation to Pyeongtaek, which local elites equated with an abrupt loss of income for the city. The second protest wave of 2013–2015 reiterated the compensation demand, this time in exchange for hosting the U.S. military for longer than anticipated. Both times, local elites ultimately blamed the heavy American presence for the economic problems of the city, which they said had been "sacrificed" for national security.

Mayor Choi Yong-soo led the first round of city-led protests, which called for countermeasures against potential economic fallouts from the 2ID's relocation, originally scheduled for 2008. He wanted the U.S. military to leave—just not too soon. With 20 percent of the local economy driven by the U.S. presence (Choi 2008), a measure that far exceeds that of Okinawa, the sudden relocation seemed to pose a serious economic challenge. The city council organized the Dongducheon City Committee for U.S. Military Affairs (Dongducheonsi migun hyeonan daechaek wiwonhoe), which mobilized some 100 civic groups in a top-down manner. According to an official account by the city, locals in these protests "spewed out their pent-up resentment" about their life alongside the U.S. military, which had been "suppressed for half a decade." The city government organized multiple trips to Seoul, bussing thousands of Dongducheon residents for rallies at the parliament and the presidential Blue House. Dongducheon elites also met everyone they could: the Gyeonggi governor; the prime minister; and Park Geun-hye, at the time the leader of the conservative ruling party and later president. They also threatened a host of reprisals, which ranged from blocking National Route 3, a national highway, to occupying the northern Gyeongwon railway line. The city had one demand: a special law for Dongducheon. The law, the mayor argued, should do two things. First, it should ease legal restrictions—imposed by the Protection of Military Bases and Installations Act—on urban planning in this heavily militarized city. Second, it should waive the costs the city is supposed to shoulder when retrieving U.S. base sites (Dongducheon City History Compilation Committee 2012, 6:64–65). The most enthusiastic backers of the campaign were small business owners catering to the U.S. presence, who make up some 17 percent of the local population (Choi 2008)—and who would be the last people to join the protests if it were not for Choi's initiation.

The campaign further heated up in 2004, following the news that some 3,000 Dongducheon-based troops were to leave for Iraq. Fearing a drop in revenue, the committee threatened "militant" action against the central government. Again, small business owners were quickly mobilized. In a city-organized event protesting the "dying" local economy, the shopkeepers wore funeral attire and carried a sign reading "In memoriam: The Special Tourist Zone," in reference to the commercial district frequented by G.I.s (*OhmyNews* 2004). The Committee also set up a tent camp for street protests (*cheonmak nongseong*), which went on for several months. In August, the city government and the city council organized a 3,500-strong rally—a large number given the city's small population, which stood at 79,200 in 2004—demanding that the central government guarantee "Dongducheon citizens' livelihood rights." At the scene, Mayor Choi and five city council members shaved their heads and, in a show of resolve, wrote a protest statement in their blood. "We have staged peaceful protests so far, but the (central) government has shown absolutely no interest," Choi said, hinting at more militant action to come (*Dong-a Ilbo* 2004). These protests ultimately led to the creation of a special law in 2006, which sought to assuage some fifty base towns across the country by partially funding the conversion of returned U.S. base sites. The mayor, having accomplished his instrumental goal of extracting economic concessions from the government, stopped protesting.

A decade later, the local government once again orchestrated top-down mobilization—this time against the delayed departure of the Americans in uniform. Mayor Oh Se-chang, of the liberal Democratic Party, took issue with the allies' decision to retain the 210th Field Brigade of the 2ID, previously slated for relocation to Pyeongtaek by 2008. The prolonged U.S. presence, he said, shattered the hope that the city could finally retake and redevelop the valuable land long occupied by military facilities. Claiming that Dongducheon residents, who have endured the "stigma" of living in a base town for decades, were about to "explode" (Song 2015), the mayor pledged to employ "any means necessary" to drive out the 2ID.

The anti-retention campaign of 2013–2015 was another elite-led effort that selectively mobilized conservative civic groups claiming to be "pro-American but anti-retention." Considering the common association between the political right and support for the U.S. military, it is hard to imagine that they would have gotten involved without elite initiation. The city government, for its part, does not want to fraternize with any group that may appear radical; appearing anti-American would be a scarlet letter for any politician dreaming of climbing the national political ladder. In the words of a city official who has lived his entire life in the vicinity of Camp Casey, the local government wants to associate itself only with "pure" civic groups "without political motives"—meaning that it wants to keep out traditional anti-base groups (Interview, anonymous, July 6, 2016). The top-down mobilization, in this regard, resurrected protest activity in the city with little involvement of typical leftist-nationalist activists, some of whom dismissed these elite-led rallies as *gwanje demo*—a term, with negative connotations going back to the authoritarian era, referring to protests engineered by government authorities. The Pan-Citizens Committee against U.S. Military Realignment (Dongducheon migun jaebaechi beomsimin daechaegwiwonhoe), a mainstay at these protests, is indeed self-professedly conservative. Han Jong-gab, who leads the group, used to chair the Dongducheon chapter of the Korean Veterans Association—one of the best-known pro-American civic groups in Korea. "We aren't saying that all U.S. forces must leave. Only a small minority of left-wingers would say that," Han said in an interview that took place at the Dongducheon City Hall, where he rubbed elbows with city officials (Interview, July 6, 2016).

Despite the opportunism on the part of the city government, the actual protests that went on were unusually fierce for otherwise staunchly pro-American participants. Protesters staged a one-person protest in front of Camp Casey for some 200 consecutive days. The city, which declared a "state of emergency" in November 2013, suspended administrative services that it had conventionally offered to U.S. base officials, such as speedier vehicle registration services available on base. Mayor Oh also threatened to block the main gate of Camp Casey, as well as the "peace road" (*pyeonghwaro*) connecting Dongducheon and Uijeongbu—a road hastily constructed in the 1970s to accommodate American leaders visiting these faraway base towns. The city claimed that the central government was "making a mockery of Dongducheon" by considering retention while awarding Seoul and Pyeongtaek—the former awaits the transformation of Yongsan Garrison into a park, and the latter now shoulders an enlarged base the size of downtown Washington, DC—economic benefits tailored for their specific needs (T. Kim 2012). In 2014, Dongducheon officials said they were considering an anti-base referendum, something that no other city government in the country had attempted. The city council threatened a riot. Large banners festooned across the city made a dramatic plea: "Let's show our anger by blocking National Route 3," a highway linking the city to the rest of the country. At city-led rallies, Mayor Oh's quips at the central government drew loud applause from such disparate groups as the right-wing Korea Freedom Federation and the Dongducheon branch of the leftist-nationalist Unified Progressive Party, as both sides sought to take advantage of the central-local elite division (Hui-hoon Lee and Sohn 2014). After years of dormancy, anti-base contention in the city was once again on the rise, with the mayor at the helm.

Compensation, at least for the mayor, apparently made everything suddenly tolerable. He got what he wanted: the central government pledged in July 2015 to fund the redevelopment of U.S. base sites and the construction of a 245-acre industrial complex in Dongducheon. City officials soon suspended protests, and as a result, base-related protests became few and far between. In the end, Dongducheon's apparently contradictory demands—opposing the relocation and then the retention—paid off each time. This single-minded pursuit of state compensation, which helps perpetuate the status quo of base politics, does not jibe with the absolutist goals favored by many traditional anti-base activists. "The city made compensation the sole focus of protests from the very beginning . . . so we stopped going to the rallies," former activists in the city, who preferred the immediate return of the base, complain (Interview, anonymous, July 11, 2016). Dongducheon, in this sense, is a microcosm of the country's anti-base scene today: the beleaguered status of traditional leftist-nationalist anti-base groups; a local penchant for government subsidies that sometimes borders on opportunism; and local elite rhetoric that, even at its most confrontational moments, stops short of fundamentally questioning the U.S. presence.

Varying Elite-Activist Dynamics

I now turn to a final set of cases that highlight two opposite types of elite-activist dynamics. First, I look at three base towns where activists maintain high-level contestation with little elite involvement: Ginowan, where both local elite allies and foes wield surprisingly little influence on the otherwise bitterly contentious base politics, and Yamato and Ayase, where elites remain aloof. What the three host communities share in common is that they are awaiting, or have gone through, base contraction: MCAS Futenma is permanently poised to leave Ginowan and move to Nago, and NAF Atsugi has offloaded its jets and troops to MCAS Iwakuni. Elite voices and influence, it seems, matter more in the context of base expansion, as we saw above in Nago and Iwakuni. Second, I look at the opposite case of Pocheon, home to Rodriguez Live Fire Complex, where grassroots activism began only after elite support became available. Of all the localities discussed in this chapter, Pocheon stands out as the only one with no history of independent community activism against the U.S. military. As discussed in chapter 4, it is also the only place where local residents repeatedly refused to join hands with professional activist groups. As a result, Pocheon residents ended up relying heavily on local elite allies, a choice that came with consequences: local elites co-opted the movement agenda.

MCAS Futenma (Ginowan, Japan) and NAF Atsugi (Ayase and Yamato, Japan): Going It Alone

In Ginowan, where MCAS Futenma perpetually awaits its departure, local leaders have come and gone without being able to shape its future. If there is one thing Ginowan mayors of different political orientations can agree on, it is that Futenma should be closed at the earliest possible date. While this may seem like a bold position to take for a mayor representing a city of 94,000, it is not enough to get them branded "anti-base" in the peculiar context of Okinawan politics. Calling for Futenma's closure in Ginowan is in line with the 1996 SACO agreement, after all, and is in no way a controversial proposition (see chapter 2). The fault line lies instead in the FRF debate, namely whether one supports Futenma's relocation to Nago.

Ironically, this bipartisan consensus on the need to shut down the unpopular base means that Ginowan mayors, whether pro-base or anti-base, do not feature as prominently as Nago mayors in Okinawa's contentious base politics. According to Iha Yōichi, an outspoken base critic who served as Ginowan's mayor between 2003 and 2010, opposing U.S. bases is "easier" when they go through drastic status changes—the kinds that herald a more intrusive U.S. presence, as in base construction or expansion. This is because municipalities have the power to grant permission for various construction projects required for base construction or expansion, as we saw in the cases of Nago and Yokosuka. Once firmly in place, however, bases become off-limits to local governments and almost impossible to monitor and regulate (Interview, June 1, 2017). For this reason, Inamine and Iha, despite being vocal representatives of their anti-base constituents, differed in their capacity to shape base politics: Camp Schwab is poised to expand, whereas MCAF Futenma is permanently on standby for departure.

The lack of local elite influence persisted even after Iha, a movement ally, was replaced in 2012 by Sakima Atsushi, a movement foe who brought conservatives to the city leadership for the first time in twenty-six years. During his tenure as mayor, Sakima, whose election was backed by the LDP and its junior partner New Komeito, maintained ambivalence about the relocation site—precisely where the battle lines are drawn. "Ginowan City doesn't really have a public stance on where the relocation site should be," said Ayako Sakugawa, a city official tasked with overseeing base affairs. "It's a decision to be made by the allies" (Interview, September 1, 2016). Such equivocation, in the context of Okinawan politics, was enough to label Sakima "pro-base." Sakima and city officials traveled to Tokyo, and even to Washington, to urge Futenma's return; but his agenda was practically redundant since just about everyone already agrees on the need to shut it down. The seemingly defiant message on a huge banner hung on the Ginowan city office, which expresses support for Futenma's early return and opposition to the Ospreys, amounted to little more than stating the obvious in the Okinawan political landscape. In this sense, Sakima did not differ much from Iha in his inability to shape base politics, regardless of their obvious political differences. Sakima's successor, Masanori Matsugawa, has also done little more than calling for Futenma's return—once again belaboring the obvious.

Local elites in Yamato and Ayase, home to NAF Atsugi, are guardians of the political status quo in their own right. They may sever "friendship ties" with Atsugi base officials, as Tsuchiya Kimiyasu did in 2000 to protest nighttime training, or oppose the fortification of base functions at CFA Yokosuka, which directly influences noise levels at NAF Atsugi. Any expression of disapproval, however, has been temporary. Local elites are happy to see the relocation of aircraft and troops from Atsugi to Iwakuni, which alleviates grievances in their backyard and dumps them on Iwakuni instead. The conditional nature of their opposition clashes with the absolutist principle of the activists, many of whom oppose the mere reshuffling of grievances.

Still, activists continue to seek out elite allies—and, surprisingly for those pursuing ostensibly radical goals, sometimes even attempt to break into institutional politics by becoming elected representatives themselves. "We always try to influence the mayor's policy stance . . . we really want to elect a mayor who will empathize with our cause and work with us," says Ōnami Shūji, a Yamato city councilman who represents the Alliance for Prevention of Noise at Atsugi Base (Atsugi kichi bakuon bōshi kiseidōmei) (Interview, October 14, 2016). In cities where anti-base activism has become increasingly routinized, predictable, and perhaps dismissable, however, finding elite allies has been a difficult task. Ogikubo Kōichi, another Alliance member, attempted to resolve this problem by running for mayor himself on an anti-base platform in 2011. His campaign centered on a more defiant local stance on Atsugi issues: a base town mayor, Ogikubo argued, should be able to negotiate directly with the U.S. military and the central government. Despite support from the SDP and a regional party called Kanagawa Network Movement (Kanagawa nettowāku undō), he trailed far behind the incumbent mayor, Ōki Satoru. The relatively high levels of local activism against NAF Atsugi continues—but without elite voices to further amplify its messages and register grievances in the political arena.

Rodriguez Live Fire Complex (Pocheon, Korea): Co-Opting "Innocent" Locals

We end with the story of a Korean border town that has gone through a drastic transition from a quiet town to an improbable anti-base battleground. The grassroots activism that emerged seemingly abruptly against the Rodriguez Live Fire Complex in 2014 coincided not only with pragmatic calls for action (see chapter 4), but also with the long-delayed involvement of local political elites. Local base opponents' consistent rejection of outside support drew them closer to local elites—who then attempted to co-opt these politically "innocent" locals.

The period of quiescence in Pocheon coincided with a period of silence not only on the part of local residents but also from local elites. For a long time, local elites distanced themselves from local grievances. The city maintained that it was "difficult to prove" that shooting exercises were a direct cause of noise, tremors, and water pollution (Yun, Choe, and Gwon 2015). A rare attempt by the city council in 2008 to create a special committee on Rodriguez-related grievances ended in failure, as council members of different political orientations—the conservative majority and the liberal minority—bickered over who should lead the team (Interview with Lee Gil-yeon, July 13, 2016). Except for occasional visits by leftist-nationalist groups that would come into town, stage protests, and then promptly leave, the firing range stood unchallenged.

When a spate of near-miss accidents beginning in late 2014 engendered a sudden outburst of anger, however, elderly residents finally found recourse in local political elites. This time around, city officials and city council members did manage to form a special committee, which pledged bipartisan cooperation. Mayor Kim Jong-chun, city council members, and a lawmaker representing Pocheon took turns staging a one-person protest at Seoul's presidential Blue House, with slogans reading "Shut down Rodriguez" and "Save Pocheon residents" (Yang 2016). The city government also established a task force to handle military-related complaints, the first of its kind created by any municipal government in Korea. Despite the fact that Pocheon also houses multiple domestic military units, officials overseeing the task force say that most of the complaints they receive are about the Rodriguez range (Interview, anonymous, August 2, 2016). In addition, the city council passed an ordinance that allocated a budget to assist anti-Rodriguez protests, bringing to the grassroots movement what it lacked the most: resources. "It was difficult to help out local protesters without the law backing them up, since helping them was technically like helping them go against the (central) government," says Yoon Chung-sik, a city councilman who leads the committee on Rodriguez issues (Interview, August 2, 2016). Gyeonggi Province, long oblivious to the local situation, began to pay more attention, with the governor visiting the affected towns for the first time in 2016.

Protesters say elite support, if long overdue, has paid off. Their complaints used to fall on deaf ears, but now they routinely hold meetings with high-ranking military officials, both American and Korean. Indeed, following a more recent accident involving a 105-mm stray shell that punctured the roof of a local man's house, a two-star general was dispatched within hours to talk to the locals and wrote them a check on the spot (Slavin 2015a)—a sea change, according to residents, from the days when a box of C-Rations substituted for apologies. *Stars and Stripes*, reporting on this particular accident, noted that the U.S. military was taking an " 'apologize first and determine the details later' approach" in Pocheon, lest the accident reignite the kind of nationwide anger seen after the Yangju Highway Incident (see chapter 3) (Slavin 2015a). The U.S. military also agreed to adjust firing positions and flight routes (Yoon and Ock 2015), and it now holds biannual consultations with the city (Slavin 2015b). All this represented progress for the unlikely protesters. "Those who refuse to join the movement say that what we're doing is like throwing eggs at a rock," Lee Gil-yeon, a protest organizer, says of a proverb describing an act of futile resistance. "But that's not true. Some parts of the rock will become dented, and some parts will get dirty" (Interview, July 13, 2016). As if to prove Lee correct, the U.S. military, much to its exasperation, has since been forced to look for alternative training options—some outside Pocheon and some even outside Korea (Sisk 2020; Gwi-geun Kim 2021).

Six decades of silence, then, was not about the local residents' inability to organize or their indifference to the din of war, but rather about their unwillingness to mobilize unless certain conditions were met: a combination of local elite involvement, which came belatedly, and a decisively pragmatist approach, which was built upon the previous failure of clunky nationalist rhetoric. This new activism, however, is still predicated on the presumed inevitability of Pocheon's fate as a base town. The reluctant protesters in Pocheon, who had long eschewed a broader alliance with professional activists for fear of adulterating their supposed innocence, became heavily dependent on elite support. With this greater dependence came greater vulnerability to elite influence. Like the elite-led mobilization in Dongducheon, calls for an economic quid pro quo, with the unspoken assumption that protests would cease in return, became a central feature of the movement. The Pocheon city council, for example, has called for state compensation of 11 trillion won ($10 billion), which they claim to be the estimated cost associated with sixty years of damage allegedly wrought by the U.S. military presence (C. Kim 2014). The city has created a seventeen-minute promotional video that features angry calls for redress. The video, complete with helicopter sound effects, presents three demands: safety measures that are "not just stop-gap measures," compensation for the damage already done, and legislation of a special law for Pocheon's economic development (Pocheon City Council 2017).

Local elite support, in this sense, seems to be a gift and a curse. By early 2019, the city government appeared to have fully co-opted the anti-Rodriguez movement. As the central government reviewed the feasibility of extending Seoul's subway line 7 to various parts of Gyeonggi Province, including Pocheon, the economic interests of the city government and the anti-base agenda of local base opponents converged. Mayor Park Yoon-guk, in demanding that the city be excluded from the feasibility study so that it could be automatically considered as a candidate site for the new subway station, pointed to the Rodriguez range as a justification for why the city deserved special treatment. At a 10,000-strong rally in Seoul in January 2019, protesters dispatched from Pocheon held up signs carrying two seemingly unrelated messages: "Move the Rodriguez Shooting Range" and "Exclude Pocheon from the Feasibility Study" (Hae-sun Lee 2019). Grassroots activists, in preemptively fending off accusations of political motives, have chosen a full merger with the local government instead. Even rare moments of city-wide mobilization, it looks like, serve as an indirect reaffirmation of the political status quo.

Conclusion

With the unwavering elite unity in interstate base politics, base opponents seek to leverage local elite support instead. While they almost universally court elite attention, activists' relationships with local elites range from mutual support to mutual disdain, with varying consequences for oppositional mobilization. In protest towns, the unusually high salience of base issues means that base opponents can occasionally forge at least brief alliances with local elites, sometimes elevating a local activist cause to a national—and potentially international—political dispute. In some quiet towns with little previous civic activism, elite involvement, and the legitimacy it confers to the anti-base movement, has proven to be crucial in turning bystanders and even some movement foes into unlikely protesters. In most places, though, local elite involvement remains at best fleeting and at worst opportunistic.

Tokyo and Seoul, meanwhile, have responded in distinct ways. Tokyo defeated the rebellious mayors with the threat of monetary punishment. State compensation served as a form of monetary coercion, as the government selectively withdrew monetary benefits that would otherwise have been automatically given out. Seoul, by contrast, rewarded the rogue mayors by conceding to their demands for economic assistance. Local government demands also varied in nature: fundamentalist or instrumental. The dissenting Japanese localities, when compared to their Korean counterparts, were more principled in their dissent. Elite enthusiasts in Nago and Iwakuni, for example, raised fundamental questions about the U.S. presence—why it must be fortified, why local input is nonexistent, and what it means for Japanese democracy—that were not conditional on instrumental, monetary interests. Central-local government conflicts in these cases expanded the scope of the local base conflict, raising broader questions about local autonomy and, by extension, the quality of democracy. By contrast, in Korea, local government demands remained more parochial, with monetary concessions as a persistent goal. Elite opportunists in Dongducheon and Pocheon, in this sense, shared common interests with the central government in limiting the scope of the central-local contest to an instrumental one about local economic grievances.

Even the most enthusiastic local elite support, as it turns out, do not always help the movement in the long run. The travails of Inamine and Ihara offer a cautionary tale: while strong local elite support galvanizes anti-base devotees and legitimates the movement agenda, such wholehearted support—and uncompromising policy stances—at the local level risks inviting retaliation from the central government. Tokyo has proven capable of "twist[ing] around" these dissenting localities with its "use of a carrot-and-stick approach" (*The Mainichi* 2017). Fearing further marginalization of their towns that are already heavily dependent on state subsidies, latent adherents are likely to withdraw their support for renegade mayors. According to Ihara, Iwakuni's collective acceptance of the enlarged American presence that came after his failed challenge is captured in a common Japanese phrase expressing a sense of resignation: *shikata ga nai* (it cannot be helped). If activists seek to win over latent adherents by courting local elites, state retaliation can render such activist efforts moot if it alienates latent adherents and makes them increasingly wary of central-local confrontation. Today, the mayors of Nago and Iwakuni remain pro-base.

Elite opportunists, meanwhile, may appear to disrupt but ultimately ensure the perpetuation of the political status quo. Emergent collective action against the Rodriguez range—led by those self-identifying as "pure" and "innocent" activists who, in a show of support for the U.S. military, voluntarily suspended protests after North Korea's saber-rattling—is proof that even the sleepiest towns may choose to break their long silence. The end of the quiescence here, however, will not necessarily mean an end to the Rodriguez Live Fire Complex. With most base opponents and their elite allies in Pocheon protesting negative externalities of the range, rather than the range itself, and with their demands largely limited to economic sweeteners rather than more fundamental changes, the 3,390-acre live-fire range is likely going nowhere. The largesse on the part of host state governments, whether used in browbeating dissenters or rewarding tantrums, is actually a "cheap cost to pay for keeping the bases and maintaining the alliance" (Interview with Tamura Jungen, September 28, 2016).

6

Conclusion

Local Voices in Contentious Base Politics

This book has sought to reconfigure the landscape of contentious base politics. The stories I tell of base towns negate both the elite disdain that trivializes local discontent and the tendency of social movement research to amplify rare cases of fervent, prolonged opposition. Instead, communities hosting twenty U.S. military bases scattered throughout Korea and Japan—both faithful, treaty-bound allies in a region of lasting strategic importance—exhibit varying degrees of discontent, resistance, and acquiescence that go unnoticed in much of the scholarly literature and policy debates. Base opponents, despite the stark power imbalance inherent in their quest, occasionally become influential enough to complicate and thwart the allies' military initiatives and operations. Wittingly and unwittingly, they also make choices that end up reinforcing the widely presumed inevitability of the American presence.

What emerges from the book is the human dilemma—too often made invisible by the master narrative of national security at the national level and alliance cohesion at the interstate level—of whether to confront or embrace life alongside machines and actions of war. Confronting the U.S. military is surprisingly difficult in these two otherwise robust democracies, especially as path dependency and inertia run deep in interstate base politics. With all the odds stacked against anti-base activists, they nonetheless seek out opportunities to build broad-based movements.

First, activists jump at the rare chance, which comes with major changes to the status quo established around long-standing bases, of shaping the future trajectories of base towns. As major status changes (e.g., base expansion) threaten to unravel the familiar normality in base towns, latent adherents, fearing the losses often associated with these disruptions, join hands with anti-base activists. Threats of land expropriation and eviction maximize these local fears. The striking similarity between the anti-base

Base Towns. Claudia Junghyun Kim, Oxford University Press. © Oxford University Press 2023.
DOI: 10.1093/oso/9780197665275.003.0006

slogan in Pyeongtaek in the mid-2000s—"Let's farm again this year"—
and the slogan heard in the 1950s in Uchinada, once a front-line protest
town in Japan—"Money lasts one year, land lasts forever" (Hasegawa 2019,
158)—is hardly a coincidence. One qualification, however, is that community responses depend on relative perceptions of the threat, rather than its
absolute magnitude. It is telling, for example, that the removal of a small,
seventeen-acre heliport site in Daegu appeased local residents more effec-
tively than the partial return—10,000 acres, the equivalent of two Kadena
Air Bases (*Stars and Stripes* 2017)—of the colossal Northern Training Area
in Okinawa. If anything, the partial retrieval of this jungle warfare training
field touched off new protests in Takae, a secluded ward in the northern
Okinawan forest, against the construction of multiple helipads as a trade-off
for the return (Kim 2021). The threat of quotidian disruption, meanwhile,
is always accompanied by a window of opportunity. As the threat begins to
materialize, the opponents' task becomes that of slowing down the eventual
status transition as long as possible. One popular delaying tactic is a practice
known in Japanese as "*gobō nuki*," literally pulling out burdock (a plant with
a long, deep taproot that is difficult to dig up), in which protesters staging
a sit-in are lifted up and removed from the protest scene by riot police, one
by one. Mobilization against status disruptions, as we saw repeatedly in
chapter 3, is a race against time.

Second, activists, even as they go after a distinctively international security target, tend to articulate their grievances in the mundane language of
the everyday. In other words, they consciously go for frames that highlight
practical, everyday grievances, as opposed to more abstract, distant frames
that align better with their nationalistic or pacifist motivations. Many
of these framing decisions have to do with the potential resonance of the
movement cause among latent adherents—the very people activists seek
to find common ground with. More often than not, latent adherents hold
grievances that are more practical and immediate (e.g., noise pollution)
than the maximalist goals that inspire many career activists (e.g., ending
militarism). A rhetorical emphasis on everyday grievances, therefore,
reflects activist efforts to subordinate their aspirations for radical changes
to the more humdrum, day-to-day issues that their fellow base town
residents want to see addressed. At the same time, rhetorical pragmatism
offers a rhetorical safe haven for activists, whose cause, supposedly radical
in their domestic contexts, routinely invites suspicions of ulterior political motives. In countries where the Old Left has lost much of its previous

appeal, anti-base activism requires conscious impression management. In Korea, student groups no longer throw Molotov cocktails on the self-proclaimed "Anti-American Day" (*banmiui nal*) of May 22—a reference to the alleged American tolerance of the 1980 Gwangju Massacre. A protest song released in 2000, titled "Song for the USFK Withdrawal" (*juhanmigun cheolgeoga*), would have found a more receptive audience in the 1980s: "The Japs were expelled, and the Yankees came . . . we'll wipe you out and march toward unification." In an ostensibly pacifist Japan, absolutist pacifism as a mobilizing force has lost much of the appeal it once had during the leftist heyday of the 1960s. Compare, for example, a 1,000-strong protest in Sasebo against a port visit by a nuclear-powered submarine in 1964 with a similarly themed protest, attended only by twenty labor unionists, four decades later (*Mainichi Shimbun* 2004). Also gone are the days of highly disruptive action reminiscent of the 1960s—firing projectiles into bases and burning tires at runways to ground fighter jets.

Third, activists court local political elites, who occasionally emerge as an unlikely veto player in domestic and international base politics. Despite some interesting contrasts between Korean and Japanese municipalities—the former wield their status as base towns to squeeze money out of the central government, whereas the latter are at the mercy of both the carrot of state subsidies and the stick of having such sweeteners withdrawn—elite involvement can meaningfully shape mobilization patterns across host communities. Especially for those wary of political participation, elite involvement has the effect of legitimating and deradicalizing the anti-base agenda. The sudden torrent of protests in Pocheon coincided with elite support that finally arrived after decades of neglect, and Dongducheon's elite-led mobilization drew the most fervent backers of the U.S. military to protest. When the central government asserts its dominance over its junior partners, as we saw in Nago, Iwakuni, Zama, and Sagamihara, local dissent takes on new significance as a test of local autonomy and, by extension, that of democracy. Local elites, however, are far from straightforward allies of the anti-base movement, even when they act as champions of the cause. Elite opportunists selectively ally with civic groups that are more moderate in their tactics and rhetoric, and they may even co-opt the movement agenda in order to use it as leverage in their demands for state compensation. On the other hand, elite enthusiasts, as loyal movement allies, invigorate the anti-base movement but risk alienating the rest of the community in the long run.

Activist Dilemmas

How activists exploit these contextual factors shapes the trajectories of the base communities. Activists in headline-making protest towns generally succeed in finding common ground with latent adherents and building relatively broad-based movements. In quiet towns, anti-base opposition tends to be either impotent (i.e., activists' mobilization attempts fail) or nonexistent (i.e., no mobilization is attempted). Local residents seem to embrace, or at least tolerate, their life alongside American military bases—even some of the most obtrusive ones. Protests, if any, are driven almost solely by professional activists, many of whom are either uninterested in building ties with latent adherents or unable to do so even if they were to try. The very quiescence in these towns, however, indirectly attests to the primacy of the local in anti-base activism. Contrary to the familiar accusations that cast anti-base activists as agitators manipulating innocent locals, it is actually those local residents who get to determine whether activists' mobilization attempts succeed or fail. Activists alone, after all, cannot build a broad-based movement. Nor can they alone win legitimacy in the eyes of bystanders, movement foes, and movement targets.

It is for this reason that most anti-base activists remain deliberately inward-looking, unlike other aggrieved local actors seeking to globalize their grievances. It is also for this reason that many anti-base campaigns are consciously localized in scope, unlike other campaigns that benefit from scaling up to national and even transnational movements. Finding common ground with latent adherents, however, often means that activists have to subordinate their maximalist aspirations to the more quotidian goals of non-activist populations. Doing so presents activists with a quandary: what helps boost latent adherents' participation can inadvertently undermine activists' goals in the long run.

First, so much of a status disruption is about delaying an eventual status transition, and as a result, activists employ various delaying tactics. In addition to physically blocking progress, as Okinawan activists have done by staging sit-ins at the gate of Camp Schwab since 2014, activists often contest procedural matters. While finding fault with procedural technicalities often buys activists time, it can also distract from what they are protesting and why they are protesting in the first place (Jasper 2006; Gordon and Jasper 1996). For example, activists have challenged the authorities to confirm whether they properly conducted an environmental assessment, a prerequisite for most base-related construction projects. They have also taken their case to court, claiming that the lack of proper procedures, for example in gaining public understanding of a U.S. base realignment project, violated local residents' constitutional rights. An overemphasis on procedural matters, however, risks misrepresenting the movement, creating the impression that activists should be happy when their procedural requirements are fully met. The authorities, for example, can easily claim that they have fully addressed base opponents' concerns as long as they do conduct standard environmental assessments.

Furthermore, delaying is not the same as stopping what is underway or undoing what has been done. While Okinawa's base opponents deserve special recognition as masters of delaying tactics, what they are ultimately doing is just that: delaying. To be sure, a series of recent attempts to further slow down the Henoko construction project do seem to have worked; in particular, the crucial revelation about the soft seabed presents yet another opportunity to extend the window of opportunity (see chapters 3 and 4). Landfill in areas that do not require additional ground improvement work has nonetheless continued, and by the end of April 2021, the government managed to reclaim 41 hectares—more than one fourth of the total area subjected to reclamation, which, according to the current plan, stands at 152 hectares. Although Henoko protesters as a whole are a remarkably optimistic bunch, others have begun to harbor doubts over what Japanese media call an "increasingly unwinnable fight" (*Asahi Shimbun* 2022). Gunsan activists, in another recent example, are pressuring the authorities to protect a 600-year-old hackberry tree in a village residents left behind to make room for new munitions storage facilities at the nearby air base. Their emphasis on the tree is an indirect attempt to obstruct, but not stop, an additional land grant to the U.S. military. Delaying tactics, in this sense, risk being seen as forlorn resistance to the inevitable outcome.

Second, rhetorical pragmatism, despite its greater mobilization potency at the subnational level, comes at a cost. Pragmatic framing, by limiting the discursive space of base contestation, keeps both activists and the authorities from asking more fundamental questions. When a stray shell lands on a local's home, for example, a pragmatic approach will ensure that she gets compensated. Similarly, in places where aircraft flying outside classroom windows is a daily occurrence, schoolchildren can get these windows soundproofed. A pragmatic diagnosis, in other words, leads to an equally pragmatic prognosis. Given the gaping power imbalance between the challengers and their target, any incremental change activists can induce is a major achievement—and pragmatic approaches best ensure this. Addressing everyday grievances will not, however, get to the issue of why American troops are there in the first place, what purposes they serve, and if current arrangements are desirable or sustainable. The dominant discursive practices in anti-base activism therefore limit what is imaginable and possible, prioritizing immediate grievances at the cost of losing sight of distant, ultimate goals—precisely those that inspire most anti-base devotees to get involved in the first place. The efficacy of rhetorical pragmatism, in this sense, is also its pitfall.

These inherent limitations notwithstanding, activists do not find it easy to simply switch to alternative framing strategies. Pacifist and nationalistic rhetoric, to be sure, does have advantages: it not only aligns better with many activists' true motivations, it also raises big picture questions about the way the United States projects its military power globally. Staying true to one's beliefs is precisely what keeps alive small groups like Sasebo Citizens' Association, which has staged street rallies every month since February 1968 despite its visibly dwindling membership over time. It is also what keeps a handful of anti-Zama protesters going, whose monthly events feature slogans like "we oppose the (U.S.-Japan) military alliance," and "weapons cannot bring peace." And yet, absolutist pacifism and its philosophical critique of the U.S. military seem to fall flat in many base towns. "If you call for the base's removal, the movement as a whole will end up getting smaller and smaller," says Tamura Jungen, a city councilman and a longtime opponent of MCAS Iwakuni (Interview, September 28, 2016). Without a modicum of pragmatism tailored to specific local grievances, one cannot even begin to build a locally grounded movement in the first place. As activists wrestle with the question of how to achieve a balance between the pursuit of resonance and their supposedly radical movement identity, their framing conundrums find no clear solution.

Third, activists courting local elites face a familiar trade-off. Elite involvement broadens the appeal of the anti-base agenda among latent adherents, which further solidifies the primacy of the local. At the same time, it also risks diluting and moderating the movement. In places with little previous activism (e.g., Pocheon) or with a dormant civil society (e.g., Dongducheon), local elites find it particularly easy to co-opt anti-base grievances and use them as leverage in negotiations with the central government. It is tempting for Pocheon elites, for example, to spin the irony of having U.S forces help

Do activists truely want the complete withdrawal of U.S. military?

fight a war, only to have them recreate the din of war in their backyard after the rest of the country has moved on, as a story of local sacrifice for national defense—a sacrifice that does not necessarily have to end, but does have to be handsomely rewarded. This opportunistic appropriation of the anti-base cause, which reduces local grievances to a simple question of economic development, often clashes with activists' maximalist stances. Notably, though, activists sometimes try to resolve the dilemma by themselves attempting to run for mayor and governor—attempting to enter, rather than reject, institutional politics as a means to shape the trajectories of base towns.

Even when local elites become steadfast movement allies, as we saw in Nago and Iwakuni, this can pose unforeseen hurdles to the movement. If local elite opportunism reduces local grievances to pleas for government compensation, local elites loyal to the anti-base cause do the opposite by elevating local grievances to a challenge to the business-as-usual politics of U.S. military bases. If the former approach indirectly helps perpetuate the status quo, as the central government can simply continue to throw money at disgruntled localities, the latter approach, seemingly an immediate boon for the movement, also comes with unexpected consequences in the long run. Activists are more likely to rally behind local leaders who seek more absolutist policy goals, as in the case of Nago's Inamine Susumu. At the same time, local elites' staunch opposition to what the authorities see as national security interests can escalate local-central conflicts in a way that makes concessions even less likely. As the central government retaliates against dissenting localities, it does its best to signal to base town residents that opposition is costly and ultimately futile. The legitimacy that local elite support initially gives to the anti-base cause wears off over time, and many latent adherents, fearing the consequences of a prolonged conflict with the government, increasingly prefer the status quo. In other words, strong elite support may galvanize anti-base devotees but alienate latent adherents over time. These inadvertent consequences defeat the very purpose of courting elite allies in the first place: attaining broad-based local support. In multiple base towns we have looked at, a transition from an anti-base mayor to a pro-base mayor followed an episode of local-central conflict over local elite dissent. Most recently, in 2022, Nago's pro-base mayor Toguchi Taketoyo, who replaced Inamine Susumu in 2018, won re-election as economic anxieties continued to prevail over base grievances even in this iconic protest town.

Thus, the very contexts in which activists and latent adherents come together may inadvertently reinforce, rather than destabilize, the political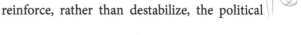

coordinations among base towns?
— new topic

status quo surrounding the American military presence. These dilemmas show that what activists typically do in order to intensify contestation and boost participation can come back to bite them, at least in the long run. At the same time, if activists did not exploit the opportunities or adopt the strategies the way they did, they would not be able to draw attention to their cause and build a movement in the first place. Activists, it seems, have to constantly juggle the tasks of initial mobilization, sustained mobilization, and attaining desired movement outcomes—even when the primacy of the local as a cardinal tenet ultimately undermines some of these essential tasks.

The Future of Contentious Base Politics

Given the vicissitudes of fortune in base towns and continuing activists' efforts to shape their future trajectories, what, then, is on the horizon for contentious base politics? As a series of U.S. initiatives dating back to the early to mid-2000s to realign bases and reshuffle grievances have largely come to fruition in many parts of Korea and Japan, protests against status disruptions have lost their initial explosiveness. As we have seen in the cases of Camp Humphreys, Camp Zama, and MCAS Iwakuni, protests either have come to an end or persist with little visibility. Even in Pyeongtaek, where militant activists organized the biggest anti-base campaign in Korea's history, the same activists are now "thinking about ways to coexist with" what has transformed into the largest U.S. military base overseas (Interview with Kang Mi, June 11, 2016). Apart from Camp Schwab in Nago, where the newly extended timeline for the FRF construction heralds an even more protracted struggle, many base towns once shaken by the latest wave of status quo disruptions will remain relatively quiet for the foreseeable future.

Another possible round of status quo changes may be in the offing, however, with the Biden administration ordering a new global force posture review in 2021. Defense analysts have singled out Japan as a potential candidate for an enhanced U.S. presence—including "more ships, more troops, even long-range strike missiles" (Gregson and Hornung 2021). If these predictions materialize in ways that makes the 56,000-strong U.S. presence even more intrusive for local populations, they are going to give Japanese anti-base activists a perfectly legitimate reason to mobilize.

In addition to the worldwide posture review that may have ripple effects in Japan, one new trend in American basing policy seems fraught with potential conflicts. While the recent U.S. force realignment focused on conventional military bases, a relatively new type of U.S. military installation has been introduced to Korea and Japan in the meantime: the missile defense system. The trend began with the deployment in 2006 of a U.S. AN/TPY-2 radar system to the northern Japanese city of Tsugaru, Aomori Prefecture. The Shariki Communications Site, where the surveillance radar is housed, has political implications that would antagonize any anti-base activist: it is the first U.S. military installation to open in Japan since the end of World War II (Cutshaw 2016), staffed not just by U.S. troops but also by private contractors working for Raytheon and Chenega Blackwater Solutions (Weaver 2007). By 2014, a similar radar facility began operating in Kyōtango, Kyoto Prefecture. Then, the U.S. military introduced the THAAD anti-ballistic missile defense system to Korea, with Seongju County, North Gyeongsang Province, as its host. All three hitherto sleepy towns mobilized in opposition to these relatively small but controversial facilities, with Seongju as an extreme outlier in terms of both its surprising mobilization capacity and the subsequent political fallout (Kim 2021). Local opponents, aside from their pragmatic, health-related concerns about radar emissions, were unsure about the purpose of the deployment: are these unfamiliar facilities meant to protect us, or are they mostly in the newfound interest of Washington? Beijing, which views U.S. bases in Asia—or "the powerful enemy's allied military bases"— as an island chain encircling mainland China (Yoshihara 2010), lashed out against what it characterizes as a new surveillance system that can peer at its own missiles. As Beijing unleashed unprecedented retaliation on Korea for the THAAD deployment, many opponents in Seongju and elsewhere could not help seeing their situation as a classic case of entrapment—or as a Korean proverb goes, a shrimp whose back is broken in a fight between whales.

As American interests as a Pacific power evolve from the defense of its allies to the management of China's rise, local skepticisms about the purpose of U.S. bases in their backyards are bound to grow. U.S. missile defense systems—a less familiar variant of the traditional U.S. military presence for most Koreans and Japanese, yet of growing importance as conventional, large bases are increasingly deemed vulnerable to attacks—risk local, and possibly national, resistance within host states, let alone costly disputes between U.S. allies and China. More broadly, these developments mirror a global trend in which it is becoming "more difficult to create a direct and enduring tie between U.S. bases and the security of a host nation" (Lostumbo et al. 2013, 103). As defense analysts bluntly put it: "[W]e have forces present in Asia, not to protect the Asians themselves, but mostly for our own American interest" (Center for Strategic and International Studies 2020). The latest case of anti-base opposition in Japan adds another data point to the trend: residents of Yamaguchi and Akita Prefectures opposed the deployment of the U.S.-developed Aegis Ashore missile defense system partially because they suspected that it was designed to protect American troops in Guam and Hawaii, as opposed to Japanese citizens (Johnston 2020). As its new, unfamiliar installations spark local doubts about the familiar rhetoric of defending the allies, the U.S. military has much explaining to do.

Rhetorical pragmatism and deliberate parochialism, meanwhile, will continue to dominate protest rhetoric, despite the more absolutist beliefs that underlie much of the anti-base activism in Korea and Japan. Opponents have repeatedly seen that pragmatic framing makes the anti-base cause more palatable to potential movement constituents, bystanders, and government authorities alike. As such, many will continue to search for pragmatically minded causes—be they coral reefs or land expropriation—that can become a unifying face of otherwise politically delicate, divisive anti-base agendas. These pragmatically presented challenges will occasionally deter policy implementations and induce policy concessions. They will not, however, unravel the business-as-usual alliance politics undergirding U.S. military bases abroad. The very palatability of rhetorical pragmatism, after all, has to do with its relatively non-threatening nature.

Of the two remaining rhetorical choices, I predict that the anti-militarist framing will be more prevalent than its nationalistic counterpart. The pacifist underpinnings of Japanese peace activism, with their corresponding pacifist frames as part of the repertoire of discursive contention, will not easily die away. Many younger activists in Korea, freer from the nationalistic baggage that defined their predecessors, have also come to see anti-base movements as part of the broader peace movement. Indeed, many career activists who joined the latest anti-base movements—the anti-THAAD movement, as well as a separate campaign against the construction of a Korean naval base in Jeju Island—self-identify as peace activists.

Still, we are unlikely to see pacifist frames gain much resonance beyond the narrow activist circles. At the national level, absolutist pacifism finds no place in the foreign and defense policies of the two host states. If anything, Japan, a country equated with an institutionalized culture of anti-militarism (Berger 1998), is increasingly aggressive in its promotion of the U.S.-led order in the Indo-Pacific region. The institutional constraints that anti-base activists assiduously defend, such as the pacifist Constitution and the three non-nuclear principles, are either constantly challenged or openly ignored. At the international level, pacifist principles do not have the same normative status and far-reaching resonance as, say, global human rights norms. The lack of a global advocacy community for anti-base causes—for example, there is no anti-base group that has the kind of international stature that some human rights NGOs have—means that subnational anti-base actors cannot easily turn to international audiences. While scholars predicted the emergence of a new transnational anti-base movement when activists launched the International Conference for the Abolition of Foreign Bases in 2007 (Yeo 2009), they lacked the resources to maintain a formal network (Vine 2019). It took a decade before activists managed to hold another international conference—the International Conference Against US/NATO Military Bases—in 2018.

On the other hand, overtly nationalistic rhetoric will persist in Korea, but on the margins of the activist scene. There will always be some indignant nationalists who define the U.S. presence as a symbol of American imperialism standing in the way of inter-Korean reconciliation. Some fringe political parties with leftist-nationalist orientations, such as the Progressive Party and the People's Democracy Party, continue to call for a complete withdrawal of "American occupational forces" (People's Democracy Party 2021). Like-minded groups, such as the Korea University Advancement Association (Hanguk daehaksaeng jinboyeonhap), occasionally remind the public of their existence with sporadic antics—like when they jumped the walls of the U.S. embassy in Seoul, demanding that Ambassador Harry Harris "leave this land" (Bellware 2019). The statue of Douglas MacArthur continues to see a smattering of protesters, including those irate enough to set it alight (and get jailed as a result). These antics, however, invite public scorn, rather than inspire opposition. These leftist-nationalists may continue to be part of larger anti-base coalitions when explosive new issues command national attention, as we saw with the nationwide coalition against the expansion of Camp Humphreys. Their pan-Korean anti-Americanism, however, will never be the public face of any future anti-base movement seeking broad-based support. Leftist-nationalists can still wish for their glorious comeback, which might, just might, come true if there is dramatic improvement in North Korean behavior and inter-Korean relations. For now, though, even they seem aware that unification is an increasingly unpopular goal, especially among younger generations; they have gone from calling for the ever-elusive unification to demanding a peace treaty (to replace an armistice that suspended, but did not formally end, the Korean War), a goal that a majority of Koreans share.

When chances arise, Korea's local political elites will opt for their rhetorically striking but watered-down opposition aimed at extracting economic concessions from the government in return for perpetuating the status quo. Most recently, Pocheon's strategy of linking the long-standing base-related grievances to the issue of winning a subway line, as well as Uijeongbu's failure to do the same, offers a telling lesson to other base town elites looking for ways to stimulate their sluggish local economies at the central government's expense. They can easily cry regional discrimination by pointing to the examples of Pyeongtaek and Seoul, the two cities for which the central government readily created special laws in order to funnel money into them, for entirely different reasons: the former for accepting its fate as a mega base town hosting the newly expanded Camp Humphreys and Osan Air Base, and the latter for converting the Yongsan Garrison site into a national park. Most Korean mayors, who are not interested in earning a reputation for chumming around with leftist-nationalists, will rely on conservative civic groups and shopkeepers for top-down mobilization. Most traditional anti-base groups, wary of co-optation, will stand by. Meanwhile, local elites who have staked their political fortune on the anti-base platform, such as Okinawa's incumbent governor Denny Tamaki, will continue to do their best to create local administrative hurdles to thwart basing policy. Indeed, Tamaki filed a lawsuit against the land ministry in 2019, accusing it of violating the Local Autonomy Act—the seventh lawsuit between Okinawa and Tokyo over the FRF construction (Ichihashi 2019). For most local political leaders, however, Tokyo's coercive compensation politics will serve as a reminder that dissent comes with a hefty price tag. Most local political elites, as a result, will only pay lip service to the ultimate ideal of the "reorganization (*seiri*), reduction (*shukushō*), and return (*henkan*)" of the American bases in their towns.

Ultimately, many in base towns will go on to demand that America's future defense policy be mindful of its local consequences. Base town residents, after all, never gave their consent to—or rather, were never given a chance to consent to—basing policies imposed from above. Those who repeat weekly gatherings and monthly marches in what some would view as a futile quest are consciously engaged in small acts of resistance, telling the world that not all is fine, after all, in their backyards. The most successful and assertive communities, where activists and latent adherents build a broad-based movement together, will force the allies to pay attention. And once they do, they should see that U.S. military bases overseas, often discussed in the rather abstract terms of American power projection, do not exist in a vacuum—and that behind every decision to move around troops and deploy another missile battery are communities and lives changed as a result. The Futenma relocation project forced a Nago man to learn how to canoe. The helipad at Camp Walker turned a Daegu grocer into an obsessive letter writer. The Rodriguez range compels Pocheon farmers to climb a nearby mountain in desperation. Most recently, even in the era of the pandemic, the absence of border restrictions for U.S. servicemen newly reminded Okinawan and Pyeongtaek residents of the invisible, and yet inseparable, link between their lives and those of the Americans in uniform. As America's far-flung military bases continue to shape the trajectories of host communities and the lives of the people in them, it is time that these varied experiences began to matter. The "interminable dialogue over parochial issues," as the American gripe goes (Dickie 2009), must continue.

Protest Events

This appendix introduces a dataset on anti-base protest events targeting twenty U.S. military bases across Korea and Japan for the period 2000–2015. It includes a protest analysis based on a zero-inflated negative binomial (ZINB) model, which shows how contentious base politics in Korean and Japanese host communities is shaped by the three contextual factors introduced in the preceding chapters.

Protest Event Data

Data Sources

The scholarly consensus on protest event data, despite some misgivings about potential reporting biases (Oliver and Meyer 1999), remains that news media offer "the best available" data that do not compromise standards of research quality (Earl et al. 2004, 76–77). I compiled a protest event dataset (N = 320, with observations for twenty military bases for the period 2000–2015) based on national and local media reports, activist-run blogs and websites, handwritten memos kept by activists, and various activist publications. For media sources, databases were used whenever available: Factiva; the Korea Integrated News Database System; and various newspaper databases, including those from the *Ryukyu Shimpo* and the *Asahi Shimbun*. Leftist-nationalist outlets, such as *OhmyNews* and *Tongil News* in Korea, and party-affiliated newspapers, such as *Akahata* of the Japan Communist Party, also contained a lot of information on protest events. Websites and blogs run by movement organizations and individual activists contained valuable information on a countless number of events that media did not cover. Keyword searches were done in Korean, Japanese, and English.

Outcome of Interest: Contestation Levels

Protest event analyses conventionally use the number of protests as a primary variable of interest indicating contestation levels. In this book, I use the number of protest participants as an alternative measure. Paying attention to large variations in protest turnout aligns with my attempt to elucidate the relationship between activists (i.e., those who organize protest events) and latent adherents (i.e., those who may or may not attend the events). There is a meaningful difference between daily protests involving three highly dedicated activists, and occasional protests attracting a crowd of 3,000, with latent adherents in the mix. If we were to focus on the number of protests, recurring events driven entirely by activists would constitute an absolute majority of events—in which case Gunsan, a quiet town that is nonetheless home to the longest-running anti-base rallies in Korea, may appear to be a protest town. A theoretical focus on the varying efficacy of anti-base frames also requires that I look at the number of participants, rather than the number of events. Linking different rhetorical strategies to varying participation levels allows us to examine the efficacy of the frames employed. By contrast, it makes little sense to link framing strategies to event counts, given that protest organizers are the ones who adopt protest frames to begin with.

The conventional focus on event counts as an outcome of interest has to do with data availability: news reports sometimes leave out information on participation numbers. Usually, the larger the event, the more likely it is for media to report on the event itself, as well as its size. The potential concern associated with missing participant numbers, however, is addressed by the fact that a relatively small number of the largest protest events make up the majority of total participants; coding large protest events accurately is therefore much more important than "worrying about the underreporting of small events" (Biggs 2018). Large protest events usually involve media, activist, and police estimates of participant counts. When multiple sources reported different participant numbers for the same event, I calculated an average. In some cases, media reports and activist-kept data provided an average number of participants for each event or the total number of participants over a particular period of time. When information on the number of participants was missing, I used the median number of participants for the events of the same types at the same base (Hutter 2014). For example, when participant information was missing for some of the recurring monthly protest marches against NAF Atsugi, I used the median from the marches where such information was available.

Counting participant numbers, of course, requires identifying protest events in the first place. By protest events, I mean public protest rallies, sit-ins, candlelight vigils, protest marches, and street campaigns. Following the disciplinary convention to account for the social, collective nature of protest gatherings, the dataset excludes events attended by fewer than three people. This decision influences event counts for Korea, where one-person protests are not uncommon; however, it hardly influences total protest turnout at a given base, and it also does not undermine the theoretical motivation to differentiate small events from larger ones. Press conferences, monitoring activities (e.g., tracking aircraft routes), and educational field trips are excluded, unless organizers combined them with overt protest action.

I collected data on anti-base protest events that took place in front of or in the vicinity of each military base, as well as in the administrative unit where each base is located. Activists sometimes choose to protest at locations in the same city with higher visibility and accessibility. For example, the Sasebo Citizens' Association (Jūkyū-nichi Sasebo shimin no kai) holds monthly marches against CFA Sasebo at a popular shopping mall, and not at the gate of the naval base. Similarly, some of the protests against Camp Humphreys took place at the busy Pyeongtaek train station, rather than in Anjeong-ri, a village across from the main gate of the base. When multiple municipalities jointly host one base, as in the cases of Yokota Air Base, Kadena Air Base, and NAF Atsugi, I counted protest events in all municipalities concerned. One important exception is Seoul, home to Yongsan Garrison; as discussed in chapter 2, I geographically restricted protest events to those taking place in the district of Yongsan. Additionally, in compiling protest events taking place in a given locality, I excluded occasional events that were exclusively about anti-base issues associated with other localities (e.g., protests in Tokyo against the FRF construction in Henoko), unless the event was organized or attended by residents from the actual community that was the focus of the protest (e.g., a protest in Tokyo about the FRF construction in Henoko that was attended by people from Henoko). Doing so helps ensure that what happens in one locality does not influence what happens in another.

Some cities host more than one major U.S. base, but only events that are related to the twenty bases under investigation were counted. In Dongducheon, for example, I focus on Camp Casey and exclude protests at Camp Hovey. In Sagamihara, only Camp Zama-related events are counted, and events related to Sagami General Depot are not. In Pyeongtaek, I distinguished protests events against Camp Humphreys from those against Osan Air Base, unless activists exclusively targeted both.

Contextual Factors

Status Quo Disruption

Status quo changes are operationalized as two dummy variables indicating expansion (as a result of new construction or expansion of existing installations) and reduction (as a result of relocation, partial return, and closure), respectively. Because these changes usually require at least several years to implement, the entire life cycle of a status transition—from announcement to completion—is coded as a status disruption.

Framing

Three separate variables reflect the three framing strategies at work: nationalistic, ideological (i.e., pacifist), and pragmatic (Calder 2007, 84). Individual protest events—each of them corresponding to one of the three frames—are annually aggregated, constituting three count variables. (For example, Base X in Year Y may have thirty recorded protest events: ten ideological, zero nationalistic, and twenty pragmatic.) Linking the varying frequency of framing strategies to the outcome variable—protest turnout—tests the resonance of the chosen strategy. Even if we were to assume that protest events are attended mostly by career activists, resonance still matters. Not many activists are willing to associate themselves with, for example, a fringe group on a crusade to physically attack military bases, like the one that fired projectiles into Camp Zama in 2002 and 2007 (Kusumoto and Little 2007).

Table 7.1 summarizes operationalization. Coding was based on activist slogans, speeches, and statements, as reported by media and activists themselves. Nationalistic frames include appeals to national pride and, in the case of Korea, portrayals of the U.S. military presence as an obstacle to reconciliation with its estranged northern brother. Ideological frames show a commitment to absolutist anti-militarist and pacifist ideals. Pragmatic frames focus on practical implications—or negative externalities—of the

Table 7.1 Operationalization of framing strategies

	Protest framing
Nationalistic	Rhetoric that emphasizes national or ethnic pride and unity against foreign (American) influence
Ideological (Pacifist)	Rhetoric that emphasizes antiwar, anti-nuclear, anti-militarist, and pacifist ideals; condemnation of U.S. global military strategy; absolutist rejection of militarism
Pragmatic	Rhetoric that emphasizes pragmatic grievances, such as environmental contamination, noise, aircraft accidents, land expropriation, and crimes

U.S. presence, such as noise, accidents, and pollution. Admittedly, it might be unrealistic to expect protest participants to say things that can be neatly pigeonholed into only one of the three categories, even at a single rally. Noting that activist discourses contain elements of all three frames, however, amounts to little more than a truism; with a focus on the frequency and efficacy of each frame, coding is based on the dominant rhetorical strategy adopted at any given event. To ensure intercoder reliability, two research assistants independently coded 100 events reported in Korea and Japan, respectively. Cohen's kappa was 0.77 for protest events in Korea (95% CI 0.656–0.880, p<0.001) and 0.85 for protest events in Japan (95% CI 0.749–0.957, p<0.001).

Local Elite Allies

The presence and absence of local political elites (i.e., mayors) in a given year at a given locality is coded as a dummy variable (0 = absence; 1 = presence). Coding is restricted to elite stances on bases located in the municipalities they govern. For example, the mayors of Yamato and Ayase, home to NAF Atsugi, did not oppose the relocation of aircraft and troops from Atsugi to MCAS Iwakuni. They, however, opposed the move to replace a conventionally powered aircraft carrier at CFA Yokosuka with a nuclear-powered one; because the functions of NAF Atsugi and CFA Yokosuka are closely linked, they feared that the deployment of a nuclear-powered aircraft carrier at the latter would increase noise levels at the former. Here, the two cities' elite stance was based on their agreement with the realignment that directly concerns NAF Atsugi, not their opposition to CFA Yokosuka. Occasional complaints filed by local elites on such issues as noise pollution and G.I. crimes, meanwhile, do not constitute sustained dissent. For multiple municipalities jointly hosting the same base, I coded the variable as 1 if at least one of them explicitly advocated for anti-base causes. When local political elites keep mum on base issues, I coded it as 0.

Controls

Trigger Events

Crimes and accidents involving U.S. military personnel have a potential to trigger protests (Marten 2005). This variable is based on crimes, car accidents, aircraft accidents, and environmental accidents as reported by *Hankyoreh* in Korea and the *Asahi Shimbun* in Japan, two national dailies commonly associated with liberal views. The number of trigger events that go unreported by media massively outweighs the number of events that manage to make headlines; national media exposure is especially a rarity and therefore is an appropriate proxy for "newsworthy" trigger events (Citizens' Coalition for Democratic Media 2007).

Crimes typically take place either near bases or in other neighborhoods offering more options for entertainment and nightlife. For example, soldiers based in Gyeonggi Province would travel to Hongdae or Itaewon in Seoul, and those stationed in Okinawa would have a night out in Naha or Chatan. Coding was based on the home base of the service members implicated in the crimes, as the backlash against crimes often comes from communities where these individuals are based. Similarly, whenever aircraft accidents cause an uproar, responses come from the communities housing the aircraft in question. The dataset excludes events reported without specifying the bases concerned, as readers will be unable to identify the exact location.

Highly publicized trigger events, a rare occurrence, may provoke protests in many different base towns. The prime example is the 2002 Yangju Highway Incident (see chapter 3), which touched off waves of protests throughout the country, including in Seoul, Daegu, and Jiinhae. I left out protest events held in one locality in response to trigger events that occurred in another, however, to clarify the relationship between the originating location of trigger events and subsequent protest levels in that very community. The only exception is when regular protest events, such as the daily protests at MCAS Futenma and the monthly rallies at Kunsan Air Base, make references to trigger events elsewhere as part of their routinized activity.

Joint Operation

Joint operation is operationalized as a dummy variable indicating whether bases jointly host the U.S. military and the host state military (0 = U.S. only, 1 = joint). The variable considers the possibility that locals might be more favorable toward U.S. bases that feature at least some domestic military presence.

Security Threats

External security threats may lead to greater support for the U.S. presence in host communities (Kagotani and Yanai 2014). To identify security threats for Korea and Japan, I collected data from the Militarized Interstate Disputes (MIDs) dataset, non-MID cases of North Korea's missile and nuclear tests, and territorial disputes concerning Korea and Japan (e.g., Dokdo/Takeshima and Senkaku/Diaoyu Islands). I calculated the distance (in meters) between each base community and the sources of security threat, based on longitude and latitude. In the case of multiple threats recorded in a given year, the distance measure was averaged. City offices and their equivalents in smaller administrative units were used as a proxy for the location of the base communities (e.g., Dongducheon City Hall for the city of Dongducheon). For bases in Japan hosted jointly by multiple municipalities, I picked the following: Kadena Town for Kadena Air Base, Yamato City for NAF Atsugi, Zama City for Camp Zama, and Fussa City for Yokota Air Base. The variable was log-transformed for skewness.

Population Size

I included the total population of each locality based on national and local government data, accounting for higher latent mobilization capacity associated with larger, more densely populated localities. When multiple municipalities jointly hosted a base, a mean value was used to avoid misrepresenting the ratio of the number of troops versus the number of local residents, a potential source of civil-military friction (Calder 2007). The variable was log-transformed due to skewness.

Local Financial Autonomy

Base towns typically receive central government subsidies, which help mitigate potential anti-base sentiments and stabilize base politics (Calder 2007, 130). At the same time, financial compensation may incentivize host communities to "highlight and exaggerate" negative externalities of the U.S. presence (Cooley and Marten 2006). Localities with low financial autonomy may be particularly motivated to press for their anti-base agenda to extract financial benefits from the central government. Korea and Japan use the same fiscal capacity index, known as *jaejeongnyeok jisu* in the former and *zaiseiryoku shisū* in the latter, which indicates the degree to which local governments can meet fiscal needs with their own revenue. This index, published by the Korean Statistical Information Service and the Japanese Ministry of Internal Affairs and Communications, respectively, is used as a proxy for local financial autonomy.

Table 7.2 offers a descriptive summary of the data:

Table 7.2 Summary statistics

Variables	N	Mean	Std. dev.	Minimum	Maximum
Participants	320	4,402.33	9,945.56	0	77,522
Status (baseline = no change)					
Expansion	320	0.25	0.43	0	1
Reduction	320	0.24	0.43	0	1
Framing (ideological)	320	8.64	19.04	0	82
Framing (nationalistic)	320	0.82	3.58	0	46
Framing (pragmatic)	320	31.28	100.79	0	728
Local allies (0 = absence; 1 = presence)	320	0.15	0.36	0	1
Trigger events	320	0.83	1.41	0	9
Joint operation (0 = U.S. only, 1 = joint)	320	0.47	0.5	0	1
ln(Distance from threat)	320	13.33	0.85	10.72	14.88
ln(Population)	320	12.68	1.19	10.94	16.17
Local financial autonomy	320	0.68	0.23	0.24	1.32

Estimation

The ZINB Model

The literature conventionally employs negative binomial or Poisson models for protest event analyses based on count data. The vast majority of the work in this tradition focuses on the number of protests as a dependent variable, which, while important and useful, comes at the cost of ignoring huge variations in protest turnout (Biggs 2018).

With the participant count as an outcome of interest, I look at two separate processes of protest participation: (1) whether protest events take place in the first place; and (2) how many people show up, once there is an event. Factors that contribute to the presence of protest events in the first place (i.e., a binary outcome) may be different from factors that influence the number of participants once such events are held (i.e., a count outcome). Zero-inflated negative binomial (ZINB) models allow us to combine these two processes (Hilbe 2011, 370–71).

It is plausible to assume that protests can be organized in response to status quo changes or trigger events. The presence and absence of local elite allies may also contribute to the initial emergence of protests, given that elites sometimes initiate top-down mobilization, rather than follow the lead of civil society. Framing strategies, on the other hand, come only after the decision to organize protests, as activists will decide on and employ protest frames only when there is an event to hold to begin with. Therefore, status changes, trigger events, and local elite allies are the variables that should belong to the logit part of the model (i.e., whether there is a protest event to begin with), and all variables—including the three in the logit part—are included in the count part of the model (i.e., how many turn out). Status quo changes, trigger events, and local elite variables are included in both parts; after initially giving rise to protests, they may also influence the level of protest turnout depending on their severity and intensity.

A Vuong test comparing a ZINB model to a standard negative binomial model shows that the former, which accounts for excess zeroes (i.e., observations with no protest event), is superior in fitting the data. A ZINB model is also preferred over a zero-inflated Poisson model when there is overdispersion (i.e., when the variance exceeds the mean), which is the case with the data in this study. The variance inflation factor (VIF) scores, meanwhile, show that the model does not suffer from multicollinearity. A separate test of autocorrelation found no evidence of serial correlation. Therefore, a ZINB model was estimated with year and base fixed effects and base-year as the unit of analysis. Considering the directional nature of the hypotheses, statistical significance reported (***$p<0.001$, **$p<0.01$, *$p<0.05$) is based on one-sided hypothesis tests.

Results

Table 7.3 summarizes ZINB estimation results. The results are divided into the inflated logit part (i.e., the presence and absence of protest events) and the count part (i.e., the number of protesters once an event is held). It is common to see different signs (negative [−] and positive [+]) associated with the variables used in the two parts of the model (Long and Freese 2006), which is the case here. Looking at the inflated logit part for factors contributing to the presence of protests, we see that status changes, trigger events, and local elite allies are positively correlated with the initial mobilization. The negative signs make substantive sense, because they indicate the lower likelihood of membership in the "protest not held" group.

The count part of the model tells us what factors contribute to the number of protesters once protests do take place. Unlike in the logit part, types of status quo changes now have opposite effects on mobilization levels: expansion increases, and reduction decreases, participant counts. Of the three frames, only the use of pragmatic frames (i.e., holding one more pragmatically framed protest) is significantly and positively associated with participant numbers. Local elite allies are also positively associated with higher protest turnout.

Among the control variables, it is notable that trigger events, while they initially give rise to protest events, do not meaningfully shape the participant count. This finding resonates with separate survey experiments showing the limited effects of trigger events in shaping public attitudes toward the U.S. military presence (Kim and Boas 2020). Distance from the sources of security threats, as well as local financial autonomy, are significantly associated with protester numbers; namely, more protesters show up in communities farther away from sources of external security threats, and protest levels are higher in less financially autonomous localities. Lastly, the joint operation variable is significant, but in the opposite direction than anticipated.

Table 7.3 ZINB estimates of anti-base protest participation (2000–2015)

Variables	Estimates
Inflated Logit (Protest not held)	
Status (expansion)	−0.992*(0.505)
Status (reduction)	−0.687(0.433)
Trigger events	−1.078***(0.29)
Local elite allies	−1.258*(0.761)
Constant	−0.836***(0.218)
Count (Number of protesters, conditional on a protest)	
Status (expansion)	0.484*(0.248)
Status (reduction)	−1.129**(0.375)
Framing (nationalistic)	0.014(0.02)
Framing (ideological)	−0.003(0.007)
Framing (pragmatic)	0.007***(0.002)
Local elite allies	0.806***(0.218)
Trigger events	0.075(0.066)
Joint operation	1.029*(0.523)
ln(Population)	0.187(0.314)
ln(Distance from threat)	0.575***(0.15)
Local financial autonomy	−2.321*(1.22)
Constant	−0.065(4.652)
Observations	320
Zero observations	48
Wald χ^2	703.25
Log pseudolikelihood	−2458.966
Vuong (z)	2.63

Robust standard errors in parentheses

***p<0.001, **p<0.01, *p<0.05

Notes

Chapter 1

1. The description in the two opening paragraphs is based on interviews with Lee Gil-yeon (July 13, 2016), Yoon Chung-sik (August 2, 2016), and two anonymous sources familiar with base-community relations (June 23, 2016).
2. There were some efforts to build a global anti-U.S. military base campaign following the U.S. invasion of Iraq in 2003, but such transnational efforts were still rooted in local experiences (Yeo 2009; Davis 2015). The global campaign has since petered out, although activists do maintain regional ties (Vine 2019; Davis 2017).

Chapter 2

1. It should be noted, however, that the Battle of Okinawa did not always serve as a source of antiwar ideology or defiance against Tokyo. In fact, the battle was once touted by Okinawans themselves as a sacrifice for "ancestral land defense" (Oguma 2014, 205–6).
2. For more on the alleged surveillance of anti-base protesters in Okinawa, see Mitchell (2016).
3. Contrary to the popular perception that the governor's action was a response to the infamous 1995 rape case, his dissent was a rejection of what is known as the "Nye Initiative"—the idea that the U.S. should retain some 100,000 troops in East Asia to maintain the stability of the region (Interview with Ōta Masahide, September 6, 2016).
4. Camp Mujuk (88 acres) and Commander Fleet Activities Chinhae (92 acres) are smaller than the other bases examined in this book. They are included for the following reasons: (1) they are identified as two of the most strategically important bases (Lostumbo et al. 2013); (2) they display low levels of contestation; and (3) these two bases—one Marine and one Navy—offer further diversity in terms of what branches of the military are represented in the study, as the Army remains the dominant service stationed in Korea.
5. To indicate contestation levels, summary statistics were calculated for the total number of protesters at each base over sixteen years (2000–2015), with the first quartile as a threshold for "low" contestation (below 13,663) and the third quartile for "high" contestation (76,350 and above). As for framing strategies, three cut-off points were used to indicate low, moderate, and high levels of pragmatic framing as a ratio of all three framing strategies used at each base over sixteen years. "Low" is operationalized as 0–33 percentile, "moderate" as 34–66 percentile, and "high" as 67–100 percentile.

Again, participant counts, as opposed to event counts, are used to measure mobilization levels. See the appendix for details.

Chapter 3

1. Given how base expansion accompanies displacements and provokes resentment, it is ironic that "very large, increasingly insular bases," such as Camp Humphreys, are at least partially meant to create some distance between service members and local residents and thereby reduce civil-military friction (Vine 2019, 169).
2. To be sure, the base was not part of the allies' 2005–2006 realignment initiatives detailed in chapter 2. The 2001 Quadrennial Defense Review by the U.S. Department of Defense, however, did state that the Navy "will increase aircraft carrier battlegroup presence in the Western Pacific and will explore options for homeporting an additional three to four surface combatants" (Department of Defense 2001). The resulting changes were closely linked to the general repositioning of other American outposts in Japan, and similarly motivated anti-base challengers to organize themselves against status disruption.
3. Other bases—Camp Kyle, Camp LaGuardia, Camp Sears, Camp Falling Water, and Camp Essyons—have been returned.
4. As of 2022, other major U.S. bases in the city—Camp Nimble, Gimbols Gun Training Area, Camp Castle, and parts of Camp Mobile and Camp Hovey—have been returned.
5. U.S. Army Garrison Daegu also includes Camp Carroll in Waegwan, just outside Daegu.
6. The land purchase campaign was styled after Okinawa's One *Tsubo* Anti-War Landowners' Movement. One *pyeong* and one *tsubo* are equivalent in size (3.3 square meters).
7. The money raised in the land purchase campaign was later spent on founding the Pyeongtaek Peace Center.

Chapter 4

1. The base borders six municipalities in western Tokyo: Fussa City, Tachikawa City, Akishima City, Musashi-Murayama City, Hamura City, and Mizuho Town.
2. A similar protest in 2003 also contributed to Hanchongnyeon's fall. On the twenty-third anniversary of the Gwangju Massacre (see chapter 2), some 1,000 student activists stopped President Roh Moo-hyun from entering the national cemetery dedicated to the victims, accusing him of "humiliating" the nation for visiting Washington and making "pro-American" statements during his meeting with George W. Bush. There was widespread anticipation at the time that Roh was going to decriminalize the student group, but a series of misjudgments on Hanchongnyeon's part increasingly eroded any remaining public sympathy.

Chapter 5

1. Interestingly, supporters of the expansion of Camp Humphreys in Pyeongtaek used identical rhetoric. The city's tourist association compared Paengseong to Jeongseon County, a financially struggling locality that symbolizes the demise of the coal mining industry in Korea (Gi-su Kim 2005, 37).

2. Parts of the Sagami Depot area, as the allies agreed in 2006, have been returned to the city. In a vexing development for local activists and the Sagamihara city government, however, in 2018 the Depot became the headquarters to the U.S. Army 38th Air Defense Artillery Brigade, which oversees missile defense batteries in Kyoto, Aomori, and Okinawa.

References

Chapter 1

Aldrich, Daniel P. 2009. Review of *Base Politics: Democratic Change and the U.S. Military Overseas*, by Alexander Cooley. *Perspectives on Politics* 7 (2): 389–91.

Allied Geographical Section, South West Pacific Area. 1945. "Special Report No. 115: Kunsan-Chonju."

Armitage, Richard L., and Joseph S. Nye. 2012. *The U.S.-Japan Alliance: Anchoring Stability in Asia*. Washington, DC: The Center for Strategic and International Studies.

Arrington, Celeste L. 2016. *Accidental Activists: Victim Movements and Government Accountability in Japan and South Korea*. Ithaca, NY: Cornell University Press.

Asan Institute for Policy Studies. 2019. "Hanmidongmaenggwa juhanmigune daehan hanguginui insik." September 2019. http://www.asaninst.org.

Bitar, Sebastian E. 2016. *US Military Bases, Quasi-Bases, and Domestic Politics in Latin America*. London: Palgrave Macmillan.

Bob, Clifford. 2005. *The Marketing of Rebellion: Insurgents, Media, and International Activism*. New York: Cambridge University Press.

Brooks, Vincent, and Ho Young Leem. 2021. "A Grand Bargain with North Korea." *Foreign Affairs*, November 12, 2021. https://www.foreignaffairs.com/articles/united-states/2021-07-29/grand-bargain-north-korea.

Calder, Kent E. 2007. *Embattled Garrisons: Comparative Base Politics and American Globalism*. Princeton, NJ: Princeton University Press.

Campbell, Kurt M., and Celeste Johnson Ward. 2003. "New Battle Stations?" *Foreign Affairs* 82 (5): 95–103.

Christensen, Thomas J. 1999. "China, the U.S.-Japan Alliance, and the Security Dilemma in East Asia." *International Security* 23 (4): 49–80.

Cooley, Alexander. 2006. *Base Politics: Democratic Change and the U.S. Military Overseas*. Ithaca, NY: Cornell University Press.

Cooley, Alexander, and Kimberly Marten. 2006. "Base Motives: The Political Economy of Okinawa's Antimilitarism." *Armed Forces & Society* 32 (4): 566–83.

Cumings, Bruce. 2011. *The Korean War: A History*. New York: Modern Library.

Davis, Sasha. 2015. *The Empires' Edge: Militarization, Resistance, and Transcending Hegemony in the Pacific*. Athens: University of Georgia Press.

Davis, Sasha. 2017. "Sharing the Struggle: Constructing Transnational Solidarity in Global Social Movements." *Space and Polity* 21 (2): 158–72.

Department of Defense. 2018. "Base Structure Report: Fiscal Year 2018 Baseline." United States Department of Defense.

Erickson, Andrew S., and Justin D. Mikolay. 2012. "A Place and a Base: Guam and the American Presence in East Asia." In *Reposturing the Force: U.S. Overseas Presence in the Twenty-first Century*, edited by Carnes Lord, 65–94. Newport, RI: Naval War College Press.

Gaventa, John. 1982. *Power and Powerlessness: Quiescence and Rebellion in an Appalachian Valley*. Urbana: University of Illinois Press.

Gillem, Mark L. 2007. *America Town: Building the Outposts of Empire*. Minneapolis: University of Minnesota Press.

Glaser, Charles L. 2015. "A U.S.-China Grand Bargain? The Hard Choice between Military Competition and Accommodation." *International Security* 39 (4): 49–90.

Gordon, Cynthia, and James Jasper. 1996. "Overcoming the 'NIMBY' Label: Rhetorical and Organizational Links for Local Protesters." *Research in Social Movements, Conflicts and Change* 19: 159–81.

Green Korea United. 2017. "Migonggae Yongsan migungji nae 84-geonui hwangyeongoyeom sago naeyeok ipsu," April 3, 2017. http://www.greenkorea.org/?p=58155.

Gullion, Jessica Smartt. 2015. *Fracking the Neighborhood: Reluctant Activists and Natural Gas Drilling*. Cambridge, MA: MIT Press.

Hankyoreh. 1988. "Juhanmigun judun 40yeonyeonui yeoksajeok uimi." *Hankyoreh*, October 11, 1988.

Harding, Shawn D. 2021. "Futenma Replacement Base Will Be Obsolete before It's Finished." *The Japan Times*, December 3, 2021. https://www.japantimes.co.jp/opinion/2021/12/03/commentary/japan-commentary/new-futenma-base-obsolete/.

Havens, Thomas R. H. 1987. *Fire across the Sea: The Vietnam War and Japan 1965–1975*. Princeton, NJ: Princeton University Press.

Hayashi, Hirofumi. 2012. *Beigun kichi no rekishi: sekai nettowāku no keisei to tenkai*. Tokyo: Yoshikawa Kōbunkan.

Hein, Laura Elizabeth, and Mark Selden, eds. 2003. *Islands of Discontent: Okinawan Responses to Japanese and American Power*. Lanham, MD: Rowman & Littlefield.

Higuchi, Naoto. 2021. "Social Movement Studies in Post-3.11 Japan: A Sociological Analysis." *International Sociology* 36 (2): 183–93.

Hincks, Joseph. 2018. "Inside Camp Humphreys: America's Biggest Overseas Base." *Time*, July 12, 2018. https://time.com/5324575/us-camp-humphreys-south-korea-largest-military-base/.

Höhn, Maria, and Seungsook Moon. 2010. *Over There: Living with the U.S. Military Empire from World War Two to the Present*. Durham, NC: Duke University Press.

Holmes, Amy Austin. 2014. *Social Unrest and American Military Bases in Turkey and Germany since 1945*. Cambridge: Cambridge University Press.

Hughes, Christopher W. 2009. "Super-Sizing the DPRK Threat: Japan's Evolving Military Posture and North Korea." *Asian Survey* 49 (2): 291–311.

Immerwahr, Daniel. 2019. *How to Hide an Empire: A Short History of the Greater United States*. New York: Farrar, Straus & Giroux.

Inoue, Masamichi S. 2007. *Okinawa and the U.S. Military: Identity Making in the Age of Globalization*. New York: Columbia University Press.

Jasper, James. 2006. "A Strategic Approach to Collective Action: Looking for Agency in Social-Movement Choices." *Mobilization: An International Quarterly* 9 (1): 1–16.

Katzenstein, Peter J., and Robert Owen Keohane. 2007. *Anti-Americanisms in World Politics*. Ithaca, NY: Cornell University Press.

Kawato, Yuko. 2015. *Protests against U.S. Military Base Policy in Asia: Persuasion and Its Limits*. Stanford, CA: Stanford University Press.

Kim, Claudia J. 2018. "Bases That Leave: Consequences of US Base Closures and Realignments in South Korea." *Journal of Contemporary Asia* 48 (2): 339–57.

Kim, Claudia J. 2021a. "Military Alliances as a Stabilizing Force: U.S. Relations with South Korea and Taiwan, 1950s–1960s." *Journal of Strategic Studies* 44 (7): 1041–62.

Kim, Claudia J. 2021b. "Scope Mismatch: Explaining the Expansion of Anti-Military Infrastructure Siting Campaigns." *Mobilization: An International Quarterly* 26 (1): 109–25.

Kim, Hakjoon. 1988. "The American Military Government in South Korea, 1945–1948: Its Formation, Policies, and Legacies." *Asian Perspective* 12 (1): 51–83.

Kovner, Sarah. 2009. "Base Cultures: Sex Workers and Servicemen in Occupied Japan." *Journal of Asian Studies* 68 (3): 777–804.

Koyama, Takashi. 2008. "'Kantō keikaku' no naritachi ni tsuite." *NIDS Military History Studies Annual* 11: 1–20.

Lipsky, Michael. 1968. "Protest as a Political Resource." *American Political Science Review* 62 (4): 1144–58.

Lostumbo, Michael J., Michael J. McNerney, Eric Peltz, Derek Eaton, David R. Frelinger, Victoria A. Greenfield, John Halliday, et al. 2013. *Overseas Basing of U.S. Military Forces*. Santa Monica, CA: RAND Corporation.

Luke, Hanabeth, Elisabet Dueholm Rasch, Darrick Evensen, and Michiel Köhne. 2018. "Is 'Activist' a Dirty Word? Place Identity, Activism and Unconventional Gas Development across Three Continents." *The Extractive Industries and Society* 5 (4): 524–34.

Lutz, Catherine. 2009. *The Bases of Empire: The Global Struggle against U.S. Military Posts.* New York: New York University Press.

Matray, James I. 1995. "Hodge Podge: American Occupation Policy in Korea, 1945–1948." *Korean Studies* 19: 17–38.

McAdam, Doug. 1982. *Political Process and the Development of Black Insurgency, 1930–1970.* Chicago: University of Chicago Press.

McAdam, Doug, and Hilary Boudet. 2012. *Putting Social Movements in Their Place: Explaining Opposition to Energy Projects in the United States, 2000–2005.* New York: Cambridge University Press.

McCormack, Gavan, and Satoko Oka Norimatsu. 2012. *Resistant Islands: Okinawa Confronts Japan and the United States.* Lanham, MD: Rowman & Littlefield.

Meyer, David S., and Sidney Tarrow, eds. 1997. *The Social Movement Society: Contentious Politics for a New Century.* Lanham, MD: Rowman & Littlefield Publishers.

Mitchell, Jon. 2016. "Contamination: Documents Reveal Hundreds of Unreported Environmental Accidents at Three U.S. Marine Corps Bases on Okinawa." *Japan Times*, November 19, 2016. https://www.japantimes.co.jp/news/2016/11/19/national/contamination-documents-reveal-three-u-s-bases-okinawa-slow-disclose-environmental-accidents/.

Molasky, Michael. 2015. "The American Occupation and Municipal Identity: Two Towns in Western Tokyo." In *Legacies of the U.S. Occupation of Japan: Appraisals after Sixty Years*, edited by Rosa Caroli and Duccio Basosi, 66–81. Newcastle upon Tyne, UK: Cambridge Scholars Publishing.

Moon, Katharine H. S. 2012. *Protesting America: Democracy and the U.S.-Korea Alliance.* Berkeley: University of California Press.

Mulgan, Aurelia George. 2000. "Managing the US Base Issue in Okinawa: A Test for Japanese Democracy." *Japanese Studies* 20 (2): 159–77.

Nexon, Daniel H., and Thomas Wright. 2007. "What's at Stake in the American Empire Debate." *American Political Science Review* 101 (2): 253–71.

NHK Broadcasting Culture Research Institute. 2017. "Okinawa Beigun kichi o meguru ishiki Okinawa to zenkoku," August 1, 2017. https://www.nhk.or.jp/bunken/research/yoron/20170801_7.html.

O'Hare, Michael, Lawrence Bacow, and Debra Sanderson. 1983. *Facility Siting and Public Opposition*. New York: Van Nostrand Reinhold.

Okinawa Prefectural Government. 2008. *Okinawa no Beigun kichi*. Naha, Japan: Okinawa-ken Chiji Kōshitsu Kichi Taisakuka.

Okinawa Prefectural Government. 2017. *Okinawa kara tsutaetai. Beigun kichi no hanashi. Q&A Book: Okinawa no Beigun kichi no gimon o wakari yasuku kaisetsu*. Naha, Japan: Okinawa Prefectural Government.

Okinawa Prefectural Government. 2020. *Okinawa no Beigun oyobi jieitai kichi*. Naha, Japan: Okinawa-ken Chiji Kōshitsu Kichi Taisakuka.

Okinawa Times. 2019. "Hondo no hantai de Okinawa ni iten Beigun kichi no rekishi, 'wakari yasuku hyōki o' senmonka ga Okinawa-ken ni chūmon." *Okinawa Times*, August 27, 2019. https://www.okinawatimes.co.jp/articles/-/462802.

Pettyjohn, Stacie L., and Jennifer Kavanagh. 2016. *Access Granted: Political Challenges to the U.S. Overseas Military Presence, 1945–2014*. Santa Monica, CA: RAND Corporation.

Posen, Barry R. 2003. "Command of the Commons: The Military Foundation of U.S. Hegemony." *International Security* 28 (1): 5–46.

Pyeongtaek City. 2018. "Migungiji yeoksa." http://sisa.pyeongtaek.go.kr.

Pyeongtaek City. 2020. "Pyeongtaek City: Covid-19 Emergency Measures." https://www.pyeongtaek.go.kr/pyeongtaek/corona_index.jsp.

Rassbach, Elsa. 2010. "Protesting U.S. Military Bases in Germany." *Peace Review* 22 (2): 121–27.

Roehrig, Terrence. 2014. "South Korea: An Alliance in Transition." In *Rebalancing U.S. Forces: Basing and Forward Presence in the Asia-Pacific*, edited by Carnes Lord and Andrew S. Erickson, 67–86. Annapolis, MD: Naval Institute Press.

Sarantakes, Nicholas Evan. 2000. *Keystone: The American Occupation of Okinawa and U.S.-Japanese Relations*. College Station: Texas A&M University Press.

Schmidt, Sebastian. 2020. *Armed Guests: Territorial Sovereignty and Foreign Military Basing*. New York: Oxford University Press.

Shimoji, Yoshio. 2011. "Futenma: Tip of the Iceberg in Okinawa's Agony." *The Asia-Pacific Journal: Japan Focus* 9 (43): no pagination.

Sisk, Richard. 2020. "Noise Complaints Force US Troops to Move Live-Fire Training Out of Korea." *Military.Com*, September 11, 2020. https://www.military.com/daily-news/2020/09/11/noise-complaints-force-us-troops-move-live-fire-training-out-of-korea.html.

Snow, David A., Daniel Cress, Liam Downey, and Andrew Jones. 1998. "Disrupting the 'Quotidian': Reconceptualizing the Relationship between Breakdown and the Emergence of Collective Action." *Mobilization: An International Quarterly* 3 (1): 1–22.

Stueck, William, and Boram Yi. 2010. "'An Alliance Forged in Blood': The American Occupation of Korea, the Korean War, and the US–South Korean Alliance." *Journal of Strategic Studies* 33 (2): 177–209.

Tanji, Miyume. 2006. *Myth, Protest and Struggle in Okinawa*. London; New York: Routledge.

Toriyama, Atsushi. 2003. "Okinawa's 'Postwar': Some Observations on the Formation of American Military Bases in the Aftermath of Terrestrial Warfare." *Inter-Asia Cultural Studies* 4 (3): 400–17.

Tsutsui, Kiyoteru. 2017. "Human Rights and Minority Activism in Japan: Transformation of Movement Actorhood and Local-Global Feedback Loop." *American Journal of Sociology* 122 (4): 1050–103.

Vine, David. 2015. *Base Nation: How U.S. Military Bases Abroad Harm America and the World*. New York: Metropolitan Books.

Vine, David. 2019. "No Bases? Assessing the Impact of Social Movements Challenging US Foreign Military Bases." *Current Anthropology* 60 (19): 158–72.

Yeo, Andrew. 2009. "Not in Anyone's Backyard: The Emergence and Identity of a Transnational Anti-Base Network." *International Studies Quarterly* 53 (3): 571–94.

Yeo, Andrew. 2011. *Activists, Alliances, and Anti-U.S. Base Protests*. New York: Cambridge University Press.

Yoshimi, Shunya. 2003. "'America' as Desire and Violence: Americanization in Postwar Japan and Asia during the Cold War." *Inter-Asia Cultural Studies* 4 (3): 433–50.

Chapter 2

Aldrich, Daniel P. 2009. Review of *Base Politics: Democratic Change and the U.S. Military Overseas*, by Alexander Cooley. *Perspectives on Politics* 7 (2): 389–91.

Arrington, Celeste L. 2016. *Accidental Activists: Victim Movements and Government Accountability in Japan and South Korea*. Ithaca, NY: Cornell University Press.

Bae, Yooil, and Sunhyuk Kim. 2013. "Civil Society and Local Activism in South Korea's Local Democratization." *Democratization* 20 (2): 260–86.

Berger, Thomas U. 1998. *Cultures of Antimilitarism: National Security in Germany and Japan*. Baltimore: Johns Hopkins University Press.

Bob, Clifford. 2005. *The Marketing of Rebellion: Insurgents, Media, and International Activism*. New York: Cambridge University Press.

Calder, Kent E. 2007. *Embattled Garrisons: Comparative Base Politics and American Globalism*. Princeton, NJ: Princeton University Press.

Campbell, Kurt M., and Celeste Johnson Ward. 2003. "New Battle Stations?" *Foreign Affairs* 82 (5): 95–103.

Carruthers, Susan L. 2016. *The Good Occupation*. Cambridge, MA: Harvard University Press.

Cockburn, Cynthia. 2012. *Antimilitarism: Political and Gender Dynamics of Peace Movements*. New York: Palgrave Macmillan.

Cockburn, Cynthia, and Naoko Ikeda. 2012. "Seeing the Whole Picture: Anti-Militarism in Okinawa and Japan." In *Antimilitarism: Political and Gender Dynamics of Peace Movements*, edited by Cynthia Cockburn, 152–79. London: Palgrave Macmillan.

Cooley, Alexander. 2008. *Base Politics: Democratic Change and the U.S. Military Overseas*. Ithaca, NY: Cornell University Press.

Cress, Daniel M., and David A. Snow. 2000. "The Outcomes of Homeless Mobilization: The Influence of Organization, Disruption, Political Mediation, and Framing." *American Journal of Sociology* 105 (4): 1063–104.

Cumings, Bruce. 2011. *The Korean War: A History*. New York: Modern Library.

Dietz, Kelly. 2010. "Demilitarizing Sovereignty: Self-Determination and Anti-Military Base Activism in Okinawa, Japan." In *Contesting Development: Critical Struggles for Social Change*, edited by Philip McMichael, 182–98. New York: Routledge.

Dietz, Kelly. 2016. "Transnationalism and Transition in the Ryukyus." In *Transnational Japan as History: Empire, Migration, and Social Movements*, edited by Pedro Iacobelli, Danton Leary, and Shinnosuke Takahashi, 211–41. Palgrave Macmillan.

Dong-a Ilbo. 1988. "Soryeon yeolgiwa banmigamjeong." *Dong-a Ilbo*, September 12, 1988.

Dower, John W. 1999. *Embracing Defeat: Japan in the Wake of World War II*. New York: W. W. Norton.

Eisinger, Peter K. 1973. "The Conditions of Protest Behavior in American Cities." *American Political Science Review* 67 (1): 11–28.

Enloe, Cynthia. 2014. *Bananas, Beaches and Bases: Making Feminist Sense of International Politics*. 2nd ed. Berkeley: University of California Press.

Figal, Gerald. 2001. "Waging Peace on Okinawa." *Critical Asian Studies* 33 (1): 37–69.

Frühstück, Sabine. 2007. *Uneasy Warriors: Gender, Memory, and Popular Culture in the Japanese Army*. Berkeley: University of California Press.

Gamson, William A., and David S. Meyer. 1996. "Framing Political Opportunity." In *Comparative Perspectives on Social Movements: Political Opportunities, Mobilizing Structures, and Cultural Framings*, edited by Doug McAdam, John D. McCarthy, and Mayer N. Zald, 275–90. Cambridge: Cambridge University Press.

Gaventa, John. 1982. *Power and Powerlessness: Quiescence and Rebellion in an Appalachian Valley*. Urbana: University of Illinois Press.

Gerhards, Jürgen, and Dieter Rucht. 1992. "Mesomobilization: Organizing and Framing in Two Protest Campaigns in West Germany." *American Journal of Sociology* 98 (3): 555–96.

Glosserman, Brad. 2005. "Anti-Americanism in Japan." In *Korean Attitudes toward the United States: Changing Dynamics*, edited by David I. Steinberg, 34–45. Armonk, NY: M. E. Sharpe.

Gullion, Jessica Smartt. 2015. *Fracking the Neighborhood: Reluctant Activists and Natural Gas Drilling*. Cambridge, MA: MIT Press.

Hankyoreh 21. 2000. "Miguneun uriege mueosinga." *Hankyoreh 21*, March 9, 2000. http://legacy.h21.hani.co.kr/h21/data/L000228/1paq2s02.html.

Havens, Thomas R. H. 1987. *Fire across the Sea: The Vietnam War and Japan 1965–1975*. Princeton, NJ: Princeton University Press.

Hook, Glenn D. 1996. *Militarization and Demilitarization in Contemporary Japan*. London and New York: Routledge.

Igarashi, Yoshikuni. 2000. *Bodies of Memory: Narratives of War in Postwar Japanese Culture, 1945–1970*. Princeton, NJ: Princeton University Press.

Iida, Yumiko. 2002. *Rethinking Identity in Modern Japan: Nationalism as Aesthetics*. London: Routledge.

Jasper, James. 1997. *The Art of Moral Protest: Culture, Biography, and Creativity in Social Movements*. Chicago: University of Chicago Press.

Jasper, James. 2006. "A Strategic Approach to Collective Action: Looking for Agency in Social-Movement Choices." *Mobilization: An International Quarterly* 9 (1): 1–16.

Joongang Ilbo. 1986. "Haksaengdeurui guho haengdong jeomcha gwagyeokwa: Daehakga geupjinseryeogui jojikgwa inyeom." *Joongang Ilbo*, April 28, 1986. https://news.joins.com/article/2047826.

Kahneman, Daniel, and Amos Tversky. 1979. "Prospect Theory: An Analysis of Decision under Risk." *Econometrica* 47 (2): 263–91.

Kang, Heon. 2015. *Jeonbokgwa banjeonui sungan: Gangheoni jumokan eumaksaui yeoksajeok jangmyeondeul.* Paju, South Korea: Dolbegae.

Katzenstein, Peter J., ed. 1996. *The Culture of National Security: Norms and Identity in World Politics.* Columbia University Press.

Kim, Claudia J. 2021. "Scope Mismatch: Explaining the Expansion of Anti-Military Infrastructure Siting Campaigns." *Mobilization: An International Quarterly* 26 (1): 109–25.

Kim, Claudia J., and Taylor C. Boas. 2020. "Activist Disconnect: Social Movements, Public Opinion, and U.S. Military Bases in East Asia." *Armed Forces & Society* 46 (4): 619–715.

Kim, Dong Sung. 2010. "Discord and Integration: U.S. Forces and Local Communities in Korea." Suwon: Gyeonggi Research Institute.

Kim, Hakjoon. 1988. "The American Military Government in South Korea, 1945–1948: Its Formation, Policies, and Legacies." *Asian Perspective* 12 (1): 51–83.

Kim, Sook. 2004. "Migun jaebaechi hanmidongmaeng ganghwagyegi." *Dong-a Ilbo,* July 29, 2004. http://news.donga.com/List/Series_70030000000093/3/70030000000093/20040729/8089194/1.

Kim, Sunhyuk. 2000. *The Politics of Democratization in Korea: The Role of Civil Society.* Pittsburgh: University of Pittsburgh Press.

Kim, Sunhyuk, and Eun Sun Lee. 2011. "'Dynamics of Contention' in Democratic Korea: The Role of Anti-Americanism." *Korea Journal* 51 (2): 229–55.

Kingdon, John W. 1984. *Agendas, Alternatives, and Public Policies.* Boston: Little, Brown.

Krauss, Ellis S., and Bradford L. Simcock. 1981. "Citizens' Movements: The Growth and Impact of Environmental Protest in Japan." In *Political Opposition and Local Politics in Japan,* edited by Kurt Steiner, Ellis S. Krauss, and Scott E. Flanagan, 187–227. Princeton, NJ: Princeton University Press. https://muse.jhu.edu/book/33334.

Lee, Chae-hoon. 2002. "Ije sopagaejeongi anin miguncheolsuda." *OhmyNews,* December 6, 2002. http://www.ohmynews.com/nws_web/view/at_pg.aspx?CNTN_CD=A0000097467.

Lee, Namhee. 2007. *The Making of Minjung: Democracy and the Politics of Representation in South Korea.* Ithaca, NY: Cornell University Press.

Lostumbo, Michael J., Michael J. McNerney, Eric Peltz, Derek Eaton, David R. Frelinger, Victoria A. Greenfield, John Halliday, et al. 2013. *Overseas Basing of U.S. Military Forces.* Santa Monica, CA: RAND Corporation.

Luke, Hanabeth, Elisabet Dueholm Rasch, Darrick Evensen, and Michiel Köhne. 2018. "Is 'Activist' a Dirty Word? Place Identity, Activism and Unconventional Gas Development across Three Continents." *The Extractive Industries and Society* 5 (4): 524–34.

Lutz, Catherine. 2009. "Introduction: Bases, Empire, and Global Response." In *The Bases of Empire: The Global Struggle against U.S. Military Posts,* edited by Catherine Lutz and Cynthia Enloe, 1–39. New York: New York University Press.

McAdam, Doug. 1982. *Political Process and the Development of Black Insurgency, 1930–1970.* Chicago: University of Chicago Press.

McAdam, Doug, and Hilary Boudet. 2012. *Putting Social Movements in Their Place: Explaining Opposition to Energy Projects in the United States, 2000–2005.* New York: Cambridge University Press.

McAdam, Doug, Hilary Schaffer Boudet, Jennifer Davis, Ryan J. Orr, W. Richard Scott, and Raymond E. Levitt. 2010. "'Site Fights': Explaining Opposition to Pipeline Projects in the Developing World." *Sociological Forum* 25 (3): 401–27.

McCammon, Holly J., Harmony D. Newman, Courtney Sanders Muse, and Teresa M. Terrell. 2007. "Movement Framing and Discursive Opportunity Structures: The Political Successes of the U.S. Women's Jury Movements." *American Sociological Review* 72 (5): 725–49.

McVeigh, Brian J. 2000. "Postwar Nationalisms of Japan: The Management and Mysticism of Identity." *New Zealand Journal of Asian Studies* 2 (1): 24–39.

Meyer, David S., and Daisy Verduzco Reyes. 2009. "Social Movements and Contentious Politics." In *Handbook of Politics: State and Society in Global Perspective*, edited by Kevin T. Leicht and J. Craig Jenkins, 217–33. New York: Springer Science & Business Media.

Ministry of Foreign Affairs of Japan. 1996. "The SACO Final Report on Futenma Air Station," December 2, 1996. http://www.mofa.go.jp/region/n-america/us/security/96saco2.html.

Ministry of Foreign Affairs of Japan. 2005. "U.S.-Japan Alliance: Transformation and Realignment for the Future," October 29, 2005. http://www.mofa.go.jp/region/n-america/us/security/scc/doc0510.html.

Ministry of Foreign Affairs of Republic of Korea. 2002. "Yeonhap toji gwalli gyehoek (LPP) hyeopjeong balhyo," October 31, 2002. http://www.mofa.go.kr.

Ministry of Foreign Affairs of Republic of Korea. 2004. "Yongsangiji ijeon hyeopjeong balhyo," December 17, 2004. http://www.mofa.go.kr.

Mitchell, Jon. 2016. "How the U.S. Military Spies on Okinawans and Me." *The Japan Times*, October 19, 2016. https://www.japantimes.co.jp/community/2016/10/19/issues/u-s-military-spies-okinawans/.

Moon, Katharine H. S. 2012. *Protesting America: Democracy and the U.S.-Korea Alliance.* Berkeley: University of California Press.

Morrison, David C. 1985. "Japanese Principles, U.S. Policies." *Bulletin of the Atomic Scientists* 41 (6): 22–24.

Mulgan, Aurelia George. 2000. "Managing the US Base Issue in Okinawa: A Test for Japanese Democracy." *Japanese Studies* 20 (2): 159–77.

National Council of Japan Nuclear Free Local Authorities. 2018. "Hikakusengen Jichitai Ichiran," March 23, 2018. http://www.nucfreejapan.com.

Oguma, Eiji. 2014. *The Boundaries of "the Japanese,"* Vol. 1: *Okinawa 1818–1972: Inclusion and Exclusion.* Translated by Leonie R. Stickland. Melbourne: Trans Pacific Press.

Okinawa Prefectural Government. 2011. "Political Situation in Okinawa." 2011. http://www.pref.okinawa.jp/site/chijiko/kichitai/documents/political%20situation%20in%20okinawa.pdf.

Okinawa Prefectural Government. 2017. *Okinawa No Beigun oyobi Jieitai kichi.* Naha, Japan: Okinawa-ken Chiji Kōshitsu Kichi Taisakuka.

Okinawa Times. 2017. "Kōanchōsachō, Okinawa no kenkyūsha o 'Ryūkyū dokuritsu seiryoku' to shiteki Matayoshi-shi-ra hanron 'henken umu.'" *Okinawa Times*, January 17, 2017. https://www.okinawatimes.co.jp/articles/-/80100.

Orr, James Joseph. 2001. *The Victim as Hero: Ideologies of Peace and National Identity in Postwar Japan.* Honolulu: University of Hawaii Press.

Paik, Nak-chung. 1993. "South Korea: Unification and the Democratic Challenge." *New Left Review* I-197: 67–84.

Pettyjohn, Stacie L. 2012. "U.S. Global Defense Posture, 1783–2011." Santa Monica, CA: RAND Corporation. https://www.rand.org/pubs/monographs/MG1244.html.

Pharr, Susan J. 1992. *Losing Face: Status Politics in Japan*. Berkeley: University of California Press.

Rhodes, R. A. W. 1999. *Control and Power in Central-Local Government Relations*. London: Routledge.

Rothman, Franklin, and Pamela Oliver. 1999. "From Local to Global: The Anti-Dam Movement in Southern Brazil, 1979–1992." *Mobilization: An International Quarterly* 4 (1): 41–57.

Samuelson, William, and Richard Zeckhauser. 1988. "Status Quo Bias in Decision Making." *Journal of Risk and Uncertainty* 1 (1): 7–59.

Shimabuku, Annmaria M. 2019. *Alegal: Biopolitics and the Unintelligibility of Okinawan Life*. New York: Fordham University Press.

Shin, Gi-Wook. 2006. *Ethnic Nationalism in Korea: Genealogy, Politics, and Legacy*. Stanford, CA: Stanford University Press.

Smith, Sheila A. 1999. "Do Domestic Politics Matter? The Case of U.S. Military Bases in Japan." U.S.-Japan Project Working Paper Series 7. Washington, DC: George Washington University.

Smith, Sheila A. 2006. *Shifting Terrain: The Domestic Politics of the U.S. Military Presence in Asia*. Honolulu, Hawai'i: East-West Center.

Smits, Gregory. 1999. *Visions of Ryukyu: Identity and Ideology in Early-Modern Thought and Politics*. Honolulu: University of Hawaii Press.

Smits, Gregory. 2010. "Examining the Myth of Ryukyuan Pacifism | The Asia-Pacific Journal: Japan Focus." *Asia-Pacific Journal: Japan Focus* 8 (37): n.p.

Snow, David A., and Robert D. Benford. 1988. "Ideology, Frame Resonance, and Participant Mobilization." *International Social Movement Research* 1 (1): 197–217.

Snow, David A., and Robert D. Benford. 1992. "Master Frames and Cycles of Protest." In *Frontiers in Social Movement Theory*, edited by Aldon D. Morris and Carol McClurg Mueller, 133–55. New Haven, CT: Yale University Press.

Snow, David A., Daniel Cress, Liam Downey, and Andrew Jones. 1998. "Disrupting the 'Quotidian': Reconceptualizing the Relationship between Breakdown and the Emergence of Collective Action." *Mobilization: An International Quarterly* 3 (1): 1–22.

Snow, David A., E. Burke Rochford, Steven K. Worden, and Robert D. Benford. 1986. "Frame Alignment Processes, Micromobilization, and Movement Participation." *American Sociological Review* 51 (4): 464–81.

Steiner, Kurt. 1980. "Toward a Framework for the Study of Local Opposition." In *Political Opposition and Local Politics in Japan*, edited by Kurt Steiner, Ellis S. Krauss, and Scott E. Flanagan, 3–32. Princeton, NJ: Princeton University Press.

Stueck, William, and Boram Yi. 2010. "'An Alliance Forged in Blood': The American Occupation of Korea, the Korean War, and the US–South Korean Alliance." *Journal of Strategic Studies* 33 (2): 177–209.

Suzuki, Shogo. 2015. "The Rise of the Chinese 'Other' in Japan's Construction of Identity: Is China a Focal Point of Japanese Nationalism?" *Pacific Review* 28 (1): 95–116.

Takahara, Takao. 1987. "Local Government Initiatives to Promote Peace." *Peace & Change* 12 (3–4): 51–58.

Takao, Yasuo. 1999. *National Integration and Local Power in Japan*. Aldershot: Ashgate.

Takeshi, Igarashi. 1985. "Peace-Making and Party Politics: The Formation of the Domestic Foreign-Policy System in Postwar Japan." *Journal of Japanese Studies* 11 (2): 323–56.

Tanji, Miyume. 2006. *Myth, Protest and Struggle in Okinawa.* London; New York: Routledge.

Tarrow, Sidney. 2011. *Power in Movement: Social Movements and Contentious Politics.* 3rd ed. New York: Cambridge University Press.

Tsutsui, Kiyoteru. 2017. "Human Rights and Minority Activism in Japan: Transformation of Movement Actorhood and Local-Global Feedback Loop." *American Journal of Sociology* 122 (4): 1050–103.

U.S. Department of Defense. 2004. "Strengthening U.S. Global Defense Posture: Report to Congress." Washington, DC.

Useem, Bert. 1998. "Breakdown Theories of Collective Action." *Annual Review of Sociology* 24 (1): 215–38.

Vine, David. 2015. *Base Nation: How U.S. Military Bases Abroad Harm America and the World.* New York: Metropolitan Books.

Welfield, John. 1988. *An Empire in Eclipse: Japan in the Post-War American Alliance System: A Study in the Interaction of Domestic Politics and Foreign Policy.* Atlantic Highlands, NJ: Athlone Press.

Chapter 3

Asahi Shimbun. 2006. "Shitsumon to kaitō Iwakuni jūmin tōhyō, Asahishinbunsha yoron chōsa." *Asahi Shimbun,* February 28, 2006.

Asahi Shimbun. 2019. "Tokyo Admits Design Change in Cards for Henoko Due to Seafloor," *Asahi Shimbun,* January 21, 2019. http://www.asahi.com/ajw/articles/AJ2 01901210036.html.

Ashton, Adam. 2015. "On Okinawa, Clash over War and Peace Began with U.S. Victory in WWII." *Sacramento Bee,* November 22, 2015. http://www.sacbee.com/news/article4 5885735.html.

Asia-Wide Campaign Japan. 2015. "Ajia kara subete no Beigunkichi tekkyo o! 2017-nen Iwakuni kichi kyōka soshi Henoko shin kichi kensetsu soshi kokusai rentai shūkai Iwakuni shiryō." http://www.awcjapan.org/.

Association for Referendum on the Homeporting of the Nuclear-Powered Aircraft Carrier. 2015. "10,000 Citizens' Questionnaire Survey on the Change in Deployment of the Nuclear-Powered Aircraft Carrier." https://cvn.jpn.org/.

Burke, Matthew M. 2012. "Marine Base Construction Brings Headaches to Iwakuni Residents." *Stars and Stripes,* August 8, 2012. https://www.stripes.com/news/pacific/japan/marine-base-construction-brings-headaches-to-iwakuni-residents-1.185103.

Burke, Matthew M., and Hana Kusumoto. 2021. "Activist Goes on Hunger Strike over Possible WWII Remains at Okinawa Base Construction Site." *Stars and Stripes,* March 4, 2021. https://www.stripes.com/activist-goes-on-hunger-strike-over-possible-wwii-remains-at-okinawa-base-construction-site-1.664517.

Calder, Kent E. 2007. *Embattled Garrisons: Comparative Base Politics and American Globalism.* Princeton, NJ: Princeton University Press.

Chugoku Shimbun. 2008. "Living with the Nightmare of Planes and Aircraft Carriers at U.S. Bases in Japan: Upgrading Iwakuni and Yokosuka." *Asia-Pacific Journal: Japan Focus* 6 (8): n.p.

Demick, Barbara. 2002. "Anti-Americanism Sweeps South Korea." *Los Angeles Times,* November 27, 2002. https://www.latimes.com/archives/la-xpm-2002-nov-27-fg-uskorea27-story.html.

Department of Defense. 2001. "Quadrennial Defense Review Report." Washington, DC: U.S. Department of Defense.

Fifield, Anna. 2017. "As North Korea Intensifies Its Missile Program, the U.S. Opens an $11 Billion Base in the South." *Washington Post*, July 29, 2017, sec. Asia & Pacific. https://www.washingtonpost.com/world/asia_pacific/as-north-korea-intensifies-its-missile-program-the-us-opens-an-11-billion-base-in-south-korea/2017/07/28/a155e34c-70b1-11e7-8c17-533c52b2f014_story.html.

Hanai, Kiroku. 2006. "Waves Build against Carrier." *The Japan Times*, October 23, 2006. https://www.japantimes.co.jp/opinion/2006/10/23/commentary/waves-build-against-carrier/.

Hankyoreh. 2010. "935ilgan taoreun Daechuri chotburi kkeojigo." *Hankyoreh*, October 7, 2010. https://www.hani.co.kr/arti/society/society_general/442607.html.

Houlihan, Sean P. 2007. "Local Leave and Pass Travel Guideline Explained." *Kunsan Air Base*, June 7, 2007. https://www.kunsan.af.mil/News/Article/414205/local-leave-and-pass-travel-guideline-explained/.

Im, Eunjeong. 2001. "Ajummaga migugeul bandaehaneun iyu." *OhmyNews*, August 31, 2001. http://www.ohmynews.com/NWS_Web/View/at_pg.aspx?CNTN_CD=A0000052094.

Inoue, Masamichi S. 2004. "'We Are Okinawans but of a Different Kind' New/Old Social Movements and the U.S. Military in Okinawa." *Current Anthropology* 45 (1): 85–104.

Inoue, Masamichi S. 2007. *Okinawa and the U.S. Military: Identity Making in the Age of Globalization*. New York: Columbia University Press.

Jeonbuk Domin Ilbo. 2004. "Gunsan seoldeungnyeok inneun ijudaechaek sigeup." *Jeonbuk Domin Ilbo*, March 29, 2004. http://www.domin.co.kr/news/articleView.html?idxno=509897.

Johnson, Tim. 2004. "Japanese Cities Anxious over U.S. Military Realignment." *The Philadelphia Inquirer*, November 1, 2004.

Kanagawa Prefectural Government. 2007. *Kanagawa no Beigun kichi*. Yokohama, Japan: Kanagawa-ken Kikakubu Kichi Taisakuka.

Kirk, Don. 2002. "Road Accident Galvanizes the Country: Deaths in Korea Ignite Anti-American Passion." *New York Times*, July 31, 2002, sec. World. https://www.nytimes.com/2002/07/31/news/road-accident-galvanizes-the-country-deaths-in-korea-ignite.html.

Kusumoto, Hana. 2005. "City Sends Protest Letter to Camp Zama about Helicopter Noise." *Stars and Stripes*, May 27, 2005. https://www.stripes.com/news/city-sends-protest-letter-to-camp-zama-about-helicopter-noise-1.33870.

Kyongbuk Ilbo. 2002. "Migungiji Pohang judun bandae umjigim beomsiminundongeuro hwaksan." *Kyongbuk Ilbo*, January 10, 2002. http://www.kyongbuk.co.kr/news/articleView.html?idxno=765112.

Little, Vince. 2007. "I Corps Establishes Forward HQ at Zama." *Stars and Stripes*, December 21, 2007. https://www.stripes.com/news/i-corps-establishes-forward-hq-at-zama-1.72618.

Lostumbo, Michael J., Michael J. McNerney, Eric Peltz, Derek Eaton, David R. Frelinger, Victoria A. Greenfield, John Halliday, et al. 2013. *Overseas Basing of U.S. Military Forces*. Santa Monica, CA: RAND Corporation.

Lutz, Catherine. 2009. "Introduction: Bases, Empire, and Global Response." In *The Bases of Empire: The Global Struggle against U.S. Military Posts*, edited by Catherine Lutz and Cynthia Enloe, 1–39. New York: New York University Press.

Maeil Shinmun. 2020. "Kaempeuwokeo damjang arae eoneu insaeng 70nyeon," December 29, 2020. https://news.imaeil.com/SocietyAll/2020122000402851701.

The Mainichi. 2017. "Iwakuni Base Expansion Accelerates as Local Heads OK Transfer of US Carrier-Borne Jets." *The Mainichi*, June 30, 2017, sec. Japan. https://mainichi.jp/english/articles/20170630/p2a/00m/0na/019000c.

Mainichi Shimbun. 2005. "Beigun saihen Kanagawa: gaman no genkai." *Mainichi Shimbun*, November 14, 2005.

Mainichi Shimbun. 2007. "Amerika, gunyō sharyō o rikuage—kanshi dantai kakunin." *Mainichi Shimbun*, October 14, 2007.

McCormack, Gavan. 2014. "The End of the Postwar? The Abe Government, Okinawa, and Yonaguni Island." *Asia-Pacific Journal: Japan Focus* 12 (49): no pagination.

McCormack, Gavan, and Satoko Oka Norimatsu. 2012. *Resistant Islands: Okinawa Confronts Japan and the United States.* Lanham, MD: Rowman & Littlefield.

Ministry of Foreign Affairs of Japan. 2006. "United States–Japan Roadmap for Realignment Implementation," May 1, 2006. http://www.mofa.go.jp/region/n-amer ica/us/security/scc/doc0605.html.

Montgomery, Nancy. 2004. "Yokosuka Citizens' Group Urges Close Monitoring of Piedmont Pier Work." *Stars and Stripes*, March 11, 2004. https://www.stripes.com/news/yokosuka-citizens-group-urges-close-monitoring-of-piedmont-pier-work-1.17498.

Nīkura, Hiroshi. 2016. *Yokosuka, kichi no machi o aruki tsuzukete: chīsana undō wa riyakā to tomoni.* Tokyo: Nanatsumorishokan.

Nishiyama, Takashi. 2014. *Engineering War and Peace in Modern Japan, 1868–1964.* Baltimore: Johns Hopkins University Press.

Park, Rae-gun. 2010. *A! Daechuri: Daechuri jumindeurui Pyeongtaek migungiji hwakjangijeon bandae tujaenggirok.* Suwon: Saramsaenggak.

Pempel, T. J. 2007. "Japanese Strategy under Koizumi." In *Japanese Strategic Thought toward Asia*, edited by G. Rozman, K. Togo, and J. Ferguson, 109–33. New York: Palgrave Macmillan.

Pettyjohn, Stacie L. 2012. "U.S. Global Defense Posture, 1783–2011." Santa Monica, CA: RAND Corporation. https://www.rand.org/pubs/monographs/MG1244.html.

Pettyjohn, Stacie L., and Jennifer Kavanagh. 2017. *Access Granted: Political Challenges to the U.S. Overseas Military Presence, 1945–2014.* Santa Monica, CA: RAND Corporation.

Rabson, Steve. 2012. "Henoko and the U.S. Military: A History of Dependence and Resistance." *The Asia-Pacific Journal: Japan Focus* 10 (4): n.p.

Robson, Seth. 2020. "Zama Museum Preserves History of Camp Serving as US Army Japan Headquarters." *Stars and Stripes*, November 12, 2020. https://www.stripes.com/zama-museum-preserves-history-of-camp-serving-as-us-army-japan-headquarters-1.651877.

Satkowski, Stephen. 2014. "New 'Footprint' Emerging in Korea for U.S. Military." *Far East District U.S. Army Corps of Engineers*, September 19, 2014. https://www.pof.usace.army.mil/Media/News/Article/499855/new-footprint-emerging-in-korea-for-us-military/.

Slavin, Erik, and Hae-rym Hwang. 2007. "Kunsan Air Base to Expand by 315 Acres." *Stars and Stripes*, June 6, 2007. https://www.stripes.com/news/kunsan-air-base-to-exp and-by-315-acres-1.64985.

Tanji, Miyume. 2006. *Myth, Protest and Struggle in Okinawa.* London; New York: Routledge.

U.S. Army Garrison Humphreys. 2018. "Welcome to Camp Humphreys, South Korea." *U.S. Army*, November 18, 2018. https://www.army.mil/article/117803/welcome_to_camp_humphreys_south_korea.

Vine, David. 2019. "No Bases? Assessing the Impact of Social Movements Challenging US Foreign Military Bases." *Current Anthropology* 60 (19): 158–72.

Williams, Brad. 2013. "The YIMBY Phenomenon in Henoko, Okinawa: Compensation Politics and Grassroots Democracy in a Base Community." *Asian Survey* 53 (5): 958–78.

Yamajiro, Hiroji, Etsuko Urashima, Yasuhiro Miyagi, Yōichi Iha, Hideki Yoshikawa, and McCormack Gavan. 2018. "Five Okinawan Views on the Nago Mayoral Election of February 2018: Implications for Japanese Democracy." *Asia-Pacific Journal: Japan Focus* 16 (4): no pagination.

Yokosuka City. 2013. "Sōgō keikaku shimin ankēto hōkokusho." https://www.city.yokosuka.kanagawa.jp/0110/upi/hyouka/documents/h25sougoukeikakuannke_tohoukokusyo.pdf.

Yoo, Chang Jae. 2002. "Juhanmigun, 'yeogin migukttangini nagara'; yeogosaengdeul, migun budae ap 'nunmurui oechim.'" *OhmyNews*, June 21, 2002. http://www.ohmynews.com/nws_web/view/at_pg.aspx?CNTN_CD=A0000079187.

Yoo, Yong-won. 2006. "Pyeongtaek migungji joseong 4-5nyeon neutchwojyeo." *Chosun Ilbo*, December 14, 2006. https://www.chosun.com/site/data/html_dir/2006/12/14/2006121400041.html.

Yun, Bo-jung. 2007. "Gunsan migungji hwakjang, je2ui Pyeongtaek doena." *Voice of the People*, July 20, 2007. http://www.vop.co.kr/A00000080581.html.

Chapter 4

Akahata. 2008. "Shii Speaks at Rally against Homeporting of U.S. Nuclear-Powered Aircraft Carrier at Yokosuka," July 15, 2008. https://www.japan-press.co.jp/modules/news/index.php?id=4386.

Akahata. 2014. "Osupurei de 'hondo no Okinawa-ka,'" December 5, 2014. http://www.jcp.or.jp/akahata/aik14/2014-12-05/2014120501_04_1.html.

Apter, David. 1984. "A 60s Movement in the 80s." *Social Text*, no. 9/10: 70–90.

Association for the Prevention of Noise at Atsugi Base. 2001. "Ikari: Bakudō 40-Nen No Kiseki."

Atsugi Residents Association to Eliminate Explosive Noise and Oppose Homeporting of the Aircraft Carrier. 2015. "Tateno tekkōjo tsuiraku jiko 50-shūnen irei," March 22, 2015.

Baek, Do-in. 2001. "Gunsan migungji banhwan jipoe 200hoe maja." *Saejeonbuk News*, October 16, 2001.

Bob, Clifford. 2005. *The Marketing of Rebellion: Insurgents, Media, and International Activism*. New York: Cambridge University Press.

Campaign for the Return of Yongsan Base. 2001. "Yongsan Migungji Banhwan Undongbonbu Gyeolseong," November 23, 2001. http://energyjustice.kr/zbxe/36800.

Cho, Kisuk. 2009. "The Ideological Orientation of 2008 Candlelight Vigil Participants: Anti-American, Pro–North Korean Left or Anti-Neoliberalism?" *Korean Political Science Review* 43 (3): 125–48.

Choi, Hae-young. 2005. "Migungji hwakjangjeoji beomgungmindaechaegwi chulbeom." *Kyeonggi Ilbo*, March 6, 2005.

Choi, Yong-hwan. 2008. "Redeployment of USFK: From the Local Society's Perspective." *Journal of International Politics (Gukje Gwangye Yeongu)* 13 (1): 39–88.

Choi, Yong-hwan. 2016. "Yeongpyeong sagyeokjang jubyeon jumin jiwondaechaek yeongu." 2016–02. Suwon: Gyeonggi Research Institute.

Cumings, Bruce. 1997. *Korea's Place in the Sun: A Modern History*. New York: W. W. Norton.

Cumings, Bruce. 2009. *Dominion from Sea to Sea: Pacific Ascendancy and American Power*. New Haven, CT: Yale University Press.

"Don't Shoot Mt. Fuji" Executive Committee. 2012. "NO! 104 jitsudan kunren, NO! Osupurei Higashifuji de shūkai to demo," September 8, 2012. http://www.pacohama.sakura.ne.jp/no12/1209higasihuji.html.

Dudden, Alexis. 2014. "Okinawa Today: Spotlight on Henoko." In *Critical Issues in Contemporary Japan*, edited by Jeff Kingston, 177–86. London; New York: Routledge.

Erickson, Andrew S., and Justin D. Mikolay. 2012. "A Place and a Base: Guam and the American Presence in East Asia." In *Reposturing the Force: U.S. Overseas Presence in the Twenty-first Century*, edited by Carnes Lord, 65–94. Newport, RI: Naval War College Press.

Fichtl, Marcus, and Yoo Kyong Chang. 2017. "South Koreans Complain about Stray Rounds, Noise from Live-Fire Range." *Stars and Stripes*, December 21, 2017. https://www.stripes.com/news/south-koreans-complain-about-stray-rounds-noise-from-live-fire-range-1.503334.

Gamel, Kim. 2018. "US Commander Apologizes for Stray Ammunition Rounds in South Korea." *Stars and Stripes*, January 12, 2018. https://www.stripes.com/news/us-comman der-apologizes-for-stray-ammunition-rounds-in-south-korea-1.506353.

Giordono, Joseph, and Song-won Choe. 2003. "S. Korean Police Arrest Rodriguez Range Protest Organizer." *Stars and Stripes*, August 21, 2003. https://www.stripes.com/news/s-korean-police-arrest-rodriguez-range-protest-organizer-1.7033.

Go, Chang-seop. 2017. "Pocheon jumindeul 64nyeon pogeum misagyeokjang pyeswaechokgu." *Pocheon Sinmun*, March 28, 2017. http://www.ipcs21.com/default/index_view_page.php?part_idx=301&idx=55773.

Gordon, Cynthia, and James Jasper. 1996. "Overcoming the 'NIMBY' Label: Rhetorical and Organizational Links for Local Protesters." *Research in Social Movements, Conflicts and Change* 19: 159–81.

Green Korea United. 2000. "Mipalgun Yongsan migungiji daryangui dokgeungmul hangange mudan bangchul," July 13, 2000. http://www.greenkorea.org/?p=10408.

Green Korea United. 2004. "Gunsan migonggungiji soeumpihaesosong seungso," January 29, 2004. http://www.greenkorea.org/?p=11090.

Gwon, Sukhui. 2015. "Gun sagyeokjang pihae 60yeonyeon sogariman haeon 'anboui ttang.'" *Yonhap News Agency*, April 3, 2015. https://www.yna.co.kr/view/AKR201504 03135900060.

Halloran, Richard. 2005. "The Politics of Assigning a Nuclear Carrier to Japan." *Japan Times*, November 9, 2005. https://www.japantimes.co.jp/opinion/2005/11/09/com mentary/world-commentary/the-politics-of-assigning-a-nuclear-carrier-to-japan/.

Hankyoreh. 2006. "Migungiji bandae '1200km teuraekteo sullye' machin gimjitaessi," January 15, 2006. http://hani.co.kr/arti/PRINT/95355.html.

Hong, Dam-young. 2016. "USFK's Off-Limits Order Deepens Conflict in Pyeongtaek." *Korea Times*, October 9, 2016. http://www.koreatimes.co.kr/www/nation/2017/08/205 _215660.html.

Hongo, Jun. 2008. "Protests Greet Nuclear Carrier at Its New Home in Yokosuka." *Japan Times*, September 26, 2008. https://www.japantimes.co.jp/news/2008/09/26/national/protests-greet-nuclear-carrier-at-its-new-home-in-yokosuka/.

Hwang, Yeong-min. 2013. "K-55 sangingwa migun tto daechi jung." *Pyeongtaek Simin Sinmun*, June 19, 2013. http://www.pttimes.com/news/articleView.html?idxno=28624.

Inoue, Masamichi S. 2007. *Okinawa and the U.S. Military: Identity Making in the Age of Globalization*. New York: Columbia University Press.

Jeon, Jun-hyeon. 2015. "Hanmiyeonham sangnyukullyeon bandae daegyumo siwi." *Kyongbuk Maeil Shinmun*, March 30, 2015. http://www.kbmaeil.com/news/articleView.html?idxno=347632.

Jinken Heiwa Hamamatsu. 2013. "Fuji o utsu na! Higashi-Fuji kōdō," September 28, 2013. http://www.pacohama.sakura.ne.jp/no13/1309huji.html.

Kim, Claudia J. 2017. "War over Framing: Base Politics in South Korea." *Pacific Review* 30 (3): 309–27.

Kim, Claudia J. 2021. "*Dugong v. Rumsfeld*: Social Movements and the Construction of Ecological Security." *European Journal of International Relations* 27 (1): 258–80.

Kim, Dong Sung, Yong-hwan Choi, Adam Evans, and Sungho Park. 2006. "The Conflict Management and Cooperation Promotion between the USFK and the Local Community in Pyeongtaek." Suwon: Gyeonggi Research Institute.

Kim, Eunji. 2012. "Hanguginman beolbeol tteoneun 'opeu rimiteu.'" *Sisa In*, August 27, 2012. http://www.sisain.co.kr/?mod=news&act=articleView&idxno=14122.

Kim, Gi-hoon. 2011. "Jubyeonsangin bandaero Gunsan migungiji jeongmunjipoe musan." *Saejeonbuk News*, June 1, 2011. http://www.sjbnews.com/news/articleView.html?idxno=369140.

Kim, Jae-soo. 2007. "'Gunsan migungiji urittangchatgi siminmoim' 500hoe maja." *Saejeonbuk News*, July 26, 2007.

Kim, Kyu-jong. 2003. "Seuteuraikeobudae hullyeonjang giseup." *Tongil News*, August 7, 2003. http://www.tongilnews.com/news/articlePrint.html?idxno=34039.

Kim, Myung-sook. 2001. "Yongsan migungiji banhwan undongbonbu baljok." *Tongil News*, November 24, 2001. http://www.tongilnews.com/news/articleView.html?idxno=13593.

Kim, Sung-woon. 2014. "Bamnajeomneun pogyeoksori obalsago deo isang mot chama." *Incheon Ilbo*, December 12, 2014.

Kirk, Don. 2000. "U.S. Dumping Of Chemical Riles Koreans." *New York Times*, July 15, 2000, sec. World. https://www.nytimes.com/2000/07/15/news/us-dumping-of-chemical-riles-koreans.html.

Kyeong, Tae-young. 2015. "Pocheon Yeongpyeong Seungjin sagyeokjang sagyeok bandae gwolgidaehoe yeollyeo." *Kyunghyang Shinmun*, April 3, 2015.

Kyodo News via Japan Times. 2012. "Osprey Crash in April Due to Pilot Error: U.S." *Japan Times*, August 17, 2012. https://www.japantimes.co.jp/news/2012/08/17/national/osprey-crash-in-april-due-to-pilot-error-u-s/.

Lee, Jong-goo. 2015. "Buk pogyeoge Pocheon jumin migun sagyeokjang ap jipoe yeongi." *Newsis*, August 24, 2015. http://www.newsis.com/view/?id=NISX20150824_0010243389.

Lee, Min-woo. 2001. "Banmiyeoseonghoe, Yongsan migungiji doechatgi suyosiwi." *OhmyNews*, July 6, 2001. http://www.ohmynews.com/nws_web/view/at_pg.aspx?CNTN_CD=A0000047016.

Los Angeles Times. 2000. "U.S. Apologizes for Dumping Chemical," July 25, 2000. http://articles.latimes.com/2000/jul/25/news/mn-58541.

Lostumbo, Michael J., Michael J. McNerney, Eric Peltz, Derek Eaton, David R. Frelinger, Victoria A. Greenfield, John Halliday, et al. 2013. *Overseas Basing of U.S. Military Forces.* Santa Monica, CA: RAND Corporation.

Maeil Business Newspaper. 2000. "Migun dokgeungmul bangnyu siin." *Maeil Business Newspaper,* July 15, 2000.

Mainichi Shimbun. 2002. "Bei genshiryoku kūbo, Sasebo ni nyūkō." *Mainichi Shimbun,* August 17, 2002.

Mitchell, Jon. 2016. "Contamination: Documents Reveal Hundreds of Unreported Environmental Accidents at Three U.S. Marine Corps Bases on Okinawa." *Japan Times,* November 19, 2016. https://www.japantimes.co.jp/news/2016/11/19/national/contamination-documents-reveal-three-u-s-bases-okinawa-slow-disclose-environmental-accidents/.

Moon, Katharine H. S. 2012. *Protesting America: Democracy and the U.S.-Korea Alliance.* Berkeley: University of California Press.

Nam, Woohyun. 2016. "Migun, Pocheon Yeongpyeong hullyeonjangseo 10ilmane sagyeokullyeon jaegae." *Joongboo Ilbo,* January 11, 2016. http://www.joongboo.com/?mod=news&act=articleView&idxno=1039149.

Nishinippon Shimbun. 2011. "Hansen no ken orosenu 66-kaime shūsen no ni Amerika kūbo nyūkō kyohi tsuranuku Sasebo no Tanimura-san 'tomodachi' kansha to betsu." *Nishinippon Simbun,* August 16, 2011.

Nishinippon Shimbun. 2015. "Sasebo kichi shūhen jūmin-ra kōgi Osupurei hirai shichō wa rikai." *Nishinippon Simbun,* March 24, 2015.

Nishitama Association for the Removal of Yokota Base. 2009. "Yokota kichi min'i jōhō." 42.

Nishitama Association for the Removal of Yokota Base. 2012. "Yokota kichi min'i jōhō." 140.

Nishitama Association for the Removal of Yokota Base. 2015. "Yokota kichi min'i jōhō." 231.

Oguma, Eiji. 2016. "A New Wave against the Rock: New Social Movements in Japan since the Fukushima Nuclear Meltdown." *Asia-Pacific Journal: Japan Focus* 14 (13): n.p.

OhmyNews. 2019. "'Kkangpae sinbu'ga gunsane yeoinsuk charin kkadak," July 11, 2019. http://www.ohmynews.com/NWS_Web/View/at_pg.aspx?CNTN_CD=A0002551792.

Park, Rae-gun. 2010. *A! Daechuri: Daechuri jumindeurui Pyeongtaek migungiji hwakjangijeon bandae tujaenggirok.* Suwon: Saramsaenggak.

Pyeongtaek City. 2015. "K-55 migonggungiji." Pyeongtaek City. 2015. http://www.pyeongtaek.go.kr/tour/contents.do?mId=0304020300.

Robson, Seth. 2015. "Training Suspended at Firing Range in Korea after Missile Goes Astray." *Stars and Stripes,* December 30, 2015. https://www.stripes.com/news/training-suspended-at-firing-range-in-korea-after-missile-goes-astray-1.386606.

Ryukyu Shimpo. 2001. "Futenma isetsu hantai de raigetsu zenkoku kyaraban." *Ryukyu Shimpo,* February 16, 2001.

Ryukyu Shimpo. 2007. "Futenma asesu hōhōsho tekkai motome seimei." *Ryukyu Shimpo,* November 15, 2007.

Ryukyu Shimpo. 2009a. "F-22 sai haibi bakuon fue seikatsu hakai." *Ryukyu Shimpo,* May 31, 2009.

Ryukyu Shimpo. 2009b. "Beigun heri okikokudai tsuiraku 5-nen hikō chūshi motome kōgi." *Ryukyu Shimpo,* August 14, 2009.

Ryukyu Shimpo. 2012. "Osupurei hantai shūkai, haibi tsūkoku masu ikari." *Ryukyu Shimpo,* September 27, 2012.

Ryukyu Shimpo. 2014. "Kenedi Amerika taishi raiken." *Ryukyu Shimpo,* February 13, 2014.

Ryukyu Shimpo. 2017. "Expert Indicates That an Active Fault Line in the Undersea Section of the Henoko Base Construction Zone Could Pose Danger." *Ryukyu Shimpo,* October 25, 2017. http://english.ryukyushimpo.jp/2017/10/31/27956/.

Schober, Elisabeth. 2016. *Base Encounters: The US Armed Forces in South Korea.* London: Pluto Press.

Shizuoka Citizens' Action for Peace and Human Rights. 2003. "1.12 Fuji o utsu na!," January 12, 2003. http://www.geocities.co.jp/WallStreet-Bull/3959/1.12higasifuzikou dou.htm.

Shizuoka Citizens' Action for Peace and Human Rights. 2004. "9.12 Higashi-Fuji Beigun jitsudan enshū kōgi kōdō," September 12, 2004. http://www.geocities.co.jp/WallStreet-Bull/3959/9.12higasifuzikoudou.htm.

Shizuoka Shimbun. 2011. "Beigun 104 kunren ni kōgi—Gotenba de shimin dantai nado." *Shizuoka Shimbun,* June 20, 2011.

Sisk, Richard. 2020. "Noise Complaints Force US Troops to Move Live-Fire Training out of Korea." *Military.Com,* September 11, 2020. https://www.military.com/daily-news/2020/09/11/noise-complaints-force-us-troops-move-live-fire-training-out-of-korea.html.

Slavin, Erik. 2015. "Protesters Call for End of Errant Shells at South Korean Range." *Stars and Stripes,* April 6, 2015. https://www.stripes.com/news/pacific/protesters-call-for-end-of-errant-shells-at-south-korean-range-1.338656.

Slavin, Erik, and Hana Kusumoto. 2013. "Nuclear Carrier Protest outside Yokosuka Draws Large Crowd." *Stars and Stripes,* September 26, 2013. https://www.stripes.com/news/pacific/nuclear-carrier-protest-outside-yokosuka-draws-large-crowd-1.243463.

Social Democratic Party of Shizuoka. 2012. "Osupurei hantai kōenkai." September 8, 2012. http://sdp-shizuoka.com/data/04/04-22.html.

Song, Jeong-mi. 2003. "8.15 janganeul banjeonpyeonghwaui auseongeuro." *Tongil News,* July 26, 2003. http://www.tongilnews.com/news/articleView.html?idxno=33603.

Spencer, Caroline. 2003. "Meeting of the Dugongs and the Cooking Pots: Anti-Military Base Citizens' Groups on Okinawa." *Japanese Studies* 23 (2): 125–40.

Spitzer, Kirk. 2012. "Still No Luck for the V-22 in Japan." *Time,* September 9, 2012. https://nation.time.com/2012/09/09/still-no-luck-for-the-v-22-in-japan/.

Tanaka, Yoshihiro. 2014. "Osupurei Beigun kichi shūhen ni hirai shimin dantai ga kōgi." *Mainichi Shimbun,* October 26, 2014.

Tanji, Miyume. 2008. "US Court Rules in the 'Okinawa Dugong' Case: Implications for US Military Bases Overseas." *Critical Asian Studies* 40 (3): 475–87.

Taylor, Jonathan. 2010. "Antimilitary and Environmental Movements in Okinawa." In *Local Environmental Movements: A Comparative Study of the United States and Japan,* edited by Pradyumna P. Karan and Unryu Suganuma, 271–80. Lexington: University Press of Kentucky.

Tetsuo, Kotani. 2008. "Presence and Credibility: Homeporting the USS 'Midway' at Yokosuka." *Journal of American-East Asian Relations* 15: 51–76.

Tritten, Travis J. 2012. "Osprey Protesters Block Gates at Marine Base on Okinawa." *Stars and Stripes*, September 28, 2012. https://www.stripes.com/news/pacific/okinawa/osp rey-protesters-block-gates-at-marine-base-on-okinawa-1.191056.

Trumbull, Robert. 1965. "U.S. Warned That Japanese Left Wing Seeks to Exploit Missile Tests on Mt. Fuji." New York Times, October 6, 1965, sec. Archives. https://www.nyti mes.com/1965/10/06/archives/us-warned-that-japanese-left-wing-seeks-to-exploit-missile-tests-on.html.

Tsutsui, Kiyoteru. 2017. "Human Rights and Minority Activism in Japan: Transformation of Movement Actorhood and Local-Global Feedback Loop." *American Journal of Sociology* 122 (4): 1050–1103.

Yeo, Andrew. 2006. "Local-National Dynamics and Framing in South Korean Anti-Base Movements." *Kasarinlan: Philippine Journal of Third World Studies* 21 (2): 34–60.

Chapter 5

Akahata. 2008a. "Iwakuni shichōsen." *Akahata*, February 11, 2008.

Akahata. 2008b. "Amerika shireibu iten hantai no taremaku Zama-shi tekkyo shimin ga kōgi." *Akahata*, August 9, 2008.

Asahi Shimbun. 2005. "Nuclear Allergy." *Asahi Shimbun*, June 25, 2005.

Asahi Shimbun. 2006. "Ukemi shisei saigo made Yokosuka shichō, Beigun no genshiryoku kūbo ukeire hyōmei." *Asahi Shimbun*, June 15, 2006.

Asahi Shimbun. 2007a. "Beigun saihen 35 oku-en 'yakusoku' torikeshi." *Asahi Shimbun*, July 8, 2007. https://www.asahi.com/senkyo2007/special/TKY200707080083.html.

Asahi Shimbun. 2007b. "Kyanpu Zama ni shin shireibu hossoku jimoto no rikai, erarenu mama." *Asahi Shimbun*, December 20, 2007.

Campion, Gilles. 2008. "Japanese Town Defies US Military." *Agence France-Presse*, February 6, 2008.

Choi, Yong-hwan. 2008. "Relocation of USFK and Dongducheon City." Gyeonggi Research Institute. http://www.gri.re.kr/.

Chugoku Shimbun. 2020. "Kokubō ni kyōryoku no tokubetsukan sosogu kichi manē, habahiroku." *Chugoku Shimbun*, July 7, 2020. https://www.chugoku-np.co.jp/column/article/article.php?comment_id=659772&comment_sub_id=0&category_id=1209.

Chūnichi Shimbun. 2005. "Genshiryoku kūbo haibi 'jimoto no ikō o mushi' Futenma ni tsuzuki Yokosuka, tsuyoku hanpatsu." *Chūnichi Shimbun*, October 28, 2005.

Daily Yomiuri. 2006. "Outcome Unclear in Iwakuni Referendum." *Daily Yomiuri*, March 10, 2006.

Dong-a Ilbo. 2004. "Seongnan Dongducheon: Migun jaebaechi gyeongje jikgyeoktan, jiwondaesang jeoe." *Dong-a Ilbo*, August 27, 2004. http://news.donga.com/List/Soci ety/3/03/20040827/8100200/1?.

Dongducheon City History Compilation Committee. 2012. *Dongducheon History of 30 Years: 1981–2011*. Vol. 6. 8 vols. Dongducheon City. http://www.munhwawon.com/down/book6.pdf.

Duong, Cassie. 2006. "U.S. Welcomes Japanese Mayor's Acceptance of Nuclear-Powered Ship." *Washington File*, June 15, 2006. https://japan2.usembassy.gov/e/p/2006/tp-20060616-01.html.

The Economist. 2007. "Overpaid to Move over Here." *The Economist*, February 22, 2007. https://www.economist.com/asia/2007/02/22/overpaid-to-move-over-here.

Fackler, Martin. 2010. "Local Vote Could Decide Japan Base Issue." *New York Times*, January 22, 2010. https://www.nytimes.com/2010/01/23/world/asia/23japan.html.

Fackler, Martin. 2014. "In a City on Okinawa, Mayor's Re-Election Deals a Blow to Marine Base Relocation Plan." *New York Times*, January 20, 2014. https://www.nytimes.com/2014/01/20/world/asia/city-on-okinawa-deals-blow-to-plan-to-move-marine-base.html.

Hanai, Kiroku. 2006. "Waves Build against Carrier." *Japan Times*, October 23, 2006. https://www.japantimes.co.jp/opinion/2006/10/23/commentary/waves-build-agai nst-carrier/.

Ishimaru, Yasuzo. 2007. "The Korean War and Japanese Ports: Support for the UN Forces and Its Influences." 8. National Institute for Defense Studies Bulletin.

Johnson, Chalmers. 1996. "U.S. Bases on Okinawa: A Case of Colonial Overlordship." *Los Angeles Times*, February 16, 1996. https://www.latimes.com/archives/la-xpm-1996-02-16-me-36493-story.html.

Johnson, Tim. 2004. "Japanese Cities Anxious over U.S. Military Realignment." *Philadelphia Inquirer*, November 1, 2004.

Johnston, Eric. 2006. "The Iwakuni Referendum and the Future of the U.S. Military Base Realignment Agreement." *Asia-Pacific Journal: Japan Focus* 4 (3): n.p.

Johnston, Eric. 2008. "U.S. Base Proponent Takes Iwakuni Mayoral Race." *Japan Times*, February 11, 2008. https://www.japantimes.co.jp/news/2008/02/11/national/u-s-base-proponent-takes-iwakuni-mayoral-race/.

Jūmin tōhyō o chikara ni suru kai. 2007. "Ikari no ichimannin shūkai apīru." December 1, 2007. http://tikaranisurukai.web.fc2.com/03/0014.html.

Kamoi, Hiroko. 2005. "Japan Peace Conference 2005 Special Reports." Japan Peace Conference, November 24, 2005. http://heiwataikai.info/past_rally/05_kanagawa/simpo/english/07.html.

Kaneko, Tokio. 2004. "Daiichi gundan wa kuru na, Kyanpu Zama ni demo to shūkai." *Rimpeace*, August 29, 2004.

Kim, Chang-hak. 2014. "Pocheonsiuihoe sagyeokjang pihae 11jo jeongbu bosang chokgu gyeoruimun chaetaek." *Kyeonggi Ilbo*, December 22, 2014. http://m.kyeonggi.com/?mod=news&act=articleView&idxno=885883.

Kim, Gi-su. 2005. *Pyeongtaek migungiji eojewa oneul*. Pyeongtaek: Pyeongtaek Simin Sinmun.

Kim, Gwi-geun. 2021. "Gukbangbu, juhanmigun hullyeon bulmane 'daegyumo hullyeonjang hwakbo chujin.'" *Yonhap News Agency*, April 28, 2021. https://www.yna.co.kr/view/AKR20210428102400504.

Kim, Tae-hoon. 2012. "Migungiji jallyu simin urong cheosa." *Incheon Ilbo*, October 29, 2012.

Kim, Yong-han. 2005. "Pyeongtaek: Jeonjaenggijinya 'je2ui Buan' inya." *Noksaekpyeongnon (Green Review)*, March 2, 2005.

Kirishima Shun. 2018. "Nago shichōsen de Koizumi Shinjirō no netsuben wa 'sōki soba, shīkwasā, awamori, Orion Bīru.'" *Aera*, February 2, 2018. https://dot.asahi.com/dot/2018020200068.html.

Kyodo News. 2016. "Diet Surrounded by 28,000 as Synchronized Protests in Japan Rip Futenma Base Move in Okinawa." *Kyodo News*, February 21, 2016.

Lee, Hae-sun. 2019. "Pocheon Residents Rally to Salvage Plan for Metro Station." *Korea JoongAng Daily*, January 17, 2019. http://koreajoongangdaily.joins.com/news/article/article.aspx?aid=3058260.

Lee, Hui-hoon, and Ji-eun Sohn. 2014. "Patannan Dongducheon, 'yangki go hom'i natda." *OhmyNews*, November 6, 2014. http://www.ohmynews.com/NWS_Web/view/at_pg.aspx?cntn_cd=A0002050297.

The Mainichi. 2017. "Iwakuni Base Expansion Accelerates as Local Heads OK Transfer of US Carrier-Borne Jets." *The Mainichi*, June 30, 2017, sec. Japan. https://mainichi.jp/english/articles/20170630/p2a/00m/0na/019000c.

Mainichi Shimbun. 2004. "Zainichi Beigun saihen: itensaki, tsuyomaru hanpatsu seifu, Beigawa ni saikentō yōsei mo." *Mainichi Shimbun*, July 29, 2004.

Mainichi Shimbun. 2005a. "Genshiryoku kūbo mondai chiji 'zettai ni sakete'—kaiken de hantai no shisei." *Mainichi Shimbun*, February 17, 2005.

Mainichi Shimbun. 2005b. "Zainichi Beigun saihen: kūbo kōkei-kan mondai Yokosuka shichō 'akumade tsūjō-kan haibi o.'" *Mainichi Shimbun*, July 28, 2005.

Mainichi Shimbun. 2005c. "Zainichi Beigun saihen: Yokosuka shichō, 12-gō bāsu enchō ninka 'tsūjō-kan shiyō no tame.'" *Mainichi Shimbun*, August 3, 2005.

Mainichi Shimbun. 2005d. "Yokosuka genshiryoku kūbo haibi: 'jiko okitara . . .' Yokosuka shōgeki shimin dantai, tsuyoku kōgi." *Mainichi Shimbun*, October 28, 2005.

Mainichi Shimbun. 2005e. "Genshiryoku kūbo, Yokosuka haibi shichō ni hantai shomei niman." *Mainichi Shimbun*, November 1, 2005.

Mainichi Shimbun. 2005f. "Beigun saihen Kanagawa: gaman no genkai." *Mainichi Shimbun*, November 14, 2005.

Mainichi Shimbun. 2006a. "Iwakuni kichimondai 'shimin ga ishihyōjisuru kikai' jūmin tōhyō, kokuji." *Mainichi Shimbun*, March 6, 2006.

Mainichi Shimbun. 2006b. "Saihen yokerarezu Zama shichō ga hatsu genkyū." *Mainichi Shimbun*, April 27, 2006.

Mainichi Shimbun. 2007a. "Genshiryoku kūbo haibi jūmin tōhyō najimanai—Yokosuka shichō." *Mainichi Shimbun*, February 6, 2007.

Mainichi Shimbun. 2007b. "Iwakuni-shi shinchōsha kensetsu hojokin mondai: kōgi shūkai kanpa, chōsha kensetsu e kifu." *Mainichi Shimbun*, December 11, 2007.

McCormack, Gavan, and Satoko Oka Norimatsu. 2012. *Resistant Islands: Okinawa Confronts Japan and the United States*. Lanham, MD: Rowman & Littlefield.

Ministry of the Interior and Safety. 2020. "Juhanmigungiji ijeone ttareun Pyeongtaek jiwon." 2020. https://www.mois.go.kr/frt/sub/a06/b06/pyeongtaekSpt/screen.do.

Mitchell, Jon. 2014. "Thousands March on Henoko Base Site." *Japan Times*, August 23, 2014. https://www.japantimes.co.jp/news/2014/08/23/national/politics-diplomacy/thousands-march-henoko-base-site/.

OhmyNews. 2004. "Dongducheon jumindeul 'migunjaebaechi daechaek' chokgu." *OhmyNews*, May 28, 2004. http://www.ohmynews.com/nws_web/view/at_pg.aspx?CNTN_CD=A0000188536.

Okinawa Times. 2018. "'Tachiba kawatta ga omoi wa onaji' Nago shichō o tainin shita Inamine-san, Henoko no gēto mae ni." *Okinawa Times*, February 8, 2018.

Park, Rae-gun. 2010. *A! Daechuri: Daechuri jumindeurui Pyeongtaek migungiji hwakjangijeon bandae tujaenggirok*. Suwon: Saramsaenggak.

Park, Sang-gyu. 2005. "Jukbong daesin chotbul deulgo migun eomneun pyeonghwasesangeul!" *OhmyNews*, December 11, 2005. http://www.ohmynews.com/nws_web/view/at_pg.aspx?CNTN_CD=A0000298001.

Penn, Michael. 2013. "Japanese Mayor Sparks International Ire." *Al Jazeera*, April 5, 2013. https://www.aljazeera.com/features/2013/4/5/japanese-mayor-sparks-international-ire.

Pocheon City Council. 2017. "Pocheonsi sagyeokjang deung pihae bosang chokgu hongbomul." YouTube, May 1, 2017. https://youtu.be/RiE8RyBMv-4.

Pyeongtaek Movement to Stop Base Expansion and Paengseong Residents' Action Committee. 2003. "Gijahoegyeonmun." *Tongil News*, September 25, 2003. http://www.tongilnews.com/news/articleView.html?idxno=35671.

Sisk, Richard. 2020. "Noise Complaints Force US Troops to Move Live-Fire Training out of Korea." *Military.Com*, September 11, 2020. https://www.military.com/daily-news/2020/09/11/noise-complaints-force-us-troops-move-live-fire-training-out-of-korea.html.

Slavin, Erik. 2015a. "Errant Shell Puts US Military's Lessons Learned in Korea to the Test." *Stars and Stripes*, April 3, 2015. https://www.stripes.com/news/pacific/errant-shell-puts-us-military-s-lessons-learned-in-korea-to-the-test-1.338245.

Slavin, Erik. 2015b. "Protesters Call for End of Errant Shells at South Korean Range." *Stars and Stripes*, April 6, 2015. https://www.stripes.com/news/pacific/protesters-call-for-end-of-errant-shells-at-south-korean-range-1.338656.

Song, Jin-eui. 2015. "Oh Se-Chang Dongducheon sijang." *Kyeonggi Ilbo*, February 16, 2015. http://m.kyeonggi.com/?mod=news&act=articleView&idxno=915084.

Takahara, Kanako. 2005. "Camp Zama Buildup Feared Inevitable." *Japan Times*, August 26, 2005. https://www.japantimes.co.jp/news/2005/08/26/national/camp-zama-buildup-feared-inevitable/#.WqfynOdG3iU.

Takahara, Takao. 1987. "Local Government Initiatives to Promote Peace." *Peace & Change* 12 (3–4): 51–58.

Tetsuo, Kotani. 2008. "Presence and Credibility: Homeporting the USS 'Midway' at Yokosuka." *Journal of American-East Asian Relations* 15: 51–76.

Tokyo Shimbun. 2006a. "Jichitai no seifu fushin 'atamagoshi' de mikata mo teki ni." *Tokyo Shimbun*, April 4, 2006.

Tokyo Shimbun. 2006b. "Yokosuka shichō, genshiryoku kūbo o yōnin 'haibi kyohi no kengen nai.'" *Tokyo Shimbun*, June 15, 2006.

Yamajiro, Hiroji, Etsuko Urashima, Yasuhiro Miyagi, Yōichi Iha, Hideki Yoshikawa, and McCormack Gavan. 2018. "Five Okinawan Views on the Nago Mayoral Election of February 2018: Implications for Japanese Democracy." *Asia-Pacific Journal: Japan Focus* 16 (4): no pagination.

Yang, Sang-hyun. 2016. "Pocheon siuihoe, cheongwadae ap 1insiwi." *Pocheon News*, June 24, 2016.

Yomiuri Shimbun. 2006. "Iwakuni jūmin tōhyō: soredemo zainichi Beigun saihen wa hitsuyō da." *Yomiuri Shimbun*, March 13, 2006.

Yoon, Min-sik, and Hyun-ju Ock. 2015. "Living in Constant Fear Bear U.S. Military Base." *Korea Herald*, December 7, 2015. http://www.koreaherald.com/view.php?ud=20151207000979.

Yoshida, Reiji. 2014. "Nago Mayor Remains Defiant over Futenma Plan." *Japan Times*, February 13, 2014. https://www.japantimes.co.jp/news/2014/02/13/national/politics-diplomacy/nago-mayor-remains-defiant-over-futenma-plan/.

Yun, Jae-jun, Jae-hun Choe, and Jun-woo Gwon. 2015. "Chimmuk ilgwanhaneun Pocheonsi." *Kyeongin Ilbo*, March 11, 2015.

Chapter 6

Asahi Shimbun. 2022. "Nago Voters, Hit by Economic 'Reality,' Re-Elect Pro-Base Mayor." *Asahi Shimbun,* January 24, 2022. https://www.asahi.com/ajw/articles/14529030.

Bellware, Kim. 2019. "Seoul Students Scale Wall outside U.S. Ambassador's Residence to Protest American Troop Presence in South Korea." *Washington Post,* October 20, 2019. https://www.washingtonpost.com/world/2019/10/19/seoul-students-scale-wall-us-embassy-protest-american-troop-presence-south-korea/.

Berger, Thomas U. 1998. *Cultures of Antimilitarism: National Security in Germany and Japan.* Baltimore: Johns Hopkins University Press.

Center for Strategic and International Studies. 2020. "The Overseas Basing Debate, Part 1." February 10, 2020. https://www.csis.org/analysis/overseas-basing-debate-part-1.

Cutshaw, Jason B. 2016. "Radar Site Celebrates 10 Years in Japan." *United States Army,* October 19, 2016. https://www.army.mil/article/176980/radar_site_celebrates_10_years_in_japan.

Dickie, Mure. 2009. "The Issues behind an Awkward Alliance." *Financial Times,* February 24, 2009. https://app.ft.com/content/7b44c626-01cc-11de-8199-000077b07658.

Gordon, Cynthia, and James Jasper. 1996. "Overcoming the 'NIMBY' Label: Rhetorical and Organizational Links for Local Protesters." *Research in Social Movements, Conflicts and Change* 19: 159–81.

Gregson, Wallace C., and Jeffrey W. Hornung. 2021. "The United States Considers Reinforcing Its 'Pacific Sanctuary.'" War on the Rocks, April 12, 2021. https://warontherocks.com/2021/04/the-united-states-considers-its-pacific-sanctuary/.

Hasegawa, Kenji. 2019. *Student Radicalism and the Formation of Postwar Japan.* Singapore: Palgrave Macmillan.

Ichihashi, Aya. 2019. "Okinawa Sues Tokyo Again to Stop MCAS Futenma Relocation Project." *Stars and Stripes,* July 18, 2019. https://www.stripes.com/news/okinawa-sues-tokyo-again-to-stop-mcas-futenma-relocation-project-1.590808.

Jasper, James. 2006. "A Strategic Approach to Collective Action: Looking for Agency in Social-Movement Choices." *Mobilization: An International Quarterly* 9 (1): 1–16.

Johnston, Eric. 2020. "Defense Ministry Blunders and Local Opposition Ruin Japan's Aegis Ashore Plans." *Japan Times,* June 21, 2020. https://www.japantimes.co.jp/news/2020/06/21/national/politics-diplomacy/defense-ministry-local-opposition-japan-aegis-ashore/.

Kim, Claudia J. 2021. "Scope Mismatch: Explaining the Expansion of Anti-Military Infrastructure Siting Campaigns." *Mobilization: An International Quarterly* 26 (1): 109–25.

Lostumbo, Michael J., Michael J. McNerney, Eric Peltz, Derek Eaton, David R. Frelinger, Victoria A. Greenfield, John Halliday, et al. 2013. *Overseas Basing of U.S. Military Forces.* Santa Monica, CA: RAND Corporation.

Mainichi Shimbun. 2004. "Amerika gensen, hatsu no Sasebo nyūkō kara 40-nen towareru anzen taisaku." *Mainichi Shimbun,* November 13, 2004.

People's Democracy Party. 2021. "Jeomnyeonggun migun cheolgeo." People's Democracy Party, January 30, 2021. http://pdp21.kr/?p=110502.

Stars and Stripes. 2017. "Japanese Government Finalizes Reversion of Northern Training Area Land on Okinawa." *Stars and Stripes,* December 27, 2017. https://www.stripes.com/japanese-government-finalizes-reversion-of-northern-training-area-land-on-okinawa-1.504170.

Vine, David. 2019. "No Bases? Assessing the Impact of Social Movements Challenging US Foreign Military Bases." *Current Anthropology* 60 (19): 158–72.

Weaver, Teri. 2007. "Tiny Base Assimilates into Japanese Town." *Stars and Stripes*, October 8, 2007. https://www.stripes.com/news/tiny-base-assimilates-into-japanese-town-1.69654.

Yeo, Andrew. 2009. "Not in Anyone's Backyard: The Emergence and Identity of a Transnational Anti-Base Network." *International Studies Quarterly* 53 (3): 571–94.

Yoshihara, Toshi. 2010. "Chinese Missile Strategy and the US Naval Presence in Japan: The Operational View from Beijing." *Naval War College Review* 63 (3): 39–62.

Appendix

Biggs, Michael. 2018. "Size Matters: Quantifying Protest by Counting Participants." *Sociological Methods & Research* 47 (3): 351–83.

Calder, Kent E. 2007. *Embattled Garrisons: Comparative Base Politics and American Globalism*. Princeton, NJ: Princeton University Press.

Citizens' Coalition for Democratic Media. 2007. "Eolloniyeo 'migunbeomjoe'e ibeul yeoreora." *OhmyNews*, May 11, 2007. http://www.ohmynews.com/nws_web/view/at_pg.aspx?CNTN_CD=A0000409769.

Cooley, Alexander, and Kimberly Marten. 2006. "Base Motives: The Political Economy of Okinawa's Antimilitarism." *Armed Forces & Society* 32 (4): 566–83.

Earl, Jennifer, Andrew Martin, John D. McCarthy, and Sarah A. Soule. 2004. "The Use of Newspaper Data in the Study of Collective Action." *Annual Review of Sociology* 30 (1): 65–80.

Hilbe, Joseph M. 2011. *Negative Binomial Regression*. New York: Cambridge University Press.

Hutter, Swen. 2014. "Protest Event Analysis and Its Offspring." In *Methodological Practices in Social Movement Research*, edited by Donatella della Porta, 335–67. Oxford: Oxford University Press.

Kagotani, Koji, and Yuki Yanai. 2014. "External Threats, US Bases, and Prudent Voters in Okinawa." *International Relations of the Asia-Pacific* 14 (1): 91–115.

Kim, Claudia J., and Taylor C. Boas. 2020. "Activist Disconnect: Social Movements, Public Opinion, and U.S. Military Bases in East Asia." *Armed Forces & Society* 46 (4): 619–715.

Kusumoto, Hana, and Vince Little. 2007. "Group Claims Responsibility for Camp Zama Explosions." *Stars and Stripes*, February 19, 2007. https://www.stripes.com/news/group-claims-responsibility-for-camp-zama-explosions-1.60500.

Long, J. Scott, and Jeremy Freese. 2006. *Regression Models for Categorical Dependent Variables Using Stata*. 2nd ed. College Station, TX: Stata Press.

Marten, Kimberly. 2005. "Bases for Reflection: The History and Politics of US Military Bases in South Korea." *IRI Review* 10 (2): 155–200.

Oliver, Pamela E., and Daniel J. Meyer. 1999. "How Events Enter the Public Sphere: Conflict, Location, and Sponsorship in Local Newspaper Coverage of Public Events." *American Journal of Sociology* 105 (1): 38–87.

Index